SIMILAR
DIFFERENCES

started
Jan — 2018

SIMILAR DIFFERENCES

BENJAMIN BERTHET

CreateSpace

First Printing, 2017

ISBN-13: 978-1976336072 ISBN-10: 1976336074

Editing and proofreading: Benjamin, Gerard, and Catherine Berthet
Cover design: Benjamin Berthet
Cover graphic design: John Laue
Interior design: Benjamin Berthet
Photos by: Benjamin Berthet

Photos printed with permission.

The writings in this book are entirely based on observations and conversations made during my seven-month long voyage around the world and on my personal interpretation of said experiences. The writings are for discussion purposes and not absolute.

To Nan Self for the gift of mentorship and spirituality she offered to me, my brothers, and countless other teenagers for over more than 30 years. She made this world a better place, and this book is a means to carry the torch.

Contents

SIMILAR
DIFFERENCES

Introduction

During my last year of undergraduate education, I decided to travel around the world for seven months. Friends and family recommended many travel destinations, and I put a long list together. I also wanted to volunteer in another country, and I found two opportunities online before departing: one in a Nepali medical clinic and one in a Thai animal park.

I soon discovered that people travel to meet new people, sightsee, have an adventure, drink, or do drugs. Personally, I wanted to travel to better understand people for their cultural diversity. I documented my trip by keeping a private journal and maintaining a public, online blog using my phone to post photos and updates. The idea to convert my writings into a book did not arise until about four months into my trip when I began to seriously value what I was observing by categorizing and relating lessons I learned and when people around me began to seriously listen to my findings along the way.

I edited my writings solely for the purpose of making a continuous story. Discussions and observations scattered across a handwritten journal and blog were rearranged into sections for this book. Dates in mm/dd/yy format mark the beginning of a blog entry that is mixed in with journaling.

Part I is a chronological detail of my journey to provide the background experiences from which discussions follow. Parts II and

III delve into topics of interest relative to human thought and behavior.

Part II: Person to Person focuses on interaction between two individuals. Individuals are complex and full of different opinions and perceptions. No two people are alike. We meet a tremendous number of people in our lives who each share with us a unique experience. You can ask two people the same question and never will the answers be identical. Grandparents often believe differently from their grandchildren. Friends disagree about what they like. Politicians debate how to best solve a legal matter. Teachers explain the same material differently. Individual people are unique. Historically, a nation's population stayed mostly within its own borders to focus on how to feed and defend itself. Today, global travel and international opportunities have placed together people who differ in more than just their opinions. They differ greatly on tangible matters like language, food, religion, and music as well as abstract matters like values, beliefs, awareness, honor, and trust. Part II identifies the differences between individuals in a multitude of topics in order to highlight the beauty of being unique. Differences between individuals also arise from the environments within which each individual develops. As no two individuals live in the same country with the same parents, teachers, mentors, friends, and life experiences, each person grows up uniquely different.

Each and every person also has his or her own mentality. That mentality is a construction of both the past environment the person was raised in and the current environment the person presently lives in. That mentality is the filter that interprets new situations in a particular way. Many individuals who share similar past and current environments find themselves sharing a similar mentality.

Part III: Person to People expands on Part II to delve into how many of these single individuals collectively form a group. Groups can be as small as a few friends or a small business or as big as an institution or a country. Groups share a common mentality which is a collective of individual mentalities. Eventually, groups come together to form societies, and those societies interact within themselves and with other societies. Groups, nevertheless, are collections of individuals I can relate to or not depending on how different their mentality is from my own. Clashes can occur when individuals raised in different environments think differently and cannot understand each other. Over the course of my trip, I encountered mentalities from environments that ranged vastly in the realms of political institutions, infrastructural development, educational levels, and cultural values. I talked with all of these people with as open and understanding a mentality as I could muster. As a result, I developed a deeper understanding of individuals and groups no matter how similar or radically different they were. I now try to balance my own mentality by averaging a wide array of values and qualities from people around the world. The most shocking discovery I made was finding out just how similar individuals are between groups.

This book arose out of my observations of people's choices and mentalities. People, including readers of this book, pick and choose what they accept, disregard, or listen to. Sometimes, it is an unconscious decision; other times, it is not. I am not writing this book to raise awareness of specific issues. I hope this book raises awareness for the value of an increased understanding between people who may vary in look, clothing, location, religion, culture, music, and basic values. Raising the awareness of other mentalities to understand why those individuals behave or react to new situations is, I believe, the first step towards reducing and preventing conflicts which people frustratingly see repeating every day. These conflicts range from small conflicts encountered during a daily routine to larger conflicts ranging over decades between warring countries. After observing as objectively as possible new cultures, values, and people, I believe all human behavior and arguments can be explained, understood, and resolved through mutual communication and understanding. People behave with reasons according to their way of thinking. People who act seemingly without reason are simply behaving with reasons outside of our understanding.

There is a saying, "When all you have is a hammer, everything looks like a nail." Another saying is that "the apple does not fall far from the tree." A hammer is a preconceived notion such that new experiences become the right-sized nails. I realized during my voyage that my own personal mentality grew to encompass all people. The hammers I was using to interact with varying cultures and languages had to constantly adapt. That mentality became a multitude of hammers which I will continue to evolve into my upcoming medical studies and practice. The tools I use to handle new situations will continue to adapt as every life experience can be a new nail or lesson. This book is about the hammers used to attack the nails that present themselves in life such as meeting new coworkers, teaching children how to handle bullying, and the willingness to try an unusual food. It is also about how far people, as apples, fall from the trees that raise and nurture them from the ground. What are the factors that push some people to fall near the values and traditions of their nurturing environment whereas others find their identity elsewhere and how do those factors interact?

This world is full of elementary thinking of "boys-only clubs" and groups that work to unite themselves and divide others. Nothing raises questions like being a white male and being denied from joining an all-Asian fraternity on a college campus. Without a doubt, people have to fight for equality before they can live as equals, but are people fighting more the external group or the internal mind? I see it unfortunate when a bisexual friend identifies herself so strongly as such that she cannot see any other friend as being neutral. Others either fit into her understanding as friend or foe such that her life will be a constant struggle unless her awareness of those around her shifts to see them as human beings rather than the dichotomy of her sexuality. To live a label is to see a world full of labels. In other words, once an idea develops into an over-generalizing hammer, it is easy to see everything as a nail whether it is a nail or not.

The mentality used to face each issue is often inconsistent, because the values employed for one issue may contradict values employed on another issue. These choices of how to face a new issue are based on past experiences. Choices are also based on affordability in the present. Can people afford to be compassionate and give a few minutes to someone who simply needs someone to talk to, even if they are running late for work and have to speed away? How did I, shivering while wearing a heavy winter jacket and winter boots, react when I saw a young child who was wearing little more than a thin sweater and pants while sitting with a piece of cardboard and freezing in the snowy wind on a city sidewalk? How would other tourists react upon seeing the child? How would a local resident react upon seeing the child? Even other things as seemingly constant as a sense of time can vary with different cultures. How individuals face a new situation is often based on the values they hold, and those values vary based on culture. Once I understood these differences, I began to understand why people behave and react the way they do to new situations. While there are many differences in behavior around the world, they ultimately all stem from values that appear to be more commonplace among all human beings than previously thought.

I wanted to call the book *Similar Differences*, because people live differently due to the different choices they make. They share the fact that their experiences are constantly changing what they become. The interactions of these choices affect how a person relates to oneself, to other individuals, and in turn between oneself and society. These interactions cross many issues people, as groups of individuals, face today.

Based on the array of both planned and spontaneous experiences with strangers turned friends from around the world, I believe the ideas presented in this book will be new for most and will stretch beyond current conceptions. All the books I know discuss a single matter: a single culture, event, time period, etc. This book is an accumulation of my experience and analysis and will attempt to make sense of all the stories I heard, both true and false, in order to discern a common theme of living and determine how similar human differences actually are.

During the course of my travels, I enjoyed reading about Robert Oppenheimer's emotional redemption after launching "the gadget" in *American Prometheus*[1] by Kai Bird and Martin Sherwin. Oppenheimer was the prominent scientific director of the Manhattan Project responsible for creating the atomic bomb during World War II. The book is an enormous biography that I started early on my trip in Asia and finished on my last flight home exactly seven months later. Never have I felt such a strong, personal connection to a book. First, I found myself emotionally drawn and tied to Oppenheimer's strong desire to learn during his early years. I saw a similar desire for education in the Nepali children I taught who were the most enthusiastic pupils I had ever seen. Second, as a passionate individual interested in both biological and sociological science, I was frustrated to see how Oppenheimer, one of the U.S.'s top scientists, could be praised as saving the Allies in WWII and banished with a seemingly personal vendetta by the House Un-American Activities Committee (HUAC) and its anti-Communist inquisition. During the Cold War and the race to the moon, scientists were then praised again, only to be banished again in my lifetime in the U.S. as science and corporate interests became mixed in, twisted, and confuddled. I cannot help but draw bridges between these stories and finding universal themes that span across conflict and disagreement. Everybody lives to the truths that they hold dear. This book could be called *Living One Trillion Lives*, for people are constantly changing and becoming different people with every new experience.

A greater understanding of people offers an unexpected solution to several conflicts between people. I look at every global leader and speaker of peace. There are patterns to the messages, but each message is isolated in its time and place. Seeing people as human beings transcends all time and place. It transcends governments and militaries. This is not like Gandhi's message to evict colonizing British or like Martin Luther King's demand for racial equality, because greater understanding cannot produce conflict of a battling sort. It is not a lesson to learn. It is a feeling, as the world speaker of peace Prem Rawat said, that must arise from within. It is not a message to be communicated in a speech. So, what exactly is a greater understanding of people? It is the same feeling and common ground that a family feels in America as a family does in Nepal and Pakistan. That is because it does not care for names, nationalities, or labels. It cares for the deepest sense of brotherhood and sisterhood that can only be shared with other human beings on Earth. The world people hope for is one in which neighbors do not kill each other and can find mutually understandable resolutions.

To read this book requires overcoming the challenge of every assumption and prediction of people's behavior that would impede the reader from seeing the message as all-inclusive rather than categorically specific. This book is also a multidimensional commentary which is void of economic and political specifics that depict the sociological and psychological grasp of people living within the realm of one society.

I hope the reader finds the ideas within this book "reasonable," courtesy from Guy, a fellow traveler I met in Goa, India. The world is neither a big place nor a small place. It is as large as one understands it, and picking sides of a two-party battle ignores the other half. If I side with too many halves, my world can shrink quite quickly. As I write this in Goa, I'm admiring the cow sitting under a beach umbrella by the crashing waves.

Similar Differences

Part I: Travel

Japan

Soon, I will depart for Los Angeles Airport from San Jose, California, to spend a day with a college Track and Field teammate, Clint. It should be fun, relaxing, and without worry about the upcoming voyage. It ended up being low-key and relaxing with a great day of body-surfing, watching television shows, and playing Scrabble.

Still, I was a bit anxious about beginning such a long trek. It was even more stressful not knowing where I would stay upon my arrival in Japan. Thankfully, Molly, a high school friend, responded to my emails and gave me information on where to meet her.

09/09/14: After an eleven-hour plane ride and a three-hour train ride, I finally arrived at Molly's place. On the flight, I sat next to a seasoned traveler who shared, to be modest, all kinds of personal, traveling wisdom throughout Southeast Asia. I don't think I will use all of it, but he definitely made the flight go by quickly. I also met a great San Diego firefighter whom I may see again in a week in Osaka. All in all, I was safe but tired after more than 24 hours of travel. Note to self: exchange money first, so I wouldn't have to ask strangers to buy train tickets and repay in USD.

No SIM card, a couple of missed trains, late in the night, no English, and no Japanese yen, but I made it. I was, however, unsure of my food situation regarding my vegetarian options. For a moment, I thought I had lost my credit cards and U.S. passport when buying a train ticket. Talk about stress. It could only get better.

09/10/14: Molly, her boyfriend, Chad, and I biked to Ushiku Daibutsu, the largest Buddha statue in the world which stands 120 meters tall. It was a beautiful bike ride through the city of Tsukuba to the surrounding towns and finally the countryside where the statue stands. We casually strolled through the site. We washed our hands as is customary before entering holy sites, stamped our tourist booklets, hit large bells, fed very eager fish, and breathed incense. We toured the interior of the statue across five floors. We saw how it was constructed, the prayer areas, and a circular room with over 4,000 small Buddha statues on the walls. It was a quiet place where time stopped, and we could just relax and walk. I began to feel somewhat grounded.

09/13/14: One more day was spent at Doho Park to process where I was and center myself, followed by Japan Aerospace Exploration Agency (JAXA), Tsukubasan (Mt. Tsukuba) and a robotics gallery. Sitting in the park and listening to birds was a great way to ground myself even more. Coming to Japan flipped my world 180 degrees. Practically no one spoke English. Thankfully, my two hosts spoke some Japanese and guided me through the city. It helped me maneuver through the next cities in Japan where I traveled alone.

These first few days were disorienting to say the least. I tried my best to calm myself and reevaluate the approach to my new surroundings. After some introspection, I came to the realization I had been living in fear. I knew what it was like not to live in fear from previous life experiences, but I realized I dug myself into a hole since then. The fear was not related to school or work but everyday social situations. It blocked me from many friendships. The fear made me feel as if every single action and breath was breaking a rule. 99% of the time that rule was self-imposed, and I shut myself down and back into a corner of inaction. I felt it tied back to the innate respect for authority that I always had. For example, I had difficulty doing a task if somebody was watching and judging. The truth was the biggest and meanest judge was myself. If I could endure my own criticism, then I could handle whatever anyone could or may say.

I think it was a great idea to visit local museums, especially science and history where national pride is involved. The narration at JAXA, some of which was in English thankfully, gave a more inclusive view on aerospace and the International Space Station (ISS), somewhat different from what I had learned in the U.S. The robotics gallery also had really cool innovations I never would have thought of.

Molly, Chad, and I took a bus to Tsukuba Mountain and its shrine followed by a cable car to the top for a great view of the local area. So many rice fields…

That night, we went out for delicious okonomiyaki which are savory pancakes. I also started taking pictures of my food. And don't forget kitsune which is fried bean curd on top of udon with tempura. Delicious!!

I had fish flakes on my okonomiyaki, and I was sure there was fish broth in my kitsune. I was not about to eat a steak or fish filet, but I began to let go of some of my vegetarian rules. Perhaps it was a sign of change. The okonomiyaki upset my stomach, but there may have been a little too much flavor and flakes for my introduction to fish for the first time in my life. On a side note, they say "okini" for "thank you" in Osaka and Kyoto, not "arigato" as they do in Tokyo.

09/14/14: I took an overnight bus as the cheapest option from Tokyo to Osaka before checking into a youth hostel. So excited! Eating instant udon for breakfast.

The youth hostel was full, but a girl offered to share her room with another person as her friend had just left. Mr. Yano, the youth hostel "Party Animal," took me, two Australian girls, and a traveler from Hong Kong on a short tour around Osaka. We stopped by a 300-year-old Japanese town replica with real furniture of that era. We also dressed in kimonos and visited each room including a pharmacy. Then we ate more okonomiyaki and noodles with shrimp. Whether to my liking or not, I just ate the noodles and the edge of okono that didn't have a slab of meat on it. It was so enjoyable to have a guide who knew the culture and language. Internally, I felt somewhat grounded to the strange place. I was unsure of what exactly I felt. After panicking before leaving Tsukuba that I would not make it through the rest of my trip, I enjoyed the tour, a full belly, and a place to sleep. I knew I would be okay.

Japanese food was yummy, but I could only have kitsune so many times. I grabbed a croissant and red-bean croissant for breakfast, making me feel comfortable and content. Udon for breakfast, lunch, and dinner pushed me to my limit. I never had to stick to a single, ethnic food before.

09/15/14: I visited the big shrines in Osaka, Osaka Castle, and had a dinner of 13 skewers in a large, entertainment district. I did not know I was not supposed to double dip from the large bowl of sauce they gave me. It was expected I would mess things up, because I was a foreigner. It was a beautiful day in the city with so much more to look forward to.

Travelers at the youth hostel were extremely sociable, and I met more Americans than I was expecting. I fed some fish and turtles with an old Japanese man that handed me bread. I saw a random beaver in the park that crawled up to me, and I found two kittens trying to sleep at a shrine. I also met a man on the bus who donated blood as a hobby with a goal to do so in every province of Japan.

09/16/14: I went to Nara with the firefighter I met on the plane. In Nara Park, we fed deer rice cakes and proceeded to get bumped by a deer wanting more. A beautiful day with perfect weather. At the main temple, there was a hole in a pillar that would offer enlightenment to the person who could fit through. One man had to be pulled back out, because he didn't fit.

I returned to Osaka in the mid-afternoon, so I walked through Dotonobori and Shinsaibashi shopping districts. That night made for an interesting time. I met two Canadians, and the three of us sat down with Mr. Yano and two Finnish travelers. We had to pick up chairs and a table from Mr. Yano's apartment across the street in order to seat everyone that had come from the hostel to eat at the restaurant. Apparently, the only reason to leave Finland was if one disliked Finland, and the Finnish travelers "hated Finland." One Canadian's job was to streamline companies in difficulty. Lately, he assisted in firing 165 people. His friend was a pickle company analyst.

Mr. Yano showed us the bathroom behind the hole-in-the-wall restaurant but not without praying to a shrine on the way. When we returned to the hostel, everybody sat around the table in the lobby. There was the American marine from Okinawa who will do embassy duty. There was Roger from Los Angeles who grew up in the system but "made a life for himself," something his friends didn't do. Then there were the two Americans that worked in Korea and a Japanese medical student.

Hearing Roger share a story made me wonder if all we had were stories. Did I just want to be a story? I looked around Osaka, the castle, the parks, and I saw so many happy, young families. I wrote while sitting in Tennoji Park, feeling free from the stress of a big city and being 7,000 miles away from home. With so many generations walking side by side in the park, I thought my parents would continue to live through me and my future through what I would be doing. I couldn't grow from just sitting on a bench.

09/18/14: I went to Kyoto for a day and a half to visit Fushimi Inari which is a mountain path of orange gates and Kiyomizudera, a large Buddhist temple. Kyoto had the most temples and historical sites I've seen. Otherwise, I wandered through a rock and moss garden, small streets, and the local life.

I had a better time living in the moment today. I was not stressed when I missed a city bus. It was merely an obstacle to overcome in time. I was proud of how I kept my stress levels down. I was learning.

I went to the monkey park and bamboo path in Arashiyama and then a cultural show with a New Zealander named James. The cultural show included a puppet show, tea ceremony, flower arrangement, harp, ancient comic play, and geisha dance. I learned my judgements were so petty and ungrounded. James looked unfashionable, dirty, and was running across the city carrying his heavy backpack. Why was my first thought of him so judgmental that I thought he did not know how to travel when in fact he was much more experienced than me? He would sleep in McDonalds and karaoke rooms to save money, but he was really insightful. He told me of the reasons the U.S. joined World War II in Europe and the devastating costs they charged Great Britain to do so. He and many English echoed the same story: Great Britain had to let free their colonies, give their intellectual property to the United States, and borrow from the U.S. a lot of money that was only repaid fairly recently. I was incredulous as I had never learned about this in my history classes, although I did wonder what happened to the colonizing empire that Great Britain once was.

After my newly-made friends had left the city, I went to dinner alone which could seem lonely, but I was ecstatic as it gave me the opportunity to meet the chef and his son. It was incredibly valuable to learn how he tried to make a good life for himself and provide for his son. He had cooked since he was 16 years old and now owned three restaurants. His son was studying economics at a famous university in Kyoto. A lack of schooling did not mean his father was not smart just like having a formal education did not correlate with intelligence.

I grabbed an overnight bus to Tokyo. Sightseeing had been a quality experience, but meeting people from all over was the other half to traveling. I was glad to be doing both.

I arrived in Shinjuku very early on the overnight bus and passed the time by walking through stores, internet cafes, and anime stores. I checked into my first capsule hotel, a hotel of long tubes to sleep in with built-in TVs and a little pull-down screen for closure at the end of the capsule. The tubes shared a common hallway, and the full baths and sauna were on a separate floor. It was a new experience I would recommend! At the hotel, I met two Canadians from Vancouver and Montreal who were studying in Singapore. We strolled through the gay district as they were studying gender relations in Japan. I feel I have grown up some since coming to Japan, and I still have so much more to do.

09/20/14: I visited different districts in Tokyo for the next three days. I could have climbed Mt. Fuji yesterday, but time was too tight. I was already exhausted and decided to wander and relax around the city including Shinjuku, a big shopping district. With Chad and Molly, I went to Akihabara and Ueno for its large anime culture, and after parting ways with my friends one last time, I stopped by another park and Shibuya.

09/22/14: I had dinner for my last night in Japan with a family friend who is a biostatistician and epidemiologist. He was kind enough to offer me to stay at his place, so I did not have to try sleeping in an Internet cafe before my flight to Singapore for which I was very grateful.

It's cliché, but the last two weeks went by so quickly, and I only had a small glimpse of what Japanese life is like. My departing thoughts on Japan were as follows: Everything was very practical and served purposes I never saw fulfilled in California. Everything was compact. There were no public trash cans. I always felt extremely safe no matter where I went. People were so trusting that they reserved tables with their wallets as they went to buy food. I was never worried about being robbed. Lastly, the clash between traditional Japanese culture, western culture, and creative anime culture was extremely visible all over Tokyo. I saw lots of dyed hair to be blonde or brunette and costumes just out and about. Overall, the people were extremely nice and modest and went out of their way to help me and others. A great experience so far.

Similar Differences

Singapore

I flew to Singapore and met my high school friend, Nick, and his girlfriend, Meg. Being the stranger among so many people made me feel like I was just one, lonely individual and how valuable it was to be with others. As for traveling, I could have stayed happily in San Jose, California, but this was an opportunity I felt I should not miss and would benefit from. I knew I needed to push forward even if I felt anxiety or fear.

My mind has been running the past few days with several thoughts, theories, and questions. Walking through Singapore was enlightening to see so many people of different faiths coexisting peacefully. I spent a good hour at a mosque discussing religion with an Australian lady who had converted a few years prior, and I received a small book as a parting gift. She said people needed religion, because "people are weak." I did see a few people litter and spit in the city despite heavy consequences, suggesting people were simply people and not saints. With strict rules against shoplifting, slurs, and foul behavior that negatively affected their fellow man, people became more inclusive of one another. Be it faith or society that established rules, people followed them. Was it good or bad? Most Singaporeans relied on government public housing, but I felt a societal comfort and trust truly unseen in the U.S.

09/23/14: I spent the day in Little India and Bugis area to see the local markets. There were so many interesting shops and amazing food with low prices. I had masala dosa for three U.S. dollars and fruit juices for a dollar each, so I bought four today to stay hydrated and happy.

There were security cameras and signs everywhere that mentioned the severe punishments for shoplifting. It was like living with Big Brother but safer and less worrisome.

So far, I've seen all kinds of ethnicities and places of worship, and everyone lived in harmony. It was an impressive feat, but it made me wonder if it was feasible only for small countries.

09/25/14: I hiked eight km through a park for a treetop walk on an elevated cable bridge. It was extremely humid and hot, and I made the mistake of not bringing any water. I wouldn't have made it had there not been a ranger's station with water fountains near the top.

I quickly visited Chinatown and the largest temples afterwards and was again impressed with their reverential adornments. I bargained for a phone case nearby and was a little too believing. I let an extra two dollars go their way, but I still paid half price at ten dollars. Oh well, it was a learning experience.

Last night, I did a night safari, apparently the only one in the world, along with two software engineers that were in Singapore for an expo. I was fascinated to see nocturnal animals from elephants, bats, lions, and water buffalo to many Asian animals I had never seen before. My only complaint was that no flash could be used so as not to disturb the animals. All the pictures were essentially useless since everything was dark. The entertaining night ended in a thunderstorm which was the first heavy rain I experienced since January.

I had a relaxing day walking along the beach past anchored ships, eating more local dishes, and taking a river cruise through the city. At night, I joined my gracious hosts at a rooftop bar called Altitude. I first had to buy pants and shoes since I was in shorts and flip flops.

I definitely left Singapore impressed. It was small enough that it could create such a harmonious and safe city, and there were so many Public Service Announcements on how to be considerate of others.

Thailand

On the plane towards Phuket, Thailand, I began to worry and fret about bargaining and going to a developing country. I was especially worried about India. Thailand itself was a new climate with so many things I did not fully understand. For example, during the Vegetarian Festival, why were lady-boys the possessed ones that acted as spiritual mediums? Some mediums were men, women, and children, but why were there many feminine boys? To be discovered.

09/26/14: Just arrived safely at the hostel. I was a bit anxious, because the hostel was empty. I had no idea what to do, but I asked the always-friendly receptionist for recommendations.

The Vegetarian Festival was conveniently ongoing, a ceremony over several days when people cleansed themselves through diet and pain and called forth the gods for good fortune.

It was my turn to eat mystery foods as there were dozens of food stands directly in front of the youth hostel, and it was all so good!! One dollar total.

I met some people tonight from the hostel, and we went out to observe massive fireworks and praying in the streets.

09/30/14: On my last morning in Phuket, I went at 5am to see the piercings before the parade. One by one, individuals approached a shrine inside the temple and entered a trance. They proceeded to get pierced with just about any metal object. Piercings became more and more intense each day, and this was far along in the nine-day ceremony. Most people had over 300 needles in their skin all over their arms and back. And that was the easy part. I watched people get pierced through lips, tongues, and cheeks. I watched one up close for too long, and I became light headed and had to walk away. Anything went from spears to arrows and giant metal rods. No anesthesia or anything. I saw questionable sterilization techniques with an antiseptic fluid of the metal objects although the needles were packaged, sterile, medical needles.

For reasons that escaped me, I thought I would come to a developing country and find a community that would be in a free-for-all survival mode whereas the community actually unified in impressive numbers to share the experience. Society appeared more friendly and enjoyable to be a part of with a sense of community.

I learned there were a few reasons behind the festival. The diet was a way to cleanse the body, originally to protect it against malaria and today to ask for the gods' blessings. People were very courteous, welcoming, and willing to converse. I felt people on average were good and trying to build a better future for their offspring. Whatever I thought of each society and culture, this was truly an experience offering lessons I could not learn back home.

I had the privilege of meeting two travelers from Winnipeg, Canada, who showed three travelers from Prague and I around the festival. I woke up at 5:30am to meet with them to go see the parade of piercings. Most people had rods, blades, or needles, but this one man had a bike frame going through his cheek. He and others were helping to hold the bike up as they walked side by side.

Phuket was truly a paradise. Besides feeling ripped off for the speedboat cruise, snorkeling and island hopping by paying the price at the hostel versus the discounted group rate an Australian family had paid, it was still relatively cheap and well worth it. The views and water were truly amazing. They were the clearest and warmest waters I had ever experienced. It was a good day.

A cool traveler from Scotland and I each rented a motorbike to tour Phuket island and visit the remote beach of Ao Sane. We snorkeled over rough coral and were cut up a little, but it was so enjoyable. We dined by the beach with a spectacular view of the nearby beaches, green hills, and teal water. We continued to ride around the island, swimming in the clearest of waters and seeing the freshest of tropical views. Six dollars for the motorbike rental and gas was a truly memorable experience.

10/01/14: I hiked into the jungle at Khao Sok Park to find a collection of waterfalls. It is a national park just north of Phuket Island with an enormous freshwater lake. I asked the guard to let me continue past where a guide was required. I hiked for another hour, only to turn around when the path ceased to exist. It was a bit daunting to be so far away on a dangerous trail as I took many wrong turns, but it was quite an experience. On my way back, I met some monks from a nearby city who claimed to be doing research in the park but seemed more preoccupied with taking photos of themselves swimming. They invited me to take a picture with them, and then we all swam together. Afterwards, they invited me for a coffee and were very gracious to pay for it. It was truly a wonder to get along so well despite them speaking very little English. I will likely not see them again, but they left me with a marvelous afternoon to remember them by.

Ead graced me with his hospitality at Khao Sok. It was an internal debate to trust someone who was making a living from my business and might take advantage of me. I could say it was my first time making friends with someone whose services I employed. Genuinely, he was a wonderful father and kind person which made me trust him. He bought me food last night and invited me for tea and coffee. He knew I was tight on money but still wanted to ensure I had a good time. I thought everything came with a price, but he was teaching me that kindness does not. Last night was a festival for the community to raise money to rebuild the local temple. Coincidentally, I was staying with one of the organizers of the festival, and he was very kind to show me around and buy me dinner.

I lived my life by drawing as little attention to myself as possible, thinking I was doing a better service to people by not getting in their way. I realized after engaging with Josh from England and the others on the lake that my life could be enhanced by being involved. Likewise, having others involved in my life only served to enhance my life as well. Oh, much would have I missed had others been as little outgoing as I had been while growing up. I felt life was worth living but only when shared with others.

Today, I had a surreal, river cruise across Khao Sok Lake. We reached the end of the water, hiked over the hill, and used a bamboo raft to reach a cave. The company of Josh and two travelers from Amsterdam, a great discussion on the bus ride, beautiful weather, warm and clear water, and magnificent mountainsides all made for a great day. With so many people from so many countries including many I may never see again, I only thought people exist on this planet together to share in its beauty and presence in the temporary moments they are together.

On my trip thus far, I found people to be happy and gracious while I fought my darker, internal battles. I believed people were good, and many acted out of habit. At the end of the day, I slept well, because I knew I was among warm and welcoming people. I was growing, and I was young. I awoke to find men and women working equally hard to prepare rebar for the extension of Ead's restaurant.

I arrived in Kanchanaburi, a city two hours east of Bangkok, in the early morning after sleeping at the bus station in Bangkok. I learned of the strong memories of the Death Railway that remain and surround the bridge over the River Kwai. Having been to the Thailand-Burma Railway Museum and Jeath Museum, I learned about the atrocities committed in order to finish the railway in 16 months. 16,000 Allied POWs died and 90,000 Asian captives lost their lives to the Death Railway. Worked to death and fed close to nil, they quickly resembled their counterparts in Europe as walking skeletons. "Forgive, But Not Forget" written over a replica of the bomb rung true. These were lessons to learn in humanity, not retaliation out of anger. The Japanese used the bridge only once before it was captured at the end of the war. Was the cost worth it? Certainly, few would contend so, but who can argue during times of war? It truly was a horrific time in which one human was being tortured and degraded by another. Learning what happened could help us identify patterns in current events. Hopefully, people have the patience and resources to learn.

I joined four French and one Italian on a 60-km trip away from Kanchanaburi. We used 125cc motorbikes towards Erawan

Falls and went up the seven tiers of waterfalls. On my return, I quickly visited the bridge over the River Kwai. The following day, I took a cooking class, received a soft, Thai massage, and began reading *American Prometheus*. I started looking at the vigor of Oppenheimer's childhood intellect, fostered and nurtured by his mentors. I also listened to the news of current events to discover the contradictory views of my generation on social, economic, and political matters. For example, there was the immediate racism towards the treatment of a Nigerian during the Ebola outbreak in West Africa. He was a human being, but his heritage and skin color defined the public perception. Furthermore, the extended despise of any West African during this epidemic was astonishing and disheartening. Another example of wrongly hating a group because of a few individuals was that Czechs facing enormous anti-Czech sentiment following the Boston Marathon bombings in 2013, and their Prime Minister had to remind the world that Czechs were not the same nationality as that of the Chechen bombers. At that moment, I realized the responses of fear and anger may be directly linked to a lack of understanding and experience with people from around the world.

10/08/14: I arrived to volunteer at the Safari Park outside Kanchanaburi. Volunteering was a lot more hands-on than I was expecting and much more than anything possible in the U.S. I fed macaques and black bears, leisured inside cages with new jackals, and helped teach a macaw to fly from my arm to someone else's arm among other things. People and animals lived in harmony. The volunteers really did a good job at changing the attitude from forceful training of animals to positive reinforcement.

During volunteer orientation, we were taught there were two dangerous animals to be on guard for. First, scorpions that liked to hide in clothing or shoes during the night for warmth, so they recommended checking our clothes before dressing. Still, an experienced volunteer was bitten by a scorpion in his shorts while cleaning a cage the second day I was there. Second, there were poisonous centipedes that could run at 30 kmph. New volunteers were told if we saw one, "Run." One night, it was raining heavily. I fell asleep after I had positioned my mattress diagonally on the floor, so the leaking roof would not disturb my sleep. I woke up in the middle of the night to go to the bathroom. The toilet and shower were in the same space around a corner in my room. While I could have gone in the dark, I decided to use my flashlight to walk around the corner. I turned the corner and startled a 30-cm long centipede that climbed from the floor halfway up the wall before I could comprehend it was the highly poisonous centipede I had been warned about. I turned around and decided not to sleep in the same room. I went outside and down a few rooms to where a friend was sleeping. I figured my knocking would mix with the heavy rain and thunder, so I made sure to knock loudly and consistently until he opened the door. I told him of the centipede and that I was staying on the other mattress in his room for the night. I was sure the centipede wanted a warm, dry place to stay out of the rain as scorpions did, but I refused to share my room with it.

I also learned of the politics of the park management. The boss had future plans that were quite different from those of the long-term volunteers, and he had the power to make waves that could tumble down and crash on his subordinates. It was unfortunate to see such opposite views in the same organization but likely a pattern I will see repeated in the future. The money may have been questionably spent, but the volunteers were happy to work with the animals. I left with wonderful memories of the people I met and the lessons I learned. The animals really were unique, kind, intelligent, and deserving of the best conditions.

10/11/14: I left the park this morning for Vietnam. My last two days at the park involved a lot more animal contact than I was expecting. I took a tiger for a walk, hand fed 4- and 7-month old leopard cubs, rode an elephant through the rain, hand- and mouth-fed giraffes, zebras, deer, and a few animals that I would never go into a cage with, especially gibbons.

Ho Chi Minh, Vietnam

10/12/14: After leaving the Safari Park in the morning, I took my motorbike back to the store, walked to the bus station, traveled by bus for a few hours to Bangkok, jumped into a taxi towards the airport, and checked in five minutes before check-in closed. All that travel took five hours. I slept on the entire plane ride over to Ho Chi Minh, Vietnam's capital. A taxi took me to the apartment belonging to my family friend Kristine.

I needed to be more assertive. I felt the taxi in Vietnam tricked me, because I stayed in the taxi after believing him say he needed to drive around the block after we passed the building accidentally when I should have just stopped him, paid, and walked out. That cost me an extra two dollars. It wasn't much, but it was a matter of principle.

Kristine, her boyfriend, three of her English students, and I went to dinner at a very fancy Loving Hut for delicious, vegan dishes of spiced mushrooms. We strolled through a park afterwards and saw people dancing salsa and tango at night with portable speakers. We ended the night with a drink on a rooftop bar overlooking the city. The traffic was much crazier than in Thailand.

10/14/14: I needed more time than I thought to visit every place I wanted to. I missed my chance to see the tunnels used during the Vietnam War, but I visited the War Remnants Museum. I saw the atrocities and results of Agent Orange that I had never seen before and truly had a hard time looking. I had no idea much of Europe was protesting U.S. involvement and brutality at the time. I had been told the museum was propaganda, but the images were not fake and were truly a difficult and striking learning experience. I then visited a Chinese market district where I did not see another single tourist. The market almost put the Singaporean, 24/7 market to shame in just sheer volume of products. Needless to say, I had two of the best hosts who took me to some of the tastiest restaurants I've experienced so far. Such a short stay, but I enjoyed every moment.

Nepal

After four flights from Ho Chi Minh City to Bangkok to Phuket to Kuala Lumpur to Kathmandu, Nepal, I finally arrived at the volunteer house after a flight delay and long customs line for an on-arrival visa. My host family was extremely kind and gracious. During 24 hours of hectic travel, I learned to stay calm and keep my stress level low, or it would have easily brought my mood down. I have realized I make better decisions when under less stress. The first day I was in the capital, I visited the Monkey Temple where I could enjoy a tremendous view of Kathmandu Valley. I also began Nepali language lessons and hoped to learn enough to be able to communicate with locals. For the first time on my trip, I did not need to plan what to eat, where to sleep, how to go, where to go, and who to speak to. While the convenience came with a price above average, the relaxation was worth it. I did not feel alone. Life was good.

10/16/14: Namaste/hello! I stayed at the volunteer guesthouse, aka a family home, for the whole week. I had language class in the morning and sightseeing in the afternoon. The city itself had terrible traffic and the roads were awful, but my host driver maneuvered the tiny spaces between cars and motorbikes. I would have had a few heart attacks driving myself. At night, the air looked like there was a medium fog, but it was all pollution. Many people wore facemasks just for that. The architecture was amazing as the houses were beautifully constructed and spacious inside. They reminded me of colored Lego pieces scattered over the ground, but none were connected. I had a lot of adventures to look forward to for the next two months. Namaste/bye!

I continued my language and cultural lessons and visited Durbar Square. The idea of "jutho," or impurity of oneself, served sanitary purposes as well as cultural ones regarding death, sharing food, menstruation, and birth. At the house, we did not share food once it or our hands touched our mouth. When it came to drinking water, sometimes there were cups and sometimes not. If not, a large bottle was placed on the table and each person drank from it "waterfall" style, so the bottle never touched the lips. Because the right hand was temporarily jhuto while eating, the left hand lifted the bottle onto the back of the right wrist as a lever and tipped down. My guide was impressed, because I was the first foreigner to do so successfully. Little did he know how I often drank that way from my water bottle back home. I adjusted to eating two meals per day of dal bhat with a small meal in the middle as the locals did. Dal bhat was the local dish of rice, lentil soup, cooked spinach, and other vegetables. Rosie, the teenage house servant of a lower caste, was calling me "brother" which my guide, Yubaraj, said was frequently done in place of names. When the rest of the family called me by the same term, I began to address them with the Nepali words for older/younger brother/sister.

10/19/14: I felt like a child speaking in basic sentences, but after each day, I could speak many basic three-word long Nepali sentences: subject-object-verb and sometimes venturing into a few four-to five-word long phrases I had learned.

I helped peel out enormous grapefruits for 15 minutes with three mothers who then mixed them into a sweet curry. We ate it in two minutes. I ate with my right hand at every meal at the volunteer home. Because I ate primarily only two meals a day, I found I consumed enormous amounts of rice with lentils and curry.

10/20/14: After class, my guides took me sightseeing to Pashupati, a holy location for one's body to be cremated, and later to a giant stupa in the city. A stupa is a Buddhist shrine that helps guide one towards enlightenment. The holy site is a must-visit during the lifetime of a Hindu. I saw my first cremation lighting. The sons walked around the wrapped body of their father three times for Brama, Vishnu, and Shiva before placing a torch on the mouth. After the fire went out and the smoke had blown around those watching including tourists, the ashes were pushed into the Ganges River. This is the same river upstream from where I will see similar ceremonies in Varanasi, India, later in my journey.

This morning at 6am, I went on a nice, hour-long hike with my guide and his friend into the hills. I wore sweats and a t-shirt, so it was not terribly cold.

When I drove in the U.S., I honked on the rare occasion someone did something dangerous or got in my way. Here, people honked all the time but merely as a non-threatening indication to announce they were coming my way.

I found myself on my rest day at the volunteer home. I relaxed and continued reading *American Prometheus* and studying Nepali. I was again conflicted with my own morals and behavior towards the local culture. I discovered I was paying, in part, a fourth of my dues into the pocket of a businessman, the same one whose residence I was staying at and who recently purchased a hotel, a hotel I later found out was to host tourists and volunteers. I came to Nepal to do charitable work, and I was offering my time and funds only to discover much of it going to a businessman.

Every temple and established religious institution I visited turned me away more and more from dogma. I felt my faith stood between myself and Spirit. Any official body or institution in between seemed to ask for money and add ceremonies to make me feel personally valued and unique. This was also troubling in regard to making local friends. I became on guard about locals who, given a period of time, would ask for money. Even this morning, I went on a hike with a friend only to end the outing with tea to discuss his new company in direct competition and cheaper than the one I was working with. Going through these countries opened me up to financial struggle to a degree I had not witnessed before. Back home, financial security seemed more binary. Home or homelessness. A lesser home was more likely a lack of opportunity than laziness. Here, the uniform struggle appeared to be to survive. Granted, the volunteer home was luxury compared to what I saw elsewhere in the city, but the nature of subjectively overcharging through bargaining with a smile was so foreign and distasteful to me. I was happy to be here, but deep down I was bothered. I could not forecast whether my travels in India would be a hoax or genuine. Even the businessman's children here at the volunteer home verbalized they did not care if I liked them. I did feel like a walking dollar sign, because of my skin color even though I, in fact, have little to my name.

10/21/14: The first of five days of Diwali, the Hindu Festival of Lights, just started, so it was decided I spend an extra day in Kathmandu to enjoy it. My days here follow the same schedule of hiking around the edges of Kathmandu Valley up to White Gumba at 5:45am, dal bhat at 10am, class from 11:00am-1:00pm, and lunch when only I ate a meal. The others had only tea and some bread for lunch as I had not adjusted yet to two meals per day. They believe in "dal bhat 24-hour power," or "dal bhat 23-hour power, one-hour sour" as a joke. 2pm-7pm consisted of sightseeing and shopping, 8pm dal bhat, and rest. Side note, bananas here had five times as much flavor as the ones back home.

10/22/14: On the second day of Diwali, many of the dogs were decorated with flower necklaces and paint. Each day, more and more lights go up in celebration. I walked through the local markets at night to see the lights. When walking home, the power went out as it did daily for eight hours, so I walked home in pitch black as there were no motorbikes around me to light the road. Thankfully, I had the flashlight on my phone.

My week in Kathmandu was really an eye-opener. While I was pessimistic before my arrival, I could see now I had simply felt hungry and seemingly isolated. Bhagawan, my driver and guide, had been wonderful to show me the local markets where I bought a solid winter coat he bargained from $65 to $35. The Nepali markets were so much more lively and enjoyable than the touristic Thamel district. The day prior, Yubaraj and Surrender took me to buy a day bag which I bargained from $10.50 to $8.00. While I was intense in my bargaining for two dollars and fifty cents, it did wonders for my self-esteem and understanding of informal markets.

I talked to a shoe salesman last night at the supermarket. He was surprised to hear how much I made as a student at $10/hr, and

I was surprised to hear he makes a little more than $100 per month. What was harder to hear was that he would not marry, because he could not provide for a wife. It was fascinating to me that while we were talking, three other salesmen stayed around to listen. I enjoyed talking with him, because he was genuinely interested in me and not trying to sell me shoes. He asked for my volunteer card and, upon seeing my name, asked which caste I was from. I had to tell him there were no castes in the U.S. and Europe. He said those were good rules. I could not even imagine living in a society which prevented the possibility of success because of a societal rule. One's caste dictated one's work, home, and relationships. It was completely opposite to my understanding of what I could do with my life in the U.S. In addition, I withdrew almost as much cash as I could in one day to pay for my "voluntourism," the combination of tourism and volunteering, as the shoe salesman made over multiple months. That was hard to believe and shocking.

I sat down content and drinking chiyaa which is the Nepali chai made of delicious milk tea with masala spices. I played my favorite Indie music. Something that impressed me was the meticulous dedication to faith Nepali people had. Christians back home seldom talked about their faith daily and attended church once a week. Here, Hindu and Buddhist temples were elaborately decorated with immense detail. I could only imagine the thousands of hours of work required to create them. People visited temples, stupas, and shrines incredibly often. It was a society raised around passionate faith.

10/29/14: I spent six days without WiFi, so I have not updated the blog recently. For three days during the main portion of Diwali, I was at a Happy Home which was sadly ironic. Happy Home was an orphanage where about 15 children ages 4-15 resided. These were children whose parents were too poor to feed and house them. I found it extremely difficult to communicate with them as English proficiency ranged from very little to basic conversation. The children lacked stimulation as many sat around waiting blankly for time to pass until their next chores of cooking and cleaning. There were few toys and objects to play with and two broken computers. There was a TV that attracted most of their attention. I never felt more at a loss with how to interact with children. With the older boys, I played football and cards and talked. All the boys I asked liked science and math, and all the girls liked English. All but one said they dreamed to move to the United States.

The neighbors in the countryside used a wooden lever to pound rice into flour on compacted dirt. Another odd observation was how a local farmer isolated rice kernels from the stalk. He had a machine that rotated and pulled out the kernels. To power it, he hung a bamboo pole with two metal prongs on the power lines running along the road. The prongs were connected to a wire which he split into two ends and placed each open wire into the portable socket of the electric motor attached to a wood plank. The neighbors were indeed living in more impoverished conditions than I was at the orphanage.

My living conditions, I would say, felt truly of the developing world. I was fortunate to have a roof, walls with windows that close, an open toilet, a sink, a cold shower, and a bed. The new part for me was the kitchen where sanitation was at the minimum. I boiled my water to drink although the children drank straight from the tap. Potato peelers were not washed after use. No one washed their hands when preparing food. Hygiene came from soaping up dishes and pots and boiling all food to a degree I trusted was sanitary. The children lived in tiny, bathroom-sized rooms, and I could smell feces as I walk through the hallway. Notions of jutho seemed less prevalent as the kids were barefoot and put their feet and hands everywhere although one girl wouldn't step over my legs while I was stretched out on the floor, because feet are perceived as dirty.

The children lacked stimulation beyond belief as they just sat quietly. The older boys played a poker-like game and bet 5 rupees at a time. Understandably, this was Diwali, so there was no schedule to follow. Yesterday, the boys went fishing, and today, I joined them swimming in the river on clay banks. I played the card game, and the businessman's son I came with relentlessly tried to cheat by fumbling numbers and fabricating winnings. His peers, likewise, peeked constantly at each other's hands and switched cards. Either this was in good fun or it was malicious, but it was exhausting for me to watch their every move. Maybe these were skills that will benefit them in an informal market. Their interactions bordered on the hostile with mild aggression being their way of expressing confidence.

During the evenings of Diwali, groups of children and adults went to different houses like trick-or-treating to dance, sing, provide worship to the gods, and maybe collect donations. One group of adults offered me roti which is fried rice flour mixed with sugar and water. I had it multiple times before that night, but this one tasted bad and right away I knew I would get sick. I did not want to reject their ritual offering, so I ate some of it and walked away to toss the remaining portion. I woke up the following morning with a sore throat and general aches. I slept most of the day, only arising when awoken to participate in the largest ceremony of Brothers and Sisters where they put a flower necklace on me and gave me a large tikka, a colored powder, on my forehead. I barely ate and returned to sleep, unfortunately only to awaken after the children had returned from singing and dancing. I was feeling a little better the next day, but I was still uneasy and uncomfortable with being able to communicate so little with so many children and with seeing them extremely disinterested in playing. To my surprise, those I interacted with the most really seemed sad when I was leaving as I think they were growing accustomed to having me around. As I left the orphanage, a boy asked if I was coming back, and a little girl that seemed distant for the duration of my stay looked genuinely sad when I said I was leaving.

I left for my volunteer project placement in Amarapuri to hopefully have better living conditions and recover. Unfortunately, I was silly upon arrival and misunderstood my new hosts when they said the government gives them filtered water. I drank from the well water storage which gave me a more intense gastrointestinal disturbance all evening and continued into the night. They showed me where the true drinking water was after I asked for clarification, and I progressively improved as the day unfolded. I did not take any medications, because I wanted to try what other travelers had told me: Get sick one time, and then the body can handle local water and food much better. I thought it would be a good idea to get sick before spending more time in Nepal and then in India. I was fortunate to say it was mild, and it only took a few days for my appetite to steadily come back. I later learned it was common knowledge locals could drink well water but not foreigners.

Being there was largely one long, cultural lesson as I interacted with locals and my host family. I went to a cow farm and helped bury a dead cow today. Because the cow is the national animal worshipped by Hindus, they had to wait for a government official to come and acknowledge the death before burying it. The most obvious cultural change was the physical contact between males. Holding hands or arms while conversing was normal. Arms around shoulders or holding hands while walking was also normal. And holding knees while sitting and talking was common, because everyone was considered either brothers or sisters.

I had a knack for picking up on the habits of others. I picked up a Scottish accent when I was hanging out with a Scot in Thailand. Here, I rapidly picked up the tilted head gesture for "yes" and the twist of the hand to add emphasis to my words. I quickly got a crick in my neck from doing it so much unconsciously. On a cultural note, the younger generation liked American music and movies although Bollywood was the most popular. Asok, my host brother and 21-year-old engineering student with great English, told me his generation will not follow traditions as tightly as their parents. For example, Grandfather lost his wife, so he would wear only white for an entire year and would not eat if someone touched him while eating. I ate outside if he was inside. Asok said his generation could not keep these strict traditions up and exposure to Western culture through the Internet and TV does not help.

More people than I expected were respectful and simply curious about me without malicious intent. I knew there would be a tiny number of people who would see me only as a walking dollar sign in developing countries, but my fears prior to visiting were greatly exaggerated. Regardless, I knew these travels were critical for my self-development, they supported every ideal I held as well as my desire to learn from the people I would encounter, and this trip would stay with me for the rest of my life.

Tonight was a fundraiser for two schoolboys who have Hepatitis B, and the entire village of about 400-500 people came to give money and watch dancers and singers. I donated and was told it was a big deal an American gave money as it had never happened before. There was a strong sense of community here, stronger than I had ever seen back home.

In Amarapuri, I am staying with Asok and his family. He was very relaxed and easygoing like me. A few interesting experiences as the day has gone by. I met a blind man who, with the help of a friendly Nepali translator, did not at first believe I was from America. Only after continued talking did he believe me. He felt my hands and arms to envision me. He was making brooms, benches, and just about anything out of bamboo and string. He lost his vision the year I was born and refused any possible corrective surgery, because he was 80 years old and planned to die in the next 10 years. Asok's younger brother ate only rice with milk since he was a child. Now, 15 years old, he looked happier and was more engaging than most Nepali. He liked civil engineering.

I volunteered in a small clinic with the doctor coming once or twice a week. The remainder of the time, different personnel took his place and offered medicine for common ailments. Because government hospitals were bigger and doctors were busier, I could receive more specific training and attention at the village clinic and saw it as an opportunity to learn more about the pharmaceuticals and some of the Ayurvedic drugs. Deepak, one of the clinic personnel, had four bachelor degrees in community health, general health, public health, and family health. He trained doctors and nurses, and I felt great relief when he showed excitement after I asked him to teach me everything.

I felt happier today ("I am feeling very happy today," in Nepali: "ekdam khusi lagyo"), because I was no longer feeling sick, and I had a routine. I watched *Basketball Diaries*, a film taking place in the U.S., with Asok which temporarily took me back to familiar places. It was pleasant to return home mentally every now and then considering I would be living in developing countries for the next three months.

I missed Halloween for the first time in my life. In a few weeks, I will miss my second Thanksgiving and thoughts came of being with my friends in San Diego, California.

I found respectful, trustful behavior in my host family. They were kind, honest, and straight-forward people who reciprocated my eagerness to learn. However, I discovered not to trust everyone I met, such as when one Nepali man working next to the clinic immediately offered me a girl and wanted to take me on his motorcycle for "cultural experiences" or when a co-worker constantly made suspicious jokes and asked for my credit card information. I was never concerned for my safety, because they understood when I dismissed their questions, but it was unusual.

10/30/14: Everybody talked about the Diversity Visa which is a lottery open to every Asian country, except India, to grant up to 50,000 green cards to the United States each year. I had never heard of this program, but I can imagine the yearning when there is a chance of a better life in the United States.

11/11/14: My days were filled with stimulating social interactions. I had not seen any foreigner in two weeks, and many of the Nepali working at the clinic were jokesters. At first, I thought they were serious only to realize later they were pulling my leg. I eventually figured that much of what people said were jokes about me hosting them in America. If I were in their shoes meeting a foreigner, I would probably have said the same things. I just had to laugh, smile, and joke in return. I learned how to play around with words and gestures as a tool to escape what I thought to be the seriousness of their suggestions. At times, the amount of miscommunication resulting from poor language skills frustrated me. I believe my inadequacy in Nepali pushed others to smile and nod blindly just as I also did sometimes rather than clarify or ask them to repeat. These interactions became frustrating when I found out later I learned some Nepali words wrong because of such miscommunication.

At my homestay, I conversed about 15% in Nepali during any given day. My experiences were definitely rural. I cut rice, lifted it onto a tractor, and carried the very heavy bags to a processing mill. I cut sugar cane and ate it raw during the last two days. More than once, I endured several days without Internet, and there had been no hot water since arriving because there was no gas and the heater was broken. The gas shop was closed, because the owner died the day before I arrived and his family was mourning. Since my arrival,

I've already watched at least six funeral processions in the neighborhood.

Many people would wake up at 4-5am to walk. I did this with Baba (Father) once. There were no lights besides the moon, and I tripped on the same speed bump both ways. We sat at the bus stop and waited for my brother and sister to leave on school buses. The fog was intense in the morning, and I could not distinguish trucks from buses. Somehow by only seeing headlights in the fog, my Nepali brother and sister knew which one was a bus and the right bus. It was still dark when I returned to the house around 5:30am to find my host mother whom I called "Shuva-mommy" cleaning bowls for worship that she then placed in a shrine and prayed to. I helped her by bringing up buckets from an outside water tap from which the government supplies drinking water for a small, monthly fee. I filled the buckets and carried them two flights of stairs to the kitchen. Because people did not own large plots of land, homes were typically narrow at the base and 3-5 stories tall including the flat roof for drying clothes.

Shuva-mommy had already milked the cow and begun cooking its milk over a wood fire. An indoor gas stove was used only for smaller pots. Any large quantity of food was cooked over a wood fire, and plastic bags were sometimes used for kindling. Everything I ate with my host family was made at home. Flour was flattened into bread and usually roasted over the fire. We fried bread once for my sister Pratikshya's birthday. I loved jheri which was deep fried flour soaked in sugar water to make a sweet crisp.

Hygiene was different too. I cut lettuce on a cutting board directly on the floor. Many grains and lentils were temporarily kept on cloths on the floor before cooking. Hygiene was resolved by boiling or steaming every piece of food. Nothing was consumed raw. Creativity was involved too. When I bought chotpot, a spicy cereal mix, it was served directly on newspaper or old homework with written math problems and I used a square spoon made of cut cardboard.

Water used for bathing and cleaning dishes came from a well which had a motor suspended in it by a rope which essentially meant unlimited, free water. It took me time to accept trash was tossed everywhere. I once finished eating a candy and put the wrapper in my back pants pocket out of habit to throw it into a trash bin later. My little brother laughed and told me to just toss it on the ground. I was told the lack of education about the environment was at fault. However, people did clean up in front of their homes and shops with small, hand-held brooms. For my host mother, I fashioned a bamboo stick to her hand-held broom made of hay to make a long handled-broom like the ones I was used to. I was proud of my contribution in that she would not have to bend over while cleaning. However, my invention was set aside a week later to reflect a different contribution as it was faster to use the hand-held broom at low level and cover more ground in a single sweep. I learned my lesson to not assume what is used in developed countries is always the best.

I usually ate inside at the table, but today, Grandfather had come in, and the rest of the family showed respect and waited until he finished eating. They did not make me as their guest wait, so they served me first. Shuva-mommy brought me food outside. My typical breakfast was dal bhat, hot milk, water, and homemade yogurt. She made the yogurt by adding a few drops of yogurt to milk and left alone to curdle overnight.

Besides volunteering, I went to a concert with a combination of Nepali pop, folk music, and dance from national artists. Simultaneously, there was a nine-day festival to celebrate the end of the harvest called Ekadashi. I spent the following day with Asok and his friend nicknamed Punks Not Dead. The latter mastered the game of fishing a ring around a soda bottle, so we won five large bottles. We ate jheri, chotpot, peanuts, oranges, and pani puri which are fried balls filled with vegetables and a spicy water mix. The highlight was seeing cars and motorcycles driven with no hands at high speed in a nearly vertical cylinder. I also went swimming with them in a small river nearby. Few Nepali knew how to swim, so no one entered the big river as the current was strong and people frequently drowned. Other times after volunteering, a large group of my Nepali brothers and sisters, actually siblings and cousins, would spend time together every night listening to music, playing cards, and drinking milk tea.

Tomorrow, I will travel to Chitwan National Park for a three-day jungle safari followed by a five-day trek to Annapurna with a day of rest in Pokhara afterwards. Then, I will return to Amarapuri to teach English.

Locals commented the government was incredibly corrupt. All the money from international sports, such as when Nepal beat the U.S. and many other countries in cricket, disappeared into the pocket of the Head of Sports instead of developing the country's infrastructure.

11/12/14: I stayed at the jungle resort in Sauraha in Chitwan National Park, enjoying huts by the river with two other volunteers from Germany and Australia. They were the first foreigners I met in two and a half weeks.

The place was extremely calm and peaceful. I enjoyed listening to the birds, admiring the buffalo grazing by the river, and watching the water rush by. I conversed with the locals in Nepali, truly prompting more conversation, insight, and humor. They immediately called me the "brother of a different color." One night, the boss shared his hospitality with us as we sat by the fire and watched the local people, the Tharu, perform their cultural dance. I was happy and feeling completely 100% myself, free of any rules but my own. The culture I was in dictated my behavior, and my personal morals guided my decisions.

My itinerary for the next four days included elephant trekking, a jungle walk, canoeing, a visit to the elephant breeding facility, bird watching, a cultural show, Nepali dancing, and more which I had yet to find out. It was very exciting to be there, yet I missed my Nepali family's company, and I knew I would miss it after leaving Nepal.

11/13/14: I started the day's activities with a 90-minute elephant trek through the jungle, and I felt the massive beast carry five people across land and water. Afterwards, a half-hour canoe ride on the river gave us the opportunity to watch many birds and crocodiles resting in the afternoon sun. We were given sticks in case crocodiles attacked our canoe, and I trusted the technique would work if needed. Then we had a three-hour walk through the jungle for a chance to view tigers and the endangered, one-horned rhino endemic only to Nepal. Unfortunately, we were in the rainy season and the grass was too tall to see them clearly. We did spot many monkeys and deer. We ended the hike at the elephant breeding center where we were quickly told to run away back across an empty field to escape a wild, male elephant which had come to mate with the domestic female, but breeding center workers had scared him away in our direction. Overall, I was overjoyed with my time at this resort. It was relaxing and the company was phenomenal.

11/14/14: Some of us went on a walk to go birdwatching at 7am. Because of its extremely varying topography between India and China with low and high altitudes, Nepal has almost 10% of the world's bird species living there. We saw egrets, herons, storks, an eagle carrying a snake, kingfishers, and others. A kingfisher, with its small and bright blue colors, had a frog in its mouth and tried to kill it by whacking it repeatedly against a log, and all we could hear was "thump thump thump." Later this morning, I went to share in an elephant bath. A local provided the experience as a gift as it was not initially planned for me. While the elephants' treatment was questionable in Asian captivity when compared to Western standards of animal treatment, it still is an experience to be sitting directly on top of a huge beast and have it spray water in the air.

I left Chitwan National Park with two German volunteers to organize our upcoming trek with other folks from Pokhara, a tourist city south of the Annapurna region.

11/16/14: I am leaving Pokhara with four German volunteers, a guide, and a porter towards Poonhill. It will be a five-day trek during which we will be staying at tea houses along the way. I had been looking forward to this hike which turned out to be the most exciting part of my stay in Nepal. Annapurna is one of the most beautiful regions of Nepal to trek in.

I am spending my first night in a tea house with Yubaraj, "Ma-nose," Max, Anna, Sabrina, and Nele. Even if guest houses had WiFi, the speed was so slow that some would say it is just not working. I clocked a 0.02 MB upload speed. It was still an amazing way for me to learn how to be friendly with people on a human level in an entirely effortless way. Two Argentinian girls at the jungle resort were courted by the locals, and they confided in me afterwards how unappealing a particularly overzealous Nepali was with them although he did have a great singing voice. I could be just myself without trying and have a fantastic time. My company was extremely pleasant and entertaining. I found we got along well comparing cultural artifacts, be they music, politics, entertainment, or history. We were accompanied by a Chinese man who contributed his cultural background. I found myself to be much more social with people than I had ever been with before. I felt so happy and at peace internally. Life truly could not be any better.

Today was the third day of trekking the Poonhill loop. The first day was spent hiking uphill to a tea house. Yesterday, we trekked stairs for seven hours up the mountain until the next guest house. This morning, we left at 5am to walk 45 minutes up Poonhill itself to watch the sunrise light the snow-capped mountain tops around 6:30am. I wore plastic bags over my feet to keep them protected from the wind. Without them, my toes would have frozen even more.

After we returned and had breakfast, we headed out in the chilly mountain air to our next mountain guest house five hours away. The following morning, I sat in the dining area of our guest house atop a hill in the Annapurna mountain range. I awoke at 5:45am to watch the sunrise light up the morning sky. It was cold again, but I really did not mind. My toes and fingers were chilled. I could have had a hot tea, but I really did not mind without it. The emerging view of a mountain village was soon defined by the majestic rising of light that happens daily, but I often failed to appreciate due to hardly ever allocating time for it. I was left completely alone with my thoughts, and I was so grateful they found me at peace. I stared at the sunrise as long as possible to burn it into my memory. It was cold, perhaps -5 degrees C or 23 degrees F, but I would not have given up my seat for anything.

11/20/14: The five days went by so quickly. The hiking was warm midday and barely negative temperature in the early morning. We trekked from village to village and stopped at small hotels to eat and sleep. We went swimming in an ice-cold creek which counted as one shower. We encountered two traffic jams on the way. One, at 5am on the morning of reaching Poonhill where about 200 foreigners woke up to see the sun rise. Two, a bunch of donkeys stopped moving in the middle of the path, so we had to shoo them aside.

Overall, I had not laughed so hard and so much with people until this trip. Everything that happened between English, Nepali, and German was absolutely hilarious. We also tried different foods every meal including a Snickers spring roll. My fellow travelers had a chicken killed for them last night. The chickens we saw wandering the mountainside were enormous as they seemed to be a cross between chickens and eagles. I stayed a day in Pokhara with the other volunteers before we split up and left to our individual projects.

11/22/14: We visited the International Mountain Museum which explained the history of the many local, ethnic mountain people and showed each people in native attire. It also compared mountaineering in Japan, Slovakia, and other countries. The museum's goal was to produce a global community and promote camaraderie on the mountaintops. There were also sections on climate change and the biodiversity crisis due to human trash and environmental degradation. The Himalayas provide a central point of water for the continental region, so too much mountain ice melting would cause drastic events.

After the museum, we went shopping and dined with the same Chinese traveler, Yu Shu, whom we met three times while trekking and once more randomly in the city. Something similar occurred with an American couple whom we encountered multiple times over multiple days on the trail. It's a small world for travelers. In Thailand, I met again a German in the city days after we took a bus together. I had so much fun that night laughing, drinking, eating, and taking photos with all of them. I really enjoyed talking with the Germans and learning about their lifestyle and culture and just how different it was to the United States. Our Nepali hosts, Yubaraj, Ma-nose, and Shanti, were all hilarious. I worked on treating everyone equally and indiscriminately. As said in the book *Into the Wild*[8] by Jon Krakauer, "happiness [is] only real when shared," and I am at my happiest when I share it evenly with everyone.

On the mountain top, I used all the Japanese I learned in one year during high school to speak with a Japanese couple and explain I had traveled to Nihon (Japan) and describe the places I visited and how much I enjoyed them. I stepped out of my comfort zone to engage in this discussion, only to be rewarded with a small yet delightful exchange. Before this trip, I treasured strong, personal connections. I always felt those connections were limited to my closest network of friends, but I now felt I could now extend them to business, social, and other personal encounters. Talking about life habits, family, or culture quickly built relationships. When this happened, I always left with a smile on my face and a new lesson learned.

How things have changed! I returned to my host family's house in Amarapuri and talked to my younger, Nepali brother, Aditya, about teaching at his K-10 private school.

11/23/14: Today was my first day of teaching. I taught mathematics at 2nd, 3rd, 6th, and 7th grade levels and two science classes for 10th grade for a total of six classes. The students were smiling and laughing and extremely enthusiastic and high-spirited. They invited me to sing and dance and asked openly for me to teach in their classroom even if it meant replacing their scheduled teacher. I couldn't help but laugh when 20 children pushed me into their classroom. Aditya said my hands were shaking the first day, but only because I lacked the trust and confidence in my newfound teaching role. As the days continued, I became more comfortable leading a classroom in discussion, lecture, or interactive problem solving depending on the class level and topic. My method was to walk into a classroom, greet them as they stood, say "Namaste," and then have a student show me their assigned lesson for the day. I would spend a minute or two overlooking the lesson and started teaching. I explained topics in depth and with a variety of real-life applications of what they were learning and why it was important.

11/25/14: I lectured in seven classes from 3rd to 10th in the subjects of science, mathematics, social studies, or health. My only break was for tea and chow mein for 30 minutes. It was a lot of fun, and I really enjoyed the company of the students and teachers. Everyone was friendly and smiling. The children were completely different from those I encountered at the Happy Home one month ago.

11/26/14: Every morning, I was greeted by all 200-300 students which means I said good morning or namaste that many times.

I appreciated that the students all wore a uniform. The school principal said some students came from poorer socioeconomic statuses than others, so the uniform eliminated potential discrimination and equalized everyone. Most students were of the highest caste, but that did not mean each family was wealthy.

In class 4, one child hit another in the neck. I separated the two, and the whole class was telling me to beat him and asking why I wasn't. I simply said I wouldn't, and their bewilderment quieted them enough for me to continue teaching.

In classes 6 and 7, I taught African geography and why much of the continent was currently undeveloped in comparison to Europe. At the end, one student asked if I had ever been to Africa.

I said "No, but I would like to."

He then asked me how I, if I had not been, knew about Africa, and I had to explain that I learned it in school just like him. I smiled as I could see his mind trying to understand before he thanked me and walked away.

Because my strengths were in science and health, the longest and most knowledge-based lectures I taught compared the impact of health and nutrition in Nepal and the U.S. I also taught stages of country infrastructure development and the importance of a government's relationship with its people. A healthy relationship encourages debates which stimulate citizen feedback. I lectured on civil, legal, and moral duties and stated that being involved never seemed more pressing. This lesson, although never formally taught in my education, acted as a personal trigger to appreciate that becoming a political bystander only benefits those writing and passing the laws. Some say a relationship is not healthy unless there are disagreements. Compliance is comparable to giving up. In the same way, I thought too many people became compliant with their government. A healthy government-citizen relationship develops when citizens support their role through voting, being involved, and protesting if necessary. I felt too many of my friends and I had become compliant and stopped striving for a better society as is our civil duty.

I had a blast with students. I taught lessons I had never learned in school but rather through life experience. I quickly learned how to teach and control a classroom as well as how to formulate my ideas using language that was age- and crowd- appropriate. I enjoyed teaching very much, but it was exhausting to come up with lesson plans on the spot. I developed much more respect for teachers.

11/30/14: After school on Friday, I stayed with a teacher, Rashmi, and her family. They believed that the "guest is God." I was treated the kindest I had ever been, and I will never forget that. After good conversations with her family, I stayed the night. Her three-year-old son was a big fan of Power Rangers, so he would watch episodes and then try to reenact characters by attacking his father.

The following morning, I met with Sabrina, another volunteer, who had come from Kathmandu. We went with two teachers to watch the river and have dinner in a restaurant. My social programs with Tikaram, Jai, Hindrijit, and Sabrina always involved some drinking to minor intoxication. We always went to obscure restaurants to sit in individual huts, and then we had to drive back at night in the cold. They were conditioned to it, so we drove no more than 30 kmph on our return. Drinking and driving is bad, but drinking and driving slowly on a Nepali highway is apparently safe.

Going out was good English practice for the two teachers. I read through a few textbooks at the school and found many English mistakes, so it was no wonder many students struggled with grammar. Afterwards, we returned home to find the family together and cooked pakoda (fried vegetables). Having the whole family together was vastly entertaining and secretly reminded me of my Thanksgiving dinners in the U.S.

12/3/14: Sabrina and I left at 6am to go to Lumbini, the birthplace of Buddha, where we met two more volunteers. I was ecstatic to visit the place, because every Nepali was very proud of having the true birthplace of Buddha in their country. It was discovered only about 100 years ago and marked by Asoka tower, a world heritage. There were temples from many Asian countries, Germany, France, Canada, and others, but none from the U.S. as I was expecting considering the U.S. likes to be an international role model. We took a local bus which turned out a much better experience than the larger, more spacious, tourist buses. Local buses were smaller, more crowded, and more interactive as I had people squeeze around me and even had a man sit in a six-inch space next to me meaning he was sitting halfway on me for the remainder of my trip. I loved how every couple of hours, the bus would pull over on the side of the highway and everybody exited. We went in the bushes to go to the bathroom as the rest of traffic drove going by. Men went right by the road and women walked a bit further into the bushes.

Sabrina said she met a Nepali who only took tourist buses because, "If it crashed, everybody cared."

A local bus though may receive less attention if it crashed. This made me very grateful when I stepped onto a local bus and saw an old driver, because that meant he survived this long. Then I became worried again, jokingly, when I changed buses to find a young driver.

Everything in Nepal was sized for Nepali people. In Nepal, I stood above the crowd at 6 feet tall. This meant I hit my head on the doorway in my home for the first few days before I remembered to duck. I also hit my head in the same spot after returning from trekking, because I had forgotten about it. I hit my head in the local bus upon entering and again on the handlebar that hung from the ceiling. I hit my head after leaving the bathroom at the school. Thankfully, at least my bed was long enough. Asok was about my height, but I am sure he already learned to duck his head.

12/4/14: Today was a singing and dancing competition among 17 schools. It was scheduled at 10am, but it started at 1pm instead. I joked that when I would go out for one hour with three friends, I counted one hour each, so we would stay for four hours. That was just how Nepali time worked. I was invited as a special guest to sit on the stage alongside principals from other schools during introductions, and later I came back on to dance while my younger brother's friend sang my favorite Nepali song, "Resham Firiri." Feedback on my dancing varied widely. The school's dancing instructor described it as "amazing and captivating."

The principal at Amar English Boarding School stated, "It's clear you have no talent, but good attempt."

Our school brought a boy singer, a girl singer, and two girl dancers who won 1st, 2nd, and 4th places respectively, so we were all very proud of them. I left at 4pm to teach English at another school to stress the importance and how-to of learning English in today's world. I told the story of my most memorable night in Nepal and had the whole room laughing for 20 minutes. I learned afterwards they may have understood only half of what I said as many were educated in government schools where education was of poorer standards than private schools.

12/5/14: Time flew by. I tried to spend as much time as I could with my family as I wanted to remember them as much as possible. I could only hope to return one day and see my brothers and sisters again, knowing that by the time I return, some of them would likely have had arranged marriages. Today was my last day volunteering at the school. They gave me a farewell ceremony and a wooden carving of Nepal in front of the whole school. Half a dozen teachers each put a red tikka on my forehead, gave me flowers, and a white cloth around my neck. The dance teacher invited me to dance in front of everyone, and I had all the students screaming with delight when I started. Later, a teacher gave me a dhaka topi which is the national hat attire worn by most men. It was a very hearty and enthusiastic way to send me off as everyone was laughing and taking pictures. After that, I left to see class 10 to say goodbye and sing my favorite song and say goodbye.

12/9/14: Before I came to Nepal, I listened to a mechanical engineer in California who had designed a fuel-efficient stove with a chimney so that people in Nepal would not have to inhale toxic particulates, black carbon, and carbon monoxide which are a serious health issue. My host family only received a gas stove 10 years ago. Electricity was not present in Nepal until 30 years ago. Cell phones suddenly became commonplace recently. The private market grew, but the public sector was very slow to provide services to the population. The engineer mentioned Nepal was one of the poorest countries. It was surprising that the government was poor as I learned it neither taxed people nor provided a constitution for government since the monarchy was overthrown seven years ago. In the capital, Kathmandu, people in the capital were rich relative to those in the rural countryside. Many people had motorcycles, nice clothes, cell phones, etc. A Nepali said no one in the country was without food. There were beggars, but they were all Indian. The Nepali had an extremely low image of Indians as "thieves and a dirty, mean people," whereas "the Nepali were all honest and kind." I was surprised to hear that as I have many kind, Indian friends in the U.S.

I stayed the evening with Rashmi again for dinner and tea, and it made her family very happy. Again, they believed the "guest is God," so I was treated with the most respect and consideration. They owned very little, but they bought me cheese, because I had mentioned once I had not had it in a long time. It was the first real cheese I had since I began traveling, and it was delicious. I spoke with her mother in their living room-bedroom-playroom-study space, and I was surprised afterwards to realize I had a whole conversation about my family, my travels in Nepal, and upcoming India trip entirely in Nepali. The same goes for the teachers at school and my Nepali host family. I understood a lot more than I expected when they spoke Nepali which left me quite pleased.

Being vegetarian was very easy. Meat was only eaten on occasion or every now and then if desired. When I told them I was vegetarian, in Nepali of course, people were agreeable, asked why, and that was it. In the U.S. over the years, every single time I declined meat, the situation suddenly transformed into an interrogation where none of my answers were good enough. That made me realize the U.S. has a strong meat culture, and people would criticize often negatively anyone or anything different from what they know regardless of its significance. Nobody cared here. The same thing was true for clothing. It was not well regarded to wear the same clothes more than two days in a row in the United States. In Nepal, nobody cared. In fact, I saw most people wear the same clothes for many days in a row. Then it became a question of hygiene. Fashion and style which I saw criticized back home were replaced to make room for practicality.

My Nepali family bought gas a week ago, and with that came hot water!! If I knew cold water was my only option, I could wash in cold water. However, if I knew I was going to have hot water soon, I couldn't take freezing showers. This fact alone was worth its own paragraph.

I woke up to go running and do push-ups at 4:40am with Asok. I could hear Grandfather blasting the radio music downstairs already. It did not wake me up as the house was concrete and acted as a good sound insulator. When we came back at 5:10am and the sun had not risen yet, we were playing music loudly from our phones, but it did not matter. Everyone was already awake either working or getting ready for school. Often, I would be the last one up when I awoke at 7:30am.

Everything was hot-wired. I was used to plugs and things, but I saw people tying wires together for rice machines, lights, and speakers. Not very safe, but it worked most of the time. Very innovative and creative.

As for voluntourism, I finally understood how it worked. It was helpful to pay a company to organize everything if a traveler was unsure about a new country. By now, I knew everybody and where and how to volunteer and how to move around, so I could do it again for 20% of what I paid. Oddly, the owner told me he barely made it by this year on volunteers' funds. He was taking care of 47 children in homes around the country and did his best to feed, clothe, and educate them even to higher standards than their peers. The money I paid went towards their care-taking. So, which to choose? Come to Nepal to be a tourist and miss all the culture and people by indulging in the natural beauty and activities or come to have an experience by volunteering and giving back? The tourists I met who had come to party in Nepal were most certainly missing out on the culture. I would recommend to simply walk into any village and express interest in volunteering rather than paying a company to organize it all. Either way, great experiences lay ahead of any trip here, and the Nepali are always incredibly nice and gracious. Last cool fact for now: if I mix milk and water, a duck can separate the two and drink only the milk.

I left Amarapuri to go rafting for three days. Then I returned to Kathmandu for a rest day before flying out to India for a month.

On my second day of rafting, I sat in a tent by the river. I ate and drank quite well with my hosts, Santosh and Deepak. We warmed up by a campfire the last night and shared some of the local drink called rakshi. I was surprised to learn about their marriages. They looked younger than me, but both were in their mid-20s and married with children. Santosh married at 20 and had a child at 22.

"Happiness [is] only real when shared." I felt down and alone at times, but I enjoyed what I learned and whom I met. My hosts would not willingly sit at the table with me the first night. I was a customer in their eyes, but it felt strange to sit alone while they talked by the fire. Still, I imagine I would sometimes like some peace and quiet.

It was the morning of my third day of rafting. The first two days were action-packed, and today was just cruising in the sun on the smooth river. It was equally cold both times since there was little sunlight in the valley between hills. Yesterday was very fun though. The guide told me to jump into the water as we were entering some new rapids. I was hesitant not knowing if he was joking or if there were rocks, but he was adamant when I asked him to repeat. Without thinking, I dropped my paddle and leapt into the freezing water in my life jacket and immediately began smiling and laughing as I bobbed up and down the rapids for 10 minutes as I watched the raft go its way and I went my way. I kept swimming around mostly to keep warm as the river moved quite fast. The water was very cold, but I was laughing and hooting the whole time that I did not feel cold until I jumped back into the raft. I rowed hard to stay semi-warm afterwards.

Life was about enjoyment, and I found I was learning how to enjoy it more. I imagined it would become increasingly important upon arriving in India to maintain low stress levels. I practiced being more calm and assertive and reduce my stress as I bargained in the streets. I was used to buying at low prices only what I needed and really liked, so I had to change and be flexible if I did not get the exact price I wanted and had to be ready to walk away. I was slightly fatigued of developing countries, but excitement and eagerness to meet people and learn new things always replaced those feelings.

I finished rafting today. Because there was more sunlight before the valley narrowed, I went upriver with another tourist and my two guides whom I knew quite well after two days. The water was calm and we appreciated the sun until someone had the idea to splash and push the others in. It was a relaxing way to spend one of my last days in Nepal. Afterwards, I hopped on a local bus and arrived in

Kathmandu at night. The last day was for doing laundry and catching up on my email, journal, and social media as I finally had good WiFi.

12/11/14: I walked in the local districts of Kathmandu like I owned the place. It was good to feel that confidence again instead of feeling like the lost, new guy in town. I went to the Royal Palace and visited where the royal family was killed in June 2001. It was a short glimpse into recent Nepali history. After the killings, Maoists and Nepali fought for control and tens of thousands died. January 22 was the deadline to have a constitution finally proclaimed, and I really hoped they would agree on one or there might be more protests.

I helped cook dinner with the neighbor as both the house worker and host mother were on their periods, and it was forbidden for them to be in the kitchen during that time because of jhuto, a concept from one of my first Nepali lessons. The mother called me to go to the kitchen to pour milk for her children and lock the kitchen door as she would not enter.

I was incredulous I still had so much travelling ahead of me. India felt like a giant wall between me and the developed world, but I knew I had to experience it. I was finding myself more and more comfortable here.

12/12/14: I flew to Varanasi, India, today. I already missed my Nepali host family that really had become my second family back in Amarapuri. I would soon miss my friends in Kathmandu that showed me the city and shared their humor with me. I do plan to return to Nepal someday.

My final thoughts were the following: the Nepali people were extremely genuine and honest. Out of the two months, only two individuals made me feel uncomfortable. People worked very hard and were very happy. The culture was family-oriented, meaning parents stayed with the children and often had cousins nearby that were equally called "brother" and "sister." Even strangers in Nepal called each other those terms of endearment to foster a positive community. It was enjoyable to travel. The country was developing rapidly despite a challenging government situation. Nepal has already changed rapidly in the last decade, and it should look vastly different when I return one day. India is going to be a vastly new experience.

Similar Differences

India

My driver picked me up from Varanasi Airport, and we arrived at the hotel two hours later due to traffic and getting lost on the way. For the first three weeks in India, I had planned to hire a driver to show me around and introduce me to the country. He had driven over 900 kilometers to pick me up, and our trip involved returning slowly westwards, day by day, back to his home region. I am a bit anxious after he warned me about the numerous cheaters I might encounter but also very excited to be in India and to have a reliable driver since his agency was recommended to me by an Indian friend back in the U.S. Japan and Singapore had very good roads. Thailand had good roads that were not crowded and easy to ride a bike on. Vietnam had nice roads in the city but overcrowded with bikes. Nepal had few good roads with only courageous drivers. India won above all others with good, overcrowded roads and drivers who followed few rules.

I enjoyed a meal at a local Indian restaurant that was delicious and priced very reasonably versus the expensive, foreigner restaurant that sold less yummy and more conventional Western or continental food. I played with fire a bit as I intentionally drank the local water with dinner instead of bottled water. My driver said it was good water...for him. I was determined to strengthen my body, because what didn't kill me would only make me stronger. I didn't become sick after one cup of local water that night, so I went back the next night and dared having two cups of local water with dinner. For dessert, my driver bought a leaf for me from a street vendor that was filled with a supari nut, sauces, gooey paste, and spices and wrapped up into a triangle. Nothing seemed more natural than that. I later discovered online this was called paan and was highly carcinogenic.

12/13/14: My first day in Varanasi started with a little over an hour-long boat ride at 6:15am with a German guy who came along with my driver and I all day, and it was all jolly good fun. Our boat guide took us by the major ghats (steps) leading down into the Ganges River and gave us the history on many of the buildings on the waterfront. We returned to eat a full breakfast. I ate so much by then since my diet had shifted from three to two meals per day. I had two enormous, delicious pancakes with bananas and honey, and a big omelette. We strolled towards the ghats to watch cremations. We later found Kashi Vishwanath Temple, one of the holiest sites in the city, but didn't have our passports as identification to enter, so we had to walk back to the hotel to fetch them. It was a discovery to walk barefoot through the narrow alleyways filled with stores and life with roaming cows, dogs, puppies, and goats. Many monkeys were scattered over the city rooftops. The hotel staff protecting us during breakfast by scaring away the thieving monkeys with sticks. I was close to being a fecal expert as there was so much everywhere that I could practically say which cows were healthy and which ones were not. Regardless, I was constantly stepping over fresh and old piles.

At the temple, we had to wait an hour to touch a holy stone of Shiva which took less than 5 minutes. The architecture was stunning yet simple, and unfortunately cameras were prohibited. We stopped for a lassi at a special lassi place for foreigners. I had a saffron cashew nut lassi. It was delicious and a bit too sweet. During the 30 minutes we sat there, three groups carried dead bodies covered in cloth past us. It was expensive to be burned at this holy city: 3500 INR ($56) for a wood fire and 500 INR ($8) for an electric fire in a crematory. I saw one face that was uncovered but otherwise saw no corpses, only fires. The water was clean of debris as far as I could see. Children played cricket on the nearby ghats. During lunch, an old lady fell unconscious for a few minutes at the nearby table amidst her concerned companions, and I thought she had died. I was wrong, thankfully.

The city was even more magical at night. It was neither as dirty nor had as many beggars as I had been warned. It was crowded, but I felt comfortable walking around. Perhaps I was getting used to these conditions, and I found it all very beautiful and peaceful. Beggars were mostly on the waterfront.

They were mostly mothers holding babies and saying, "No money, only milk," prompting me to fill up an empty nursing bottle at the store.

At Lumbini, a traveler had told me that it was a scam as they returned to the store and sold the milk back. The same scam went for children in "need" of textbooks. Most hassling came from every other Indian offering boat rides or trading goods. At night, the offerings were all sorts of drugs. One guy offered his services as barber before shaking my hand and refusing to let go. He started to massage my hand and said he was also a masseur, so I tugged my hand away. Needless to say, I turned down many offered hands after that.

12/14/14: Humor section: I saw a t-shirt that said, "French America," and had a giant British flag below it. Always trust Asia to make the best shirts. Playboy was an entertainment brand I saw on trucks, bikes, earrings, shirts, bracelets, flip flops, and some people did not know what it was or did not care. Still a funny brand to see surprisingly often.

Health section: My driver bought a second paan for me which made me constantly spit red. It was the reason why so many sides of buildings and roads were stained red.

Covered bodies in Varanasi were nothing compared to what awaited us this morning. We were driving to the city of Khajuraho which turned out to be an 11-hour ordeal and still faster and more reliable than trains when we saw a crowd of people around a fallen bike. I scanned the ground and found two, separate brain hemispheres on the pavement and the body pooling out blood. My driver said more than half of people die because of road accidents. Whether that was true or not, it was his impression of how grave road accidents were in the state.

Civil rights: I saw a dog kicked yesterday. Another man hit another dog with a four-foot bamboo stick as hard as he could, because the dog was approaching the table. It explained why the dogs were so frightened of people and fought amongst themselves much more than with people. An analogy of power dynamics between social classes could be applied here.

Sports: Besides children playing cricket on the ghats, I played a game of chess with a few Indians. What I soon found out was that it was group chess of four versus four as most of my moves came from my teammates. The game ended in a draw.

Culture section: I watched part of a Hindi action film of a robot cop shooting people. Likely because I hadn't seen action films in so long, I was confused why he had to kill them and was disturbed enough to want to change the channel. The same was true for a few minutes of a familiar American movie where killing people occurred repeatedly, and I wasn't enjoying the film as I would before in the U.S. I found it bizarre how my tastes changed so quickly and that they even had changed at all. With some knowledge of Japanese, Thai, and Nepali, I could speak a few Hindi words to get around, but it was different enough to cause confusion that I had to rely on my driver to speak for me.

People section: Should people donate to beggars? Westerners often did out of guilt or empathy, and beggars targeted those feelings. There were a multitude of scams, so was it best to disregard everyone or pick and choose one or two? To disregard everyone was to stop seeing them as human beings and begin to see nuances. Sometimes people gave money to make themselves feel less guilty rather than truly caring about helping the child or mother. I read articles supporting not giving as it would not help the local economy, yet people always felt a need to support those in need. Was that feeling always felt every time people saw a beggar in the developed world? I heard most agreed it was better to give food or clothes directly instead of money which could be pocketed, used for other things, or handed over to someone profiting off the beggars. Food for thought.

12/17/14: My driver and I left for Khajuraho. It was a very small city but full of beautifully constructed temples that took many decades and over 15,000 people to build. Just as we were about to drive towards Orchha, I encountered two Swiss-Germans and an Italian lady were all about to take a tuk-tuk to a train to another tuk-tuk to reach Orchha. I invited them to join in my car since I was going to the same place. We had a great car ride full of good conversations and laughter then had dinner together. We parted ways the morning after I visited the fort. The building was just magnificent with its sandstone structures. My driver and I left early to reach Agra before dark. Apparently after dark, bandits hold up at gunpoint any car on the road and police won't venture into the countryside. Trucks can get through but only in a caravan of trucks that wouldn't stop for anything.

12/19/14: In Agra, artwork on the Taj Mahal palace was built with all white marble carvings beautifully inlaid with colored stones. It was very beautiful especially in contrast with the red sandstone of adjacent buildings and the green lawns.

I am in my hotel in Ranthambore. I became sick just before leaving Varanasi and am finally feeling good six days later. My judgement may be affected by my illness, but this trip in India so far has been an ongoing experience of contrasts. The artwork and architecture were stunning and unique without a doubt. Perhaps my patience for poor infrastructure was running low, but I found it frustrating when some of the nicer, tourist hotels frequently failed to have hot water. TV channels were nearly all in Hindi with unknown repeats on English speaking channels. WiFi was slow. Traveling alone, being sick, and hopping between the car and hotels was no fun either. My driver spoke little English, so any topic beyond his understanding elicited a "Yes, yes sir."

Facilities were lacking at every single hotel I visited thus far. I felt most hotels tried to cheat me for some service whether it was charging for free wi-fi or included breakfast, or pressuring me with dubious questions and ignoring me when I asked them why they asked. It struck me as dishonest and mischievous. Smiles were a job contract requirement but little more. Customer service did not seem to exist. Cities were dirty, smells were overwhelming, and people stared at me everywhere. Cows, buffalo, dogs, pigs, goats, and their respective bodily functions filled the streets. Add stronger petrol fumes, smells of tobacco and paan emanating from the red stains spat out, and muddy trash smashed into the red dirt. Beggars were always present. I thought ignoring worked, but one child knocked and shook the car for two minutes before I told him no and he walked away. Persistency was a tool. So was loud volume and aggressive facial expressions. I do not use these tools to meet my needs, but I understood that desperation caused that behavior which I found to prevail here. Poverty was not a culture shock after Nepal, but the additional dishonesty felt unsettling. People were dishonest, because dishonesty was rewarded. Police and governments were corrupt, because corruption was possible. Good behavior was rare only because it was difficult to make ends meet when surrounded by people who cheated to survive. I still felt optimistic about people. In Nepal, poverty did not cause the desperation I saw in India where overcrowding turned people hostile and aggressive for resources.

I became tired of being targeted as a tourist, tired of being seen as a toy with greetings as a game, tired of being disrespected by many standards, and tired of being stared at. It was bearable in Nepal, but it was much worse in India. Positive interactions with people were hard to find and rare enough that I could feel the desperation as well. It was stifling. Period. The structure of this tour was also too isolating, touristic, and removed. Yes, I was traveling alone, but driving for hours almost every day was not a vacation. 5% of my time was worthy sightseeing with 95% of my time being a hellish wait for the 5%. To top it all, I haven't had a good, hot shower yet despite the fancy hotels.

I went on two jeep safaris today. One at 7am and another at 3pm. I saw so many animals and more species than in Nepal. We spotted a baby owl, a baby crocodile 12 inches long, huge "deer" that were not quite deer, parakeets, green pigeons, wild boar, peacocks, monkeys, and more. Many people came for days and never saw a tiger, but my jeep was lucky this morning as an adult came walking within ten feet of our open jeep. I was a bit worried as nothing was between it and myself. The tiger was walking along the road, and we watched for at least 10 minutes before it departed.

In a village, I met an old grandfather who was mute and only spoke via hand gestures. I was the first foreigner he had ever seen.

He had never seen a TV. It was a hilarious conversation, because I could speak more with him through hand gestures than I could with those surrounding us. My driver also helped translate where I could not understand. It was a bizarre yet memorable conversation.

12/26/14: In Bundi, I saw two step wells; the Queen's narrow step well and the other being the large, four-directional step well I really wanted to see. An Indian asked me to take his photo. I enjoyed watching kites being flown from many of the rooftops and saw several kites stuck on telephone lines instead of tied shoes as in the U.S. In the city palace, paintings struck me much more than the architecture for their intricacy, quality, and sheer volume painted over 300 years ago.

I talked with a good, honest man at my hotel in Bundi tonight who reinforced my idea that education matters. People were learning their aggression was disliked and gradually becoming ineffective. He mentioned Prime Minister Modi was making huge changes and he felt the country will be much better in five years. I am having dinner in a big hall, my sole companions being my food, my beer, and my ice cream. Writing in this diary was clearing my head of my negative thoughts. In the U.S., my family was preparing to get together for the holidays, and I was alone in India. I hoped to video-call them soon. This was an odd time in my travels. It was the first time I felt so alone and isolated from friends and family. I would have enjoyed being on my couch back home watching movie after movie, but then I thought every experience here was new for me. Whether good or bad, I was learning and becoming the stronger and more confident person I wanted to be.

Today was my first day without any stomach illness, respiratory infection ignored, after nearly two weeks with diarrhea or upset stomachs between Nepal and India. It humbled me to see the power of my health over every aspect of my life, one reason I initially found a strong interest in medicine.

My day consisted of calling home, visiting the city palace of Udaipur, and playing cards with Hakum, my driver, for over an hour as the sun went down over the lake. I had spent so much money just to be here, but my happiest memories arose from a few dollars spent here or there. The other 90% of my expenses were for just room and transport. This was a unique manner of travel. I had a lot of time to be alone with my thoughts.

My breakfast at my hotel in Udaipur was by far the best I've had in India. They offered Nutella, cereal, hot milk, honey, juice, coffee, peanut butter, butter, toast, mango juice, and the neon, red jam that I could only bizarrely describe as tasting equally neon.

My driver bought biscuits to feed puppies at his hotel. One night, I had dinner at his hotel with other Indian drivers who stayed there at rates one tenth that of my tourist hotel. I ate home cooked food with the drivers who were not in their right, sober minds but made for a very fun night! They were extremely friendly and engaging.

I found the artwork most fascinating in the Udaipur fort. The detail in carving marble and sandstone never ceased to amaze me. There was stained and colored glass in perforated walls which, when illuminated by the sun, lit up in great color. The artwork was simple and very elegant.

There were TripAdvisor reviews in the official Udaipur city palace. These reviews were sacred in India as everybody followed them to the letter. All businesses asked for good reviews on TripAdvisor, because it was the main way to get more tourists and business.

While driving through a small village on the way to my next destination, my driver stopped to show me how two oxen walked in a circle to turn gears that eventually lifted buckets of water from the river. The cart driver gave me his stick, and he verbally commanded the oxen to walk.

From what I understood from Hakum, there were two major Jain temples in northern India, and I saw the first one in Khajuraho. Another one I saw on the road from Udaipur to Jodhpur was even more impressive than the already impressive first one. It was a temple made entirely from carved marble.

At my traditional home stay in a mud hut with electricity, hot water, and an attached bathroom in Jodhpur, my hosts dressed me and an Italian family in typical Rajasthani attire before we sat to eat homecooked dinner together.

I admired the combinations of red and yellow sandstone with marble in the architecture. Inside the fort of Jodhpur was a museum displaying seats placed on elephants, seats with long sticks to be carried by servants, and highly ornamented swinging baby beds from a long time ago. There was also painted artwork done on paper in similar style to what I found on the walls in Bundi.

After leaving Jodhpur for Jaipur, we stopped by a cow barn along the highway and fed them rolls of grass, because my driver said, "If they are happy, the gods are happy." I fed them too.

It was Christmas day in Jaipur, India. I started my morning by calling the family and then sightseeing. Upon returning in the evening, I bought a tailored Cashmere, wool jacket. I treated it as my Christmas present.

Amer fort was an enormous fort placed on the hill including amazing glass hallways and large, geometrically designed courtyards. I also visited the Turkish baths and latrines used back in the day. And I thought I had it bad now. All jokes aside, the fort was stunning for its sheer scale and preservation.

Ignoring someone's presence seemed to involve more alienation at its foundation than anything else, a step I disliked immensely. It was something I personally vowed not to do as people were always human beings to me. Perhaps that was why I found India disenchanting. The sights were spectacular, but I had to alienate people to get by. I had to turn down greetings, ignore approaching people, and look past begging children as if they were a nuisance. It was wrong, but strangely necessary so that I could function in such a chaotic place. I met a German at Amer fort who shared my sentiment.

At the Jaipur royal palace, I saw many galleries of textiles, weapons, and royal artifacts. The armory was cool as I saw guns, swords, and daggers I had only seen in video games. Some guns were like handheld cannons. I walked through clothing galleries including descriptions of royal attire, ceremonial dresses, different kinds of turbans, saris, and polo uniforms worn by the Jaipur polo team when they won internationally and consistently for several consecutive years in the 1930s. A nearby courtyard had four, beautifully decorated doors which represented the seasons of monsoon, summer, winter, and spring that were both extremely intricate and visually confusing.

I also visited Jantar Mantar next to the royal palace. It included different sundials and astronomical instruments used 300 years ago. There was the biggest sundial in the world and many smaller versions that were accurate down to 20 seconds. A trip to India would have been incomplete without a snake charmer that stopped after a few minutes to ask for money.

I continued my India travels by plane from Delhi to Aurangabad with a new, executive class ticket as my first economy ticket was canceled. I was upset at first to spending money unnecessarily on executive class, but the lounge before the flight and spacious seat on flight quite literally gave me the space to relax. I am rested, fed, and my bag was packed well. I was ready for the next adventure in India.

Many kinds of people in the world seemed to exist. I was meeting many types I liked and admired as well as their opposites. At the heart of meeting everybody was my perspective, me, analyzing and learning through observation.

01/01/15: Ajanta caves were magnificent caves carved right out of the rock and still holding some of the paintings done 1400-2200 years ago. I had to stay in one room for a long time just to absorb all the work that had gone into carving and painting every intricate design. It was hard to convey the mystique of being here in words. Ellora caves were the second group of temples carved right out of solid rock. Many were unfinished and I presumed never would be. There were only enormous carvings instead of paintings.

When people are overcrowded on their land, they become accustomed to pushing, shoving, and using quite forward tactics to get what they want. Pressure, pressure. Here I was, standing in line with kids and adults pushing me from behind and touching my back to go forward when I was already pressed against the people in front of me. Their understanding of my culture was elementary and their English only sufficient enough to ask my age, country, name, and marital status.

Everyone received my respect initially for being a human being, and it either grew or vanished depending on one's actions and reasons for such. I was grateful to have so many friends and family in my life that helped foster such strong, positive relationships in my life. These were basic lessons I found to be human in nature, and they surpassed culture. This is why I found India frustrating. 99% of my social interactions depended on breaking these basic lessons to function. I was highly likely biased now to new experiences as I made up my mind after multiple encounters where I was disrespected and objectified by basic, human standards, not just Western ones. I knew I focused on the negative, but it was overwhelmingly recurring.

Money seemed to buy kindness as kindness disappeared once the transaction was finished. Greed spurred lies and acted to confuse and pressure me to buy rather than let me choose if I liked something. Bargaining, in its very nature, was designed to take advantage. Paying 10R for an Indian and 250R for a foreigner was the perfect example that not all lives matter equally. Salesmen cared only about customer service until the bill was paid. If they were particularly aggressive which I found most to be, they kept talking, pulling me to and fro, and showing one product after another. The only way to manage such a situation was to ignore the salesman. He was no longer a person but an annoyance. They were too overwhelming for the senses, so my attitude adjusted to the sensory repetition the same way my body did: it ignored them. It felt horrible, but this country made me understand the quality of human life. There were too many people doing too many things. Foreigners were not seen as people either. We were walking ATMs. It was not unique to see foreigners this way, but it was unique to India to dehumanize each other the way I had felt. The history, art, and architecture were stunning, but people were frustrating.

I stopped writing momentarily as the train was bumping around. The train was the best option to travel along the coast. While it was a great experience with cots, meals, and beautiful scenery, it was not the best environment to write in.

Most would argue it was just the way things existed, but I knew it was better elsewhere under similar conditions. There were good people here, but they were greatly outnumbered by the desperate. In the West and in Nepal, as I can speak after having lived somewhat in both, the good people far outnumbered the few extremely desperate people. Before taking the train, I paid for my driver's tea in Aurangabad, and I did not receive any acknowledgement.

While I gained significant stares in Nepal, I earned even more here. The most degrading act was having me pose for photos like a show. One father grabbed both of my hands, placed a hand from each of his two children in my own, and had a third, smaller child stand in front of me. When the third child would not focus on the camera, the father picked him up and placed him in my arms. What was supposed to be a friendly act turned into a ridiculous sideshow. Parents asked to take photos of me for their children, mothers for their families, and children asked like it was a game. Many people put out their hand to shake mine then walked away without courteous engagement. Maybe it was just the way things were, I had a chip on my shoulder, or there was something fundamentally wrong with how people viewed one another in general. I was grateful to be aware of my own risk, but I could see how someone could easily self-generate stereotypes.

I ignored my nutrition during my stay here as it seemed to be high in carbs with rice and low in the vegetables that I liked. I just felt unhealthy even when I did not have diarrhea. India was in between extreme desperation and rapid development. I knew it needed the latter, and I expect the humanitarian crisis grew as the country sped towards growth.

01/05/15: These writings contained cultural lessons across the countries I visited. The purpose of the lessons was not to say which cultural customs were good or bad but to begin to understand the root causes behind a culture and society as it existed in the present. Observations helped me understand a people and the environment that shaped them. Certainly, any country I could have been born in would have greatly shaped what I am. I was not putting a hierarchy on the cultures, but rather I was learning about different rules so that I could apply a new, more inclusive perspective on the rules I lived by.

Locals told me that India was not as brutal in the past. I could only imagine rapid development accelerated business at a rate that people had to catch up to and further development would change people again in the upcoming years. It was a transition phase. The same thing happened elsewhere. The U.S. had rapid industrialization before people realized the environmental and health impacts of unchecked industry. This next government, as I understood it, would be adding more regulation and removing corruption.

I sat on a train in the early morning in Aurangabad. I should arrive this evening in Mumbai and catch another train at midnight to arrive in Goa the following afternoon on New Year's Eve. My bag was filled to the brim with some new clothes and a few souvenirs.

I arrived in Agonda Beach in Goa. I checked in and met an Englishman, Guy, whose group I joined for the rest of the evening. We ended up at a restaurant that had tables out on the beach. We had candles lighting our dinner, fireworks going off, music, people dancing, and several fire lanterns releasing into the sky. The change of pace was refreshing from moving around constantly in north India.

Happy New Year! I arrived in Goa yesterday and checked into my room which lacked hot water as I expected it by now, bed sheets, towels, soap, or toilet paper. I went downstairs for dinner and met a "f****** Australian," in his words. He struck me as a hippie, bitter at the world and finding enjoyment by escaping to Goa, but my impression was irrelevant and didn't matter as he had as much right to be there as I did. I also met an Englishman whose party of three I joined for the night. I spent my night pleasantly drinking beer and cocktails and having intellectual conversations with the group, something I missed dreadfully.

One of the women had some advice for a young fellow such as myself.

One, "Don't sweat the small stuff." This sounded like solid advice, and I agreed at the time. The next day though, I realized I focused on the small things to address them before they grew into larger things. Normally, after a severe mistake, I would say, "Never again," but my life would put me through the same or similar experience again at which point I would use my past experience to make a better decision. Letting small symptoms pass would allude to a brewing disease.

Two, "Have lots of sex." Some would argue against this, but one's approach to sex is based on personal values.

Three, "Travel to Asia to clear your mind." I agreed coming to Asia was good for the mind. Leaving behind all familiarity forced the traveler to reexamine everything through a baby's innocent eyes. All filters, if defined as the mentality used to approach new situations, were gone. Those filters were designed for the developed world with its developed problems. Either for a first time or repeating visitor, changing filters was a great reality check. It was the best reality check I ever came across. Her advice session ended when she kicked her leg in the air. Much to her friend's failed attempt and dismay, she justified her success by joking, "My hips are quite open." I moved slowly the next day towards breakfast and fell asleep repeatedly on the beach while attempting to go out for a swim. I eventually went swimming and then watched a football match on TV in between power outages.

I joined Guy on his rented, blaring Royal Enfield motorcycle as we headed 90 km south to Gokarna. We found the religious city too busy and crowded to enjoy, so we headed onwards to Om Beach where we spent the night. The water was green and murky but very warm, and the beaches were so nice to fall asleep on. For almost one-eighth the price I paid for booking my Agonda Beach hotel online, I had a beach hut that had a bed, mosquito net, and a sand floor. The light didn't work, but I didn't really need it. Food and drinks cost between one to three dollars each which meant I could live like a king on my budget.

Guy and I didn't like Om Beach, so we left for Kudle Beach the next day where we paid an extra dollar per night to have a clean hut with a hard floor. However, the bamboo and straw door, chained together with a tiny padlock, offered little security considering the other side of the door was held to the hut with two pieces of string. Still, there were hammocks right outside the hut and a freshwater shower. A freshwater shower sounds normal, but my shower at Om Beach tasted pretty salty. Daytime consisted of eating leisurely, sunbathing, swimming, bodysurfing, and warding off the many peddlers selling trinkets and cheap jewelry. There were more hippies than I imagined, many of whom I imagine stayed there months at a time. I already met a few people who spent six to nine months in the area which seemed the perfect amount of time to detach from the real world.

I had a great time at every meal as Guy and I discussed many topics. He was laid back and avoiding politics and economics, but his insight was full of depth, intellect, and reason. He rationalized several highly sensible and practical arguments. This was in sharp contrast to most conversations of limited English I had had over the last few months. I shared my most personal philosophies and was content to find he found my rationale as sensible and practical for my world. I did learn the importance of connecting with people. A lack of awareness could lead people to be immature and not know what was best even if they thought what they were doing was good. People were foolish. Guy asked for my life advice. I came up with 1) treat everyone with respect, because they are human beings until they prove they do not deserve respect, 2) treat people as one would hope to be treated, and 3) live so one can sleep well at night. At the end of the day, I was content I slept well at night.

I learned from Guy a lot about how people and governments, defined as organized groups of people, operated. Take Indians for instance. While most north Indians were considered cheaters by Nepali and even north Indians themselves, they were all trying to work for a better life the best way they knew how. Those that worked with foreigners understood respectable interactions which they preferred to overaggressive scams. "No good," as my driver would say about these scams. Governments worked just well enough to get what they wanted and changed just enough to keep their popularity. Guy's cynicism about politicians and businessmen did spill over understandably. Governments and politicians were self-centered, and they focused only on their own well-being and justly so, at least in today's short-term agendas. The world was a dirty place where people suffered, but those people wanted a better life. Westerners did not argue and fight like Indians did. No, they schemed and planned to take down their competitors while appearing and sounding pretty to the untrained eye, because that was exactly what Westerners wanted to see. Westerners tuned out of news, because it was repetitively depressing. They could afford to ignore the world's atrocities. The world became a beautiful place only after working hard to make it a beautiful place. People wanted better lives. People attempted to do so using ethical or unethical methods. Groups of people led to good or bad things depending on their goals. Either way, this was home.

One last of Guy's points stood out: "We all deserved equal opportunity to be unequal."

Society was inherently structured into a ladder. While it was easier to step down than up (oddly, the same felt true for a student's GPA), there would always be a hierarchy, because there existed a hierarchy of hopes and aspirations. People coming from one kind of family were likely but not limited to live a life similar to that of the family they came from. The fear of everyone flocking to the top tiers of society was ungrounded. It had never happened in history. Not everyone wanted a college degree. It was like a train ride. Everyone stepped on in the beginning, and people stepped off at stops along the way. In the end, only a few people were left at the terminal station. The analogy assumes there is an end-stop to learning, and while people build skills their whole life, formal education is fairly linear with an actual end stop.

We cruised back to Agonda Beach but not without stopping first to visit Palem and Palolem Beaches that I had heard so much about. I found them barren and extremely overcrowded, respectively. Agonda beach cemented itself in my mind as extremely relaxing. The beach was enormous at about 3 km long and populated with just enough people to not make it feel empty and not nearly enough that it felt overcrowded. Shopkeepers said, "Good morning," "Good night," and, "How are you?" without trying to sell things. If they did try, it was not pushy. The travelers were equally relaxed and friendly. There was nothing better than having the most down-to-earth conversations with good-thinking people. On the whole, this was one of many highlights of my trip. It was an escape from reality without a doubt, but who doesn't need a relaxing vacation from time to time?

North Goa was full of drugs and dancing which the Indian and foreign newspapers complained were bringing down its respectability. Still, Goa was completely artificial. Tourists came to the beaches to avoid winter and shopkeepers came from Kashmir in northern India to avoid the cold. No one was here in summer during monsoon season except for fishermen. The Russians were typically the main attendees, but their numbers dwindled greatly this year due to the economic boycotts. The area was much emptier than previous years.

01/06/15: My days were spent reading *American Prometheus* and *Three Cups of Tea* which are very intense and emotionally charged books, swimming out in the warm water, sunbathing, writing, and eating and drinking with different groups of people. Most people were older than me, and it was really enjoyable to talk with new minds and learn new ideas from their vastly different ranges of their life experience. I spoke with Kashmir shop owners who were dissuaded of Prime Minister Modi's primarily Hindu government. They were Muslim, but the issue arose when a member of the new government stated that he wanted India to be only Hindu and purged of Christians and Muslims. Kashmir wanted to develop, but the Indian government did not want it to because then the locals would demand rights. So, the only jobs were for women to make textiles and men to sell them. Pakistan wanted to claim Kashmir for itself, and India wanted it too. The shopkeepers in south Goa, 99% being from Kashmir, just wanted to be left alone from the fighting on both sides and to live peacefully. It was a simplicity of life I found existing in every country I visited and every story I heard; people wanted to live safely and provide a better life for their children.

I left Goa after a full week of sunbathing on the beach and swimming into the ocean as far as I could and back. Leaving Goa, my taxi driver was pulled over for not wearing a seat belt. He paid 100 rupees and continued driving without a seatbelt, because the ticket protected him for 24 hours from receiving another ticket for the same offense. Laws didn't mean much if people did not understand why they existed.

I took a 13-hour train from Margao to Alleppey. I spoke with more English people on the train, so the ride went by quickly. There were many English in India which was good, because I picked up their words like "tickety-boo." I woke up at 1:20am and saw some fellow passengers had vanished. I fell back asleep only to be awakened at 2:00am by other English people who knew I was getting off at Alleppey. If they had not woken me up, I would have slept right on through to the last stop. The state of Kerala was safe, so I thought I would sleep a few hours at the train station until daylight to find a hotel. A tuk-tuk was available at 2:30am to bring me to a hotel recommended to me by guests from Agonda beach. The hotel keeper woke up and seemed okay with the whole matter of a random guest arriving unexpectedly in the early morning when he saw I was carrying his hotel's business card. I thought I would have had to sleep outside if it was closed. So, I am safe and sound in a simple, quaint room that has a bed and bathroom. Provided was just a bed sheet on top for the mattress with no top cover. I did get one, but only after asking. It was really hot and humid this far south unlike Agonda where it cooled at night. I planned to take the famous houseboat of Kerala around and spend a day experiencing Ayurvedic detoxification.

01/10/15: Alleppey was like a larger, more natural and green version of Venice, Italy. I took a canoe ride with four other people and lounged in covered seats all day. There was a group of about ten people split among four canoes, and we stopped together for breakfast, fresh coconut, and lunch. It was a great day under the hot weather to cruise around big waterways and narrow ones too narrow for larger houseboats. The nice thing about canoes was that I didn't have to listen to a loud motor the whole time. It was a wonderful way to sit all day and absorb the atmosphere.

On the canoe, I was with a Swiss lady and two Aussie girls around my age. One worked for an NGO, and she explained how competition was fierce in charity. That sounded so foolish to me as in who can prove to be the better good person. It seemed to be another example of picking and choosing who deserved the most charity with each group prioritizing one group over another. Why not join forces? Some charities had agendas. The case of Rosie, the Nepali house worker, came to mind in which she converted to Christianity to receive healthcare. Of course, this was a one-dimensional view of the matter as there were surely more reasons to remain a Christian, but why did helping someone require that he or she belong to a particular group? The two Aussies did not like the statement that a charity could be biased, and I could hear their tension with me rise in their voices. When they brought up gun laws in the U.S., they could not understand why gun violence continued. After a shooting in Australia, the government bought back as many guns as it could. After I brought up the Second Amendment, they were delighted to inform me, both having a Masters in Politics, the second sentence of the amendment says "arms for a militia". When I suggested I have never heard it discussed in any argument for gun rights as a reason it did not hold much bearing, they were quick to say all Americans were so stupid and didn't even read their own rules. I couldn't discuss much more as their minds were made up before we even started talking. As bright as they were in the textbook, I felt their awareness shrank the more they learned and settled within their ideology.

No common ground could ever be found if one party wasn't willing to step into the middle ground. People could be happy to learn new ideas, but learning should not stop. It would be crippling to decide any current state of affairs was perfect, because there were always better ideas out there, be they social, political, or technological. I mentioned how fascinating Singapore was. With enough rules about hate speech and hateful acts, the city was extremely peaceful and harmonious even with a highly concentrated amount of religious and ethnic diversity. The two Australian girls retorted with the atrocity of having Big Brother watching and controlling people's behavior. I had a single dimensional view of the city after spending a few days there, so it was possible there were Big Brother atrocities being committed I was unaware of. Still, I would have happily lived in the happy, diverse, and thriving nation I witnessed if I had to. I may not feel my heart lay in Singapore, but the country lacked much of the hatred that plagued many other countries and I felt much safer. All the people I met living in Singapore spoke only of good things.

Back to the charity topic, I thought it was better to treat people by their individual actions instead of those of their group. People acted as their group expected them to, because it was safer to do so. Fields of study consisting of individual topics had intricacies that could easily be overlooked by internal beliefs. The reality of studying a controversial topic to its core understanding and causes, whether consciously recognized or not, was why new departments in universities arose.

A Tibetan guy I met in Alleppey was so adamant about visiting China, repeating the same glory and national pride with Wikipedia-like facts as the first Chinese traveler told me back in Nepal. It made me wonder how much of what he said was rhetoric he had heard and how much was true from personal experience.

I arranged for an Ayurvedic treatment center to give me three days of treatments and teachings on the old form of healthcare. I had a lesson from one of the staff before the treatment. He taught me about the ancient medicine and its practice. I took a general treatment as I was not acutely ill, but there were specific oils and herbs used for specific ailments. Ayurveda, from what I learned, targeted the root of the issue over a period of time. It was a time-lengthy medicine which is why many Indians I asked revert to allopathic, primarily Western, drugs if they caught a cold in order to quickly alleviate symptoms within hours or days. Ayurveda could take days to weeks, because it was functioning on a deeper level. There were no side effects or potential harm. The treatment was profoundly eye-opening to an entirely different world of medicine than the one I was familiar with. It had been practiced for thousands of years and was an equally valid form of healthcare in its own way. Bringing what I experienced back to the U.S. could face cultural challenges with the degree and time constraints of full treatment, but the philosophies and practices were sound. There was a convenience of time efficiency to Western medicine and scientific backing. Ayurvedic medicine could not be held to the same reference as it operated on multiple levels all at once. It was a different medicine, but I did take some notes I would be bringing home about the treatments.

I had the first session yesterday. It was an entirely new experience. The facilities inside the room were a big wooden table carved for oil drainage and different instruments for administering herbal and medicated oils. All I wore was a T-shaped cloth. At first, he instructed me to undress, so I went down to underwear. Then he wrapped the cloth around me and said to remove the remaining clothing with not so many words. I would say about 98% of my body was exposed while wearing the one piece of cloth. The first treatment was called abhyangam swedhanam and was a full body, oil massage. This sounded pretty straightforward, but my senses were on alert after feeling somewhat vulnerable. I could honestly say I had no idea what to expect. The goal was to relax, improve circulation, and prepare the body for the subsequent treatments. The next treatment was kizhi, a bundle of herbs, leaves, and powders placed inside a cloth. I was unsure if the man was a doctor or masseur, but he rubbed the bundle in the oil sitting over a flame before pounding it gently and rubbing the medicated oil against my skin. The oil he used, I could only describe, made me smell like a very well-seasoned, Italian pasta. He successfully focused around the joints for any pain I had. At this point, I was covered from the neck down in different kinds of oil which made turning over unusual as I would just slide around rather than lift my body to rotate. This was a cultural experience for me, but worth the full exposure, pun not intended, to learn about this traditional medicine and compare its philosophy to Western medicine. The third treatment was sirodhara meaning head-oil. Cloth was placed over my eyes and in my ears in case of oil dripping onto my face. A pot of warm oil was suspended over my head with a wick trailing from a hole in the bottom to allow oil to slowly and steadily stream onto my forehead. While he was heating the big pot of oil, he spilled it all over the floor. I couldn't see because of the cotton over my eyes, so I just waited and listened to him wiping it up. During the treatment, he swayed the pot back and forth gently, so that the oil eventually covered my head on all sides. After time was up, he rubbed in the fact, pun intended, I was covered in oil by smearing even more oil over my hair. He then wiped away excess oil, and I got dressed to leave around 9:30pm. My body was still drenched in oil as it didn't wipe off easily. I had trouble washing it away. Ironically, the treatment was to induce relaxation and rejuvenation, but I slept horribly. I inhaled strong, Italian pasta smells and a few mosquitoes terrorized me all night. I woke up too late for the backwater canoe ride, had breakfast instead, and then returned to sleep for two and a half hours. Despite mixed feelings about the whole ordeal, I knew it was a first impression. I went back again today for the second day of treatment, and it went much more smoothly. I planned it earlier in the day, so I could have time to wash properly. I was not as oily afterwards, and I did feel very relaxed. I was unsure if my mood was from the oils or the long massages.

01/11/15: After breakfast and my last Ayurvedic lesson this morning, I went to the train station in Alleppey to catch a train to Kanyakumari, the southernmost tip of India. It was the site where one could see an ocean sunrise and sunset from the same point, but the train schedule was too tight. After some thinking, I changed plans and decided to go solely to Trivandrum, spend the night re-laxed, and see south Indian temples to compare them to the ones I saw in north India. Then I could easily check out of the hotel and go to the airport with no stress for time.

While waiting for the train, I took a walk to the beach, had a sweet lassi and tea, and wrote some of my thoughts down from the previous day. Just before leaving, I struck up a conversation with a Muslim I identified by the heavy beard. He was very friendly and wasn't the first one to reiterate what others have made clear in every country I had the opportunity to discuss; terrorists were not Muslim, because they could not both kill and follow a faith of do no harm.

I returned to the railway station to catch my train when I met a fellow traveler who was about to get on too. We walked down the platform for a few minutes past cars packed with people. I had bought a ticket that morning for the sleeper class in order to have extra space and a bed, but that did not guarantee an easily available seat. Eventually the two of us found a compartment with three empty beds on top, so we threw our luggage on one and climbed onto the other two. We talked until he left at Varkala to go to the beach. I wrapped myself with my bags and fell asleep to music. I woke up in Trivandrum to a line of people getting off the train. I joked with one local walking down the aisle that everyone was going to let me sleep, and he laughed and said he was about to wake me up. I got off the train still groggy and had a 7-rupee tea that helped wake me up. I had no idea where I was going and was not going to take a rickshaw if I didn't know what hotel to go to. I took off into the city searching for a cheap hotel. I had 1300 rupees ($21) on me and was destined to make it last until I left the following afternoon. One driver saw me looking at my map and offered to help. I told him I needed a hotel, and he said he knew one for 1000 R. I told him the price was too high, so he said he could go for 900. Based on previous experience, drivers didn't know prices for hotels. They just wanted a fare, so I took off walking. Two hotels were full, and one only had expensive doubles. The fourth one only had an air-conditioned room for 1600 R, but with a 15% discount and tax, the total came to a sweet 1400 R. I didn't want to pay that and actually couldn't and not starve. I asked where cheaper hotels were, ready to walk out. Magically, he pulled a key and had the doorman check a room to see if it was empty. He came back, said a single non-AC room was available for 620 R. I checked the room, and it was huge with two twin beds, a couch, desk, TV with English movies, a closet, and a huge bathroom with hot water. This was nicer than some rooms I had paid a lot more for elsewhere in India. And the hot water finally worked perfectly! I was happy and could catch up on a few things before waking early to visit the wonders of Trivandrum before leaving for Dubai.

01/12/15: This was not the first time it happened. I was having breakfast in a restaurant with lots of empty tables, and a local sat down at my table to eat. I was not sure what to make of it as he didn't speak English, but it was friendly to have company. The restaurant where I ate dinner and breakfast was super cheap. I paid 75 rupees for dinner and 35 rupees for a full breakfast, fractions of what I thought was cheap previously, because they were actually the local prices. No other foreigners were around.

I went to Padmanabhaswamy temple this morning. Unfortunately, non-Hindus were not allowed inside, and visitors to the premises were required to wear the traditional robe as pants and t-shirts were not allowed. A group of cheerful, young Indian men approached me outside while I was looking at the temple, and they were so impressed when I fulfilled their curiosity by showing them a U.S. $20 bill and my passport. One of them took a photo of the bill. They wanted a $1 bill, and I wished I had one to give. They said most Indians hardly left their state their entire lives.

I jumped in a rickshaw to the local park with museums, but Monday was a holiday so it was closed. The rickshaw had a meter in it! It was the first meter I had seen in India, and the driver agreed to the verbal price I had been told at the hotel without any bargaining at all. The meter came within a few rupees of the price making me content and relaxed at the hassle-free nature of transport in the city.

I sat on a bench in the quiet park and conversed with another Indian man on the bench. He asked a lot of questions about the U.S. and knew quite a bit about American politics too. He asked about different ethnic groups and their places in society, and I tried to dispel some of the stereotypes he had. Another man from this morning asked me if Michelle Obama was Barack Obama's wife or sister.

The people I met in south India were genuine and nice. I walked down the street and exchanged smiles and greetings with everybody. Kerala was the only people-elected, socially communist government in the world, and it worked pretty well. Everyone was educated and unbelievably friendly and roads were developed. It was really pleasant and safe to travel. The man working at the hotel desk in Alleppey was about my age, had only a high school education on paper, and was the brightest, most politically and socially savvy person I had met in a long time. He was fully updated with American current events and even knew about the recent two-year-old toddler killing his mother accidentally with the gun in her purse. It was heartwarming to meet such good people and connect with the outside world through current events.

I recently clocked in four months of travel with most of it in developing countries. I had the time of my life with the people I met, and I would do it all again in a heartbeat. My only changes would be avoiding small, naive mistakes I made as an inexperienced traveler. I treasured the memories and hoped to return one day to travel more, and I will definitely visit my Nepali family again. I am so excited for upcoming Dubai, St. Petersburg, and Europe. I am also very happy weather reports in St. Petersburg show only a few degrees below freezing rather than the expected 20-30 degrees below zero in January.

I checked my itinerary a dozen times in the last month to verify and re-verify the airport, time, and date of departure. Needless to say, it did not register until I was about to leave for the airport that a 4:30 departure time meant in the morning and not 4:30pm. I was incredulous I made the mistake considering I ran on European time for years. I let myself panic and rushed to the airport in hopes of talking to an agent to catch the next flight to Dubai, because my flight to Russia left Dubai a few days later and I could not miss that. Guards armed with machine guns outside the empty airport let me talk to the airport manager who just had me call the airline to sort it out. No options were available to reach Dubai without paying an outrageous amount of money before my flight to Russia. I returned to my hotel for WiFi, searched flights, and found seats in economy class opened up on the same flight 24 hours later, so I only had to miss one day. I quickly called the airline again, and with the no-show fee, the price came out to extremely acceptable. I was so lucky this was not worse financially, and my heart finally began slowing down.

I tried to relax in the afternoon before leaving for the airport to catch the 1:00am flight. I dined at the same restaurant as before. The owner of the restaurant sat down at my table and started a conversation. He was a very interesting man. His son about my age, Vidhu, later stopped by and was excited to speak to a native English speaker. The three of us talked until I had to leave for the airport. Vidhu graciously offered to drive me so I would not have to take a tuk-tuk. I was incredibly grateful for the hospitality both he and his father showed a random traveler who ate in their restaurant.

Hopefully, farewell to cold showers, men peeing just about anywhere, and low prices. I was ready for good cheese, wheat bread, non-neon colored jam, toilet paper, cold weather, new sights, new people, and my family.

Similar Differences

Dubai, United Arab Emirates

01/13/15: After sleeping on and off at the airport and on the plane, I arrived at the hotel in Sharjah around 8:30am just outside the main city of Dubai. I took a plane, a cab, a bus, a boat, and a train that day. I sat on the hotel bed thinking I would take advantage of the hotel's sauna to relax, but I never had time.

The Los Angeles-like traffic to enter the city in the morning and leave it at night was terrible. There were so many things to see and I was sad to have already lost a day, but that just meant a three-day schedule was crammed into two. I started by visiting a heritage village to see traditional homes. I entered the Grand Mosque, one of the oldest in Dubai, and observed the empty prayer room from the doorway to be respectful based on my experience in Singapore. I went to the Dubai Museum which showed the complete development of the city from nomadic Bedouins to traders and artists in bronze, pottery, herbs, textiles, pearls, tailoring, foods, medicine, carpentry, camels, falcons, fishing, and more. It was an impressive feat after looking at how well they optimized natural resources. Development boomed when the country discovered oil I think back in the 1960s. The museum was very well organized and creative with the right amount of traditional artifacts, interactive videos, and dressed mannequins to constantly captivate my interest. In the fishing exhibit, the ceiling was built like I was underwater and looking up at the feet of a swimming man. The museum is situated inside the original fort of Dubai with walls 50 cm thick made of coral stone. Afterwards, I went to a juice shop my father had visited while on a business trip. I had a mango and date milkshake with a panini. The fruit juice was equally delicious as another lime juice and grape juice freshly made for me in India last night.

I hitched a boat ride across the canal to see the Gold Souk market, and I can only say the amount of gold was both overwhelming and impressive. Dubai is named the City of Gold for a good reason. I walked down the long street staring at one half of the storefronts then returned gazing at the other half. There was a world record sized ring and more gold attire than I could process. After my astonishment settled, I continued towards the Dubai Mall and Burj Khalifa tower to appreciate its size. I can honestly say I never thought a building could continue into the sky so high, and I really wanted to know what it would be like to be that high over the city. It stood at least twice the height of other skyscrapers. I booked a ticket to go up to the 125th floor at 10:30pm. Afterwards, I realized I had barely slept, my feet were hurting, and I hadn't eaten a full meal that day in my excitement to see the city. I decided to return to the hotel to recover, because tomorrow's plan would be even more packed.

The Dubai market was entertaining to watch, because the city was so developed, but the markets looked like a mix between standardized, fixed pricing and fun bargaining. The markets reminded me a bit of Singapore, the last developed city I visited three months ago. That was a shocking realization. I walked down one street where everyone was selling cashmere shawls and scarves, the same products made in Kashmir and cheaper in India I had no doubt. I had to smile when literally every shopkeeper tried to throw their scarves around me and would not take them back willingly, so that I would have to stop and talk. It was kind of my fault as I made eye contact and smiled at everyone, because I was happy. On the way back through the street an hour later, I decided to try something. I looked down at the floor and walked in the street, and sure enough, not one person approached me. I was surprised it worked and how simple the signs were for them to catch a likely customer.

01/15/15: My second and last day in Dubai deviated from the original plan. I left at 6am for the bus into the city. I met Seth, a Ghanan who was at heart a musician of six instruments, but he came to Dubai to work in the steel industry. He told me about how safe Ghana was, how there had been repeated public elections in the country without violence, and how beautiful and full of natural resources the country was. What surprised me was how the lack of education was a big hindrance to creating peace. He said those without schooling tended to find solutions through violence rather than negotiations. The good aspect of Ghana was that many conflicts were resolved in courts. Still, he said education needed to be more widespread. Building schools was not the only problem. He said most people didn't see the need for school when they could make money working. Also, seeing high school or college graduates fail to attain good jobs in the country was not a great model for children. The educated traveled abroad to work and left the lower skilled workers behind, an issue I found very common in Nepal and India. This slowed economic growth and development. It was good to hear a new perspective on some of the things I observed.

I headed onwards to Mall of the Emirates where there was an indoor ski slope. The Mall partnered with Disney's *Frozen* to make an enormous winter experience with real penguins to play with. I smiled seeing workers bundled up in winter clothing as the space remained at -6 degrees Celsius. It reminded me a bit of Las Vegas, Nevada, being entirely artificial and constructed out of the desert for human benefit. I went back outside and headed towards the Palm Jumeriah to see the water and bask in my last day of warm sunlight before I traveled to colder climates. I had to take a tram to the end of the artificial resort. On the way, I saw neighborhoods squeezed between GPS-plotted beaches much in the same way intestines fold into themselves to increase surface. No number of trees could replace the feeling of human construction that took place to create this paradise. I was so intent on enjoying the warmth that I stayed too long. I tried to reach the pick-up point for a desert safari, but I missed it. Instead, I went to the Museum of Islamic Civilization which wasn't as glamorous as blazing over sand dunes, but I became giddy in the science section where I saw many of the discoveries with demonstrations that Arabs had discovered for use in the West. These were in the fields of geometry, trigonometry, chemistry, engineering, medicine, and astrology. Europe would not know about Aristotle had it not been for the Arabs protecting his manuscripts during the Middle Ages. One scientist also contributed to vision neuroscience, a field I did research in. The museum displayed several achievements of astronomy and had many replicas throughout the museum of Jantar Mantar, the astronomy park I had visited in north India. There were also exhibits of artifacts from century to century, but I found most interesting the merging of cultures, art and ideas from different times between the Islamic world and Europe or Asia.

The shopping mall exhibited a very interesting blend of Arabic and Western influence. People wore hijabs, veils exposing only eyes, dresses, suits, white robes, dress shirts, t-shirts, and more. Different mannequins in storefronts illustrated this diversity. The cutest thing I saw was a father I glimpsed from the corner of my eye. My initial thought was that he was swinging two pieces of black cloth back and forth, but after looking, he was holding the hands of two fully covered, giggling little girls as he swung their arms back and forth as they walked. My initial perception was way off.

The grocery store was enormous. It was the first one I had seen in months and illustrated the luxury of food availability and diversity that was lacking elsewhere in the world.

I caught dual shadows of myself while walking during the day. It made me stop in the street to look at it. Light from the sun formed one shadow and also reflected off of glass buildings to give me a second shadow. A simple light trick, but I never had two shadows during the day before.

I really liked the sunset over a mosque as a man called to prayer over loud speakers. Apparently, there was another mosque near my room, because the call to prayer was loud and really cool to hear and remind me I was in a different world. There were many ethnicities and languages present in the city, and it was very safe.

I headed over to the internationally-constructed Burj Khalifa to see the city at night. There were still many floors above me, but the height over the city was unprecedented. There were digital telescopes that showed a live feed with details on whatever it was centered on. It also contained prerecorded images of the city at night, during the day, and a historical view showing what the city looked like decades ago. The elevators felt like a theme park ride with music and lights. I returned to the hotel at 1:30am, awoke at 5am, and headed over to the airport to fly to Russia.

I spent most of my time in transit. I left Dubai which showed me several remarkable feats of human construction. From a ski slope to artificial beaches to the Burj Khalifa, it showed mankind could create whatever it wished.

Similar Differences

St. Petersburg, Russia

01/16/15: I remember a few comical things about coming to Russia. First, I was the only traveler to have my visa double checked before boarding in Dubai perhaps because I had an American passport. Second, I stepped onto the plane surrounded by Russians and thought I was now surrounded by every movie villain I had ever seen since movie villains were often Russian in American movies. Third, all drinks were complimentary on the flight, and people were drinking heavily at six in the morning. Fourth, people started getting up after landing to grab their luggage before the plane had stopped despite the stewardess' protests. Fifth, everyone changed from shirts and sweaters to heavy winter jackets within a matter of seconds. I turned around and saw children that had now become marshmallows melting away into their jackets, scarves, and gloves. Sixth, I exited the bus at the metro station to see a woman with high boots, a warm jacket, and nothing but skin between the boots and jacket. That was fashion I could not keep up with. Seventh, buying a metro ticket was confusing at first as the ticket was a token that happened to be the same color and shape as the rest of the change. Eighth, I took a train to Pushkin whose smell brought back repressed memories of train museums I went to as a child. I asked my friend if the train was from World War II, and she informed me it wasn't. I asked how old she thought it was, and she honestly said around 50 years which was not that far off from the war. Ninth, it was the off season for tourism, so while there were others in the hostel, my entire 10-bed dorm room was empty, leaving me to sprawl my belongings out. Tenth, the ruble currency was down, so everything was really cheap. The grocery store had become a dollar store, and I bought camel wool socks from a metro peddler for $4. These were the ones I remembered from early in my stay, and there were many more things that made me smile while I was here.

I arrived safely at my youth hostel. It was only a few degrees below freezing making the jacket I bought in Nepal more than warm enough. Seeing a city in snow made me smile and nostalgic for when I studied abroad in Montreal. I missed walking bundled up in the cold. The experience was new, cool, and beautiful.

My first night in Russia involved buying groceries and cooking pasta at the youth hostel. I was so tired having lacked a good night of sleep during the previous three nights that I went to bed at 8pm. After waking up slowly and cooking breakfast, I was surprised it was only 10am and the sun had not yet risen.

I walked to the Hermitage Museum to discover an English group tour available later in the day. For being one of the greatest museums in the world, it only cost me a few dollars for the tour with student discount. Oddly enough, there were few visitors, and I was the only person in the tour meaning I had a personal tour guide for two hours. She was very good at telling the narratives behind art pieces and offering the history about the multiple buildings themselves and their architecture. After spending an entire day there, I saw just about as many pieces as I could process. I quickly walked through Greek, Egyptian, and Asian sections as I recognized many of the art pieces and had seen similar pieces recently. The European art from each country, including French and medieval art on the other hand, were new to me. The history of the art, including works by Leonardo da Vinci and Rembrandt, astonished me. Each painting had a story and purpose, and having learned both, I appreciated the pieces even more. Afterwards, I treated myself to a fancy Russian restaurant called "The Idiot" which I was unaware was named after a famous book by Russian author Fyodor Dostoyevsky. I had Russian borscht and pelmini which turned out to be dumplings. I came back to the hostel and talked late into the night with hostel staff and a French PhD student, Jean-Philippe, who lived a few kilometers from my family in France. The world was truly a small place.

The city was so beautiful and littered with a wealth of historical palaces and monuments of Peter the Great and Catherine the II. I extended my stay by two days to absorb more of the city. Yesterday, I went to Pushkin with Jean-Philippe and Elvira, a "Kyrgyzstani St. Petersburger." Jean-Philippe was the man with the plan, she was our translator, and I was assigned to tell jokes. The buildings in Pushkin were so striking and elegantly adorned. It was a memorable excursion.

01/18/15: We took a train to the city and walked the park where the palace and its adjacent stables, kitchens, and Turkish baths were located. There was a frozen lake with an island in the middle. I was absolutely thrilled to walk onto a frozen lake for the first time. Snow sprawled over the serene park. The interior of the palace was extremely well decorated, and I was stunned by its elegance and luxury in spite of having visited royal places before.

I walked inside Kazan Church near the hostel. I discovered it was a functioning church and filled with at least a thousand people. I checked my phone and realized it was Sunday at about 1pm. Priests walked around ceremoniously and blessed water that they then proceeded to throw at the people. Water was stored in multiple large, silver containers throughout the church. People also waited in line with empty bottles to fill them with what I assumed to be holy water. Bottling the water to take home reminded me of my driver in India who bottled some water from the Ganges and stored it in the trunk of his car so that he may splash some over his head before daily prayer. The fervor and emotions I could see in people's eyes and faces when they were touched by the water was the exact same I saw at temples in India. Instead of lighting incense, people lit candles. The choir's singing beautifully echoed throughout the interior. An eerily strong energy perfused the room. What I felt in the church had the same strength of faith I felt standing within a large mosque or temple.

After the church, I continued onwards across canals and through a frozen park to the Church of Spilled Blood, the famous exterior of which was outstanding. I would return the following day to visit the interior. The beautiful appearance from the outside masked the enormous murals inside. The entire interior was made of several murals, and the shocking part was the details of facial expressions. The stones were placed together in such a way that they could have been paintings.

I returned to the hostel temporarily before leaving to see the Best of Russian Ballet at the Hermitage Theater. It contained popular dances and live orchestra pieces from Swan Lake, Don Quixote, Nutcracker, Sleeping Beauty, and others. Both sexes moved with such dexterity that I was in awe of their unparalleled talent and expertise as they made their movements that seemed inhumanly possible yet were performed flawlessly. Their movements demonstrated the full potential of the grace and beauty of the human form in what it can achieve.

01/21/15: After sleeping in the next day, I woke up slowly and ate a full breakfast of toast with butter and honey, cereal, oatmeal, and toast with cheese. To top it off, I made chai that tasted just like milk tea in Nepal.

Full and warm, I dressed and walked over the main river to an unexpected sight near Peter and Paul fortress. January 19th was the celebration of the baptism of Jesus for Russian orthodox believers. People plunged three times into the icy river in front of a small shrine with a photo of Jesus. Priests entered with their robes, and then people followed in their underwear. No one made a sound or showed any distress like athletes did during ice baths. People were poised and solemn as they entered the water and crossed their chests in between dips.

I toured the fortress and more of the north island before returning to the hostel. Back at the hostel, I met Max, a Latvian who had come to the city to purchase a red dress for his new, short film. Max and I went for breakfast at an amazing vegetarian restaurant. I found it funny that when he talked about temperatures, he would assume we knew he was talking about negative temperatures. He would just say, "20 degrees," for example, and not "negative 20 degrees," because it was often so cold in Latvia. In this city, people threw food onto icy canals for the pigeons.

Afterwards, Max walked with me to see Mariinsky Theater and the submarine north of the island. After sightseeing, we stopped at a formal coffee shop for a double Americano. It was an enormous cup of extremely dark coffee. I did not add sugar, and for the first time, I really enjoyed the bitter flavor. The following day was my last full day in the city and also the coldest at -17 degrees Centigrade. I took the metro to a church cemetery complex five km away. It was nice to appreciate this aspect of Russian culture as it varied from other countries. I strolled into the church and made a circle over my heart with a line down the middle upon entering. To me, the gesture symbolized the unity in the world that I hoped to experience. It was sweet to see a mother lift her son, so he may kiss the paintings of Jesus and other saints. Outside, I walked through the cemetery and stopped at different graves, but mostly those that looked the most abandoned. It was touching to be there and communicate with people who defied time by being there in the present yet had managed to escape the recent horrors of history. They lived in a different world. I took a long walk back to the hostel in the cold which I did not mind as I soaked up the city one last time before my departure. I was wrapped up in my jacket and shawl so that the cold didn't bother me. That evening, I saw The Nutcracker at Mikaelhovsky Theater. While the first piece of ballet I had seen a few days ago had struck me for its talent, this piece was mind-boggling. I sometimes forgot the dancers were human, because they were moving so gracefully. It was especially impressive to see 20-30 dancers on stage coordinating majestically all at once while supported by a large, live orchestra. Photos of the show were prohibited, but the theater was oozing beautifully with history.

In the evening, Max, our French friend, and I went to a karaoke bar. It was a lot of fun, because I sang Hotel California and Californication with different Russians who bragged through the microphone about how I was from the U.S., and the whole bar would cheer me on. The really cool part of the night was meeting a Russian seaman from the Navy who had just returned from Crimea. He said the area was peaceful with no shooting. He continued that while Putin said there were no Russian soldiers there, the troops were indeed there sporting the green Russian uniform, but the stars, rankings, and titles on the uniforms were stripped off. He and his friend were not Putin's staunchest supporters as the leader created trouble for the people. He also admitted many Russians were fierce supporters, because they did not readily access news sources outside of what they were told which sounded familiar to me. I really liked it when I suggested a toast, and he was the first one to toast to peace. Every single person was very nice and friendly. I felt no animosity for being American here despite the conflict we hear between the governments. It would seem people and their government are two separate entities in that regard.

While I was in St. Petersburg, it was quite cold albeit warmer than I expected. Still, cold weather did not detract one bit from my joy of being there in the city with the beautiful snow and ice around me.

Prague, Czech Republic

01/23/15: A really cool Czech named Vasek whom I met in Phuket, Thailand, picked me up at the airport and let me stay on his couch. All was good! We bought some beer, bread, and cream cheese. After finishing the food and drinks, I took a nap for two hours to add to my three hours of sleep the night before. Come late afternoon, we drove into the city for a tour of Prague. Searching for parking in Prague struck me as a foolish way to spend our time, only because my recent experiences did not include sitting in a rolling metal box to find where to leave it so that we could begin to enjoy the evening. The city was smaller than St. Petersburg, but that did not lessen the elegance of cobblestone streets and narrow alleys under snow and street lights. The night started with two beers at a flagship shop, meaning the beer company owned and supplied the shop daily with their one beer. Apparently, the Czech Republic has a larger beer culture than Germany. It was cheaper than soda and water and available everywhere. After that, we walked through the city at night towards a vegetarian restaurant. It was full, so we continued walking in search of veggie food as Czech food was not at all conducive to my diet. We finally stopped for dinner at James Dean, an American-themed restaurant. The music and environment was heavily American 1960's themed. I had mac and cheese and mashed potatoes. It was refreshing to be surrounded by American artifacts for the first time in a long time. The bartender was shocked I ordered two plates of food as one was not big enough. I took it as a challenge to eat it all which I managed to do. Afterwards, he brought me two free pancakes which I managed to gulp down as well.

I parted ways with my host who had work early the next morning to go out with an English girl and two German guys I met that night. She came to the city to see the six-story club with an ice bar. It was so much fun dancing with them to different music on different floors. One floor had amazing lights and ironically the worst music.

After sleeping in the next morning, I visited the old castle in Prague, the main church, and the surrounding neighborhoods. I had the chance to stumble upon the changing of the guard.

I already felt a slight culture shock coming back to the developed world. I had a heightened awareness of being in a nice car on paved roads. Walking on cobblestone streets was a delight because there were no potholes in downtown Prague. I also drank tap water which had been unthinkable the last few months. And even though prices were higher, I thought less about paying more than I did in Asia, because I knew the prices were equal for everybody without bargaining.

Vienna, Austria

01/26/15: I stamped my EuRail Train Pass for the first time and took the train to Vienna. It was a little cold with sprinkling rain, but I still walked the 2 kilometers from the train station to the hostel instead of taking a taxi. I enjoy walking through a city at any time under any weather as well as to save money from a taxi which would otherwise rob me of the opportunity to enjoy the narrow streets.

I joined two travelers I had just met, a German-Australian, Andrew, and a Swiss, Stefan, to visit the Schonbrunn Palace. Its structure was similar to the Versailles palace. The palace and entry courtyard were enormous and beautifully adorned in fresh snow. We toured the facility walking through snowy gardens and admiring the maintenance of said gardens. Outstanding fountains aesthetically bordering between ruin and art were scattered along the pathways. They looked like movie sets. Behind the palace stood a large hill with an elegant building on top that had a cafe inside. The snow was fresh, and the three of us had a bit too much fun with it between building a snowman and rolling a giant ball of snow and ruining the snowy hillside as it exposed the grass below. I had fun reenacting a scene from the film *300* with a snowman.

"This…is…Vienna!" I roared as I kicked the stacked snow-balls down the hill.

We enjoyed a Chinese buffet, but I filled myself so much on veggie spring rolls and noodles that I had to nap afterwards. The following day was very slow as I did not sleep well after my three-hour nap. I left the hostel at 3pm to visit a graveyard hosting people from all religions and countries. I went with a group of about eight or so travelers that became my friends for the next few days. There were Jews, Buddhists, Christians, and Muslims all buried there. The Muslim tombstones all lay in one direction; I assume towards Mecca. The sun had set and the gates were locked, forcing us to jump the wall to exit.

01/27/15: I saw Madame Butterfly opera last night with an Englishman, John, who had tickets for the standing section for four euros. We arrived two minutes before the opera commenced. There were about 40 of us standing in the back of an immense chamber of at least 400 people. I had trouble understanding what was happening as I stood in the aisle without a screen offering translations. That meant I listened to an hour of opera without a clue as to what was happening. One woman fainted and fell down. I imagined she found it extremely moving or she couldn't stand the opera. It was worth the experience to decide whether I preferred opera or ballet. Sadly, we both absorbed enough opera after one hour that we left at inter-mission to enjoy apple strudel with cream with two German medical students who were studying in Hungary. I went skiing the next day with the same gentleman in Semmering, a small village an hour southwest of Vienna. I hadn't skied in at least five years. I was very sad to return to Vienna to realize I lost the Nepali shawl I had bar-gained for, because it reminded me of my Nepali family and my entire experience there.

01/29/15: After a night of skiing, I went to dinner at Pla-chutta with the medical students. It was a very classy restaurant with pictures on the wall of famous people from George Lucas to Putin that had eaten there. It was supposedly the best schnitzel in town, but the meat was beyond my culinary tastes. Still, the vegetable mix-tures formed one of the tastiest meals I ever had. It was crazy to think among my cohort that my meal was the cheapest at $25 when I bought a tasty meal in Nepal for 25 cents a few months prior. We proceeded from a somewhat slow dinner conversation to a McCafe, shamefully, for dessert. It was surprisingly good as my friends had macaroons, and I had a marzipan tart. The Englishman was in his

10th and last year of his medical studies, and I had never met such a book-smart man who had particular social skills which surprised me. I thought his personality came from so much experience working with patients rather than speaking with them. He asked questions about parents' work or siblings, topics I would not normally discuss over dinner with new friends.

I was sad to see the two groups of people I had explored the city with over multiple days were leaving or have left Vienna. Consequently, I finally had quiet time to myself which I didn't realize I had been missing. I had a nice walk around old Vienna, stopping by the museum of modern art and the giant ice skating rink in the park. The streets in Vienna looked similar to those in Prague, but the statues blew my mind. I had never seen veins detailed into stone before. I returned to the hostel and made pasta with avocado and a delicious pepper sauce. Yesterday was a detox for me, so I ate plenty of avocado and lettuce and drank plenty of fruit juice. I messaged a Nepali student that I was taking care of my sore throat, and he told me it was because of too much soda. It was more the lack of sleep and the cold weather, but I liked his explanation.

Similar Differences

Bratislava, Slovakia

I walked to the train station and walked straight onto the train for Bratislava. Having a train pass was handy. I was pretty sure Bratislava was in another country, but I didn't know which one, and I didn't look it up on WiFi before leaving. I spent the whole day not knowing which country I was in. I walked a few kilometers from the train station to the quiet and pleasant old town. I took a detour accidentally and found myself walking through a snowy park parallel to the highway. I even took the wrong bridge into the city. Still, it was nice to lose myself with a really great audio book I finished and not think of anything else. Putting myself into a void from any familiarity was a great way to clear my head. I had done the same thing before when hiking deep into a Thai jungle alone and swimming as far as I could straight out into the Indian Ocean.

Bratislava was surprisingly quaint, and the castle had a plain architecture. The style reminded me I was no longer in India with highly decorated and carved castle walls. The scary part of the day was realizing I lost my phone with my credit card in the snow about 100 m away from the castle! My heart really jumped. I had foolishly put it in the horizontal pocket in my jacket, and it must have slid out when I jumped up a step. I later had a grilled circle of Camembert cheese on top of salad to settle myself.

I toured through a World War II memorial for the Slovakians just before leaving the city. It was the third cemetery I had visited recently although I was not sure why. Before, standing in the same place beside people who had lived in a different world with different problems felt mystical. For the first time, walking through this one made me angry. I think I didn't fully understand the exact conflict they experienced to end up in the cemetery, so their deaths seemed slightly more futile than those I understood. I hopped back onto the train in the evening to Wien, so I could make dinner and finish the food I bought.

Budapest, Hungary

After three days in Budapest, I finally had an afternoon to sit down and write my thoughts. I've been more focused on my thoughts these last few days as I struggle to remember them before writing in this journal. Travel days changed from long days and casual evenings to short days and long nights.

02/01/15: My schedule always seemed to fill up with newly-made friends to meet and new places to visit. I ate mushroom tacos that first night there, the first time eating a familiar food since leaving the U.S., and it put me back in San Diego for 15 minutes of joy. I met a few Portuguese folks who were visiting friends studying here in the city. I spent the next few days with them as we explored the city together. One fun night was spent ice skating and then in an escape room trying to solve puzzles to figure out how to exit. We had an hour to put clues together, and even with four hints, we exited with just five minutes to spare. And don't forget Turkish food and kebabs on every street corner! Thanks to inflation, my two falafel Pitas cost 700 Hungarian forint each or about three dollars.

I went on a walking tour of Buda and Pest, the two sides of the river and vastly different environments. Buda was on the hill with the castle and Pest was flat and had an organized street layout. The architecture was a mixture of many styles from around the world and was reminiscent of the different groups in power over time. I did not take many photos on the tours as some parts looked similar to things

I had seen, meaning I could soak in more the atmosphere of simply being there. I went on the Communism walking tour where I learned additional history of life before, during, and after Communism. The first tour was filled with Hungary's history and dry yet clever humor. It was interesting to learn the many ways of manipulating people under Communism once the Russians had liberated the country from the Nazis and stayed for 45 years. It was also interesting to realize that it wasn't the first time I had heard of such techniques being used as many continue to be in use today.

02/03/15: The Parliament building looked strikingly as the one in London, England, and the Chain Bridge looked like the Tower Bridge there too. Metal shoes on the river bank acted as a memorial to the Jews that were made to stand there as the Nazis shot them one by one and their bodies plunged into the river. There was a dark history in this country made of immigrants, Hungarians, Jews, and gypsies. As the tourist guide admitted, locals supported the wrong side of the war by standing with the Nazis. Then they underwent Russian liberation and occupation. The tour guides emphasized, before their respective tours, they wished to stay as objective as possible and let attendees decide for themselves what they liked and believed. When guides added opinions, they clearly stated it was personal opinion and not fact, but the personal anecdotes of family life under Communism added a good sense for what life was like during that time in history. Democracy came in 1989, so there was a young government in place, and people were happier. The Liberty Statue was put up in 1947 in dedication to Soviet liberation. From the statue atop the hill, there were amazing views with Buda on the left and Pest across the river on the right.

02/05/15: I slept in again to let my body recover some energy. After slowly preparing myself for the day, I headed off to an Italian restaurant a kilometer north. As I was leaving Nepal, an older lady came to the volunteer house to begin her own volunteering experience. I was well adjusted to the local lifestyle, so I helped explain and host her with Nepali tea and advice for getting around. Her son lived in Budapest and offered to take me to lunch, so we arranged a lunch. It was very good food, and it was nice to feel how small the world really was.

Afterwards, I visited the House of Terror. It was a museum within the same building used as a headquarters during both Nazi and Communist regimes. Inside were remnants of the era, video interviews of survivors, and examples of the control tactics and propaganda used to eliminate popular support for democracy in 1947 and promote communism. I descended floor by floor to eventually reach the basement where they kept any enemy of the state for torture, interrogation, or execution. Some prison cells were too small to stand or sit in. There were wooden structures used to hang people by their hands. At the end of the exhibits were over a thousand photographs of the victimizers as in those involved in perpetuating these criminal acts over the years. Usually, museums focus only on the victims, so it was powerful to see the faces of the perpetrators who could not be distinguished from the faces of their victims. The scariest part of the whole experience was not the horrific acts committed against Hungarian civilians in the name of a dictatorship, but how many parallels I realized between their tactics to control a population and those I continue to see in use by countries which promote equality and safety for their citizens.

02/06/15: I woke up the next day and rushed to the Jewish tour. I learned more specifics about the treatment of Jews by Hungarian Nazis and then life under Communism. A scary anecdote was how the German leader overseeing Hungary at the time was surprised at how enthusiastic the local people were to do their job of tracking down Jews. I walked by the second largest synagogue in the world and the mass graves in its backyard. I walked by part of the ghetto wall although it was rebuilt in the same location to resemble the original. There was a plaque thanking the Russian liberators who, for those suffering under Nazi rule, truly were liberated. While there was only criticism for the Communist rule that ensued, Nazi removal was a lifesaver for many. And now Hungarians believed they were on the wrong side of both World War II and the Cold War. In retrospect, it was not a radicalized community that targeted itself and sold its neighbors for not clapping loudly enough at pro-government, Communist rallies but rather ordinary people believing the rhetoric handed down to them. Every government did this to flourish, but I felt it was the people's responsibility to be educated and aware of what was happening in society at any time to ensure evil acts do not occur unnoticed. Ideally, people could see how history repeated itself and avoid making the same mistakes again which was why I enjoyed learning about the history of the city and country.

Traveling to Russia while the ruble was half of what it was six months prior was fantastic for a tourist which made prices so much cheaper relative to the dollar. I arrived in Europe to find the euro at its lowest point in the last decade which lowered my costs too. Either I was the smartest traveler as I followed economic disasters or an evil one as economic disasters followed me.

I had a last lunch with my Portuguese friends to celebrate our goodbye. My last few days in Budapest were spent with two Brazilian travelers, a Slovakian student who knew six languages, and a German student. We met at Szimply, a ruins bar, and made plans for the following night. We swam in thermal baths which were giant, outdoor baths when the weather was below freezing. Walking from one pool to the other was brutally cold, but we stayed for three hours or so talking and playing in the artificial whirlpool. It was within a beautiful building with marble statues and fountains overlooking the baths. That night, we all went out for dinner and a drink, and then I had to say goodbye to them as well.

One tour guide pointed out a fantastic mural that showed the city of Budapest in black and the Jewish quarter in red, saying there was more to see in Budapest and its surrounding areas than this small area. It was a good point to make, because this quarter had boomed in the last few years for entertainment, nightlife, shopping, and I can say most of my time was spent around these neighborhoods. Budapest was an amazing city with a conflicted past, but it was growing into a vibrant community. No matter where I went and what country it was, everyone was friendly and helpful.

Belgrade, Serbia

I decided this morning I would go to Belgrade, Serbia, instead of Brasov, Romania, because a stranger told me it was beautiful. Belgrade sounded cool, so I hopped onto the night train. The train ride was an interesting night filled with passport checks leaving Hungary, another entering Serbia, and finally ticket control.

I arrived at Nina's apartment in the city as part of my first couch-surfing experience. Walking through the worn-looking city, I passed a street peddler with fox fur and various animal skins on the street. Once had I settled in, I returned to the city to explore further!

From what I saw and heard, the city was living back in the 1950s. The downtown was mostly cement buildings with some bombed buildings preserved in the southern part of the city. The mentality was strongly patriotic and resistant to change despite poor education and infrastructure. When I arrived at the tiny train station, there were men with hammers to verify the wheels had not cracked along the way. I had a nice Americano coffee at a classical Dorian Gray café with Nina's boyfriend, but the rest of the city looked a bit weathered down. Some may wonder why I came here, but the remnants of the nation's history under Communism were even stronger than in Budapest. The previous cities had been well maintained and developed, but this was truly a step back in time with a different people with vastly different mentalities.

There was some Serbian hatred of Albanians and Croatians over a relatively recent conflicted past. There was also anger with NATO as they bombed Belgrade in 1999, because the government would not share land with people in the South. My host thought so many aspects of the country were catastrophic. While newspapers talked about whether the country should join the EU, half the people were struggling to simply earn a living. These were the same, pressing issues I heard over and over again in every country I visited.

02/07/15: I went on a small sightseeing escapade today. I saw additional bombed buildings from the 1999 NATO bombings for not giving Kosovo, a southern city, its independence. I walked through a 1000-year-old fortress that had been partly demolished 500 years ago. Several city buildings were built with cement. Granted, it did not seem like the most appealing city. People recommended it to me, and afterwards I realized that it was humbling to be in a city that didn't seem to be growing as quickly as other cities. It really felt like a blast into the past or a black and white movie as weather was cloudy, cold, snowy, windy, and rainy. I had walked back into a different decade, and. I did not find many of the social niceties I had experienced in the rest of Europe.

I met with the grandson of the sister of a family friend named Stanko. He was a really bright interior designer in school and about my age. I liked how he mixed up the English words "ponytail" with "horsetail" and "rabbit foot" with "bunny paw." It was mind-blowing that within 12 hours my family friend in California informed me she had family in Belgrade on the other side of the planet and for Stanko and I to set up a meeting.

I was walking through the city with Nina when a cab driver started yelling at another driver and saying some pretty over-the-top cusses according to Nina's translation. Nina said a taxi driver could call his friends to come beat up a customer who wouldn't pay the exorbitant price they charge foreigners. Nina said to be a man was to be as macho as possible. Balkan women were supposed to be very feminine. This meant many women looked plastic and Barbie-esque. It was a very polarized world to be in, especially for younger people.

Nina had a very interesting story. As a child, her father told her she was a mistake, and her mother said her father was a liar and cheater. The parents separated, and her mother paid for Nina to go to a private, American high school in Serbia where Nina loved her classes and did very well. Her mother refused to pay for an American university, so Nina went to a local university where classes were of lower standards, and her interests and motivations dissipated. She started working with disabled children, because she felt she could help them escape a traumatic childhood like her own. It was too depressing for her, and she had to change jobs. Later, she became pregnant. She wanted to keep the child. While she was three months pregnant, her father had pre-paid a doctor to assist in an abortion after telling the doctor lies about how the boyfriend beat his daughter. When the father pointed out some health issues about the pregnancy, he took her to the doctor. She was in such distress, and she was asking her doctor if the baby would be okay. The doctor said yes and had her sign a form to help the baby as she was of a unique blood type. She did not read the form but was told she had to sign it. The doctor then gave her a spinal tap and performed an abortion. After the abortion, her spirit and heart were gone as she lost the child she wanted and would never have again. She took him to court, but her signature, signed under manipulation and distress, inhibited her from any legal retribution. Her father also defended himself by going to the hospital and having false medical reports made of how she assaulted him with forks and bats. Even the police were skeptical of his reports due to her small stature and his large size, but what could they do? Her friends tried to offer their support, but the father soon made false police reports of how her friends threatened and stalked him at his home.

It was a false and master manipulation of a system that was built to defend people in need. She had since cut off all ties from both parents and had not received news or concern of their well-being. She told me this as I hoped to become a family doctor, and I share this here as a lesson that abuse can take even the most pervasive forms, and mental abuse or trauma had little, legal defense from what I know. Abuse was very difficult to prove. Still, the most beautiful thing was that while stories like this one could produce drug addicts or criminals, she was kind-hearted, sane, and working hard to make a happy life for herself. Part of growing up involved bad experiences to learn from, and my experiences didn't even begin to compare to what she had gone through. It was unbelievable to see a flower grow out of darkness.

02/09/15: I took the night train from Belgrade to Sofia, Bulgaria. Nicknamed "The Night Train from Belgrade" by my fellow travelers and I, it was the weirdest possible train trip imaginable. I walked up the aisle and felt like I was in Alfred Hitchcock's film *The Lady Vanishes*. Each person was an extreme caricature of bizarre looks and behavior. I had no doubt that our sitting on this night train in Serbia looked like the beginning to any number of thriller films. I sat with the same two Germans I met on the train towards Belgrade as well as two Swiss. We saw one man dressed like a pilot with a cigarette lazily hanging from his mouth. He made us believe we were on a plane, creeping along anywhere between 5 km/hr and 80 km/hr. There were frequent random stops that we assumed to be brake checks. There were no food carts, only plausible ammo carts. Our plane had no wings for aerodynamic purposes, and it was headed towards another airport. Perhaps it was because I did not want to close my eyes until 5am that everything was so hilarious. Reaching the border with frequent, unexplainable stops took 10 hours. The Germans made a joke that we had historical train museums in the West, but Serbia lacked them. Why? All the trains were still being used. None of us had prepared for such a long trip, so all we had to drink were a bottle of wine with a bottle cap, a single water bottle, and a large thermos of tea.

The Bulgarian morning met us with cold air and snow-capped forests. The train became very warm as there was no air flow. Our part of the train was non-smoking, so the airy compartments between cars apparently became the smoking section. Everyone respected the rule except the pilot-looking guy. Passport control into Bulgaria involved an official taking everybody's passport and disappearing for 30 minutes. When he returned, he had to play the game of find-your-passport-in-this-huge-stack-of-passports-that-I'm-carrying with each passenger. I flipped through mine to find no stamp or anything. Brilliant. I awoke after 2 hours to find myself in Sofia. The strangeness of the night seemed like a dream, but I knew we had been laughing all night on "The Night Train from Belgrade."

Bulgaria

02/11/15: I headed to the hostel in Sofia, Bulgaria, checked in, and napped for another two hours. The hostel was a renovated, old inn that used to host travelers over a century ago. The new part was that they served free breakfast and dinner.

I awoke to join a free walking tour in the 6,000-year-old city which I learned had a fascinating history. There were ruins from ancient Rome, medieval times, and modern day, each constructed on top of the previous time period. The city was a mixture of Roman rule, Ottoman rule, Communism rule, and democratic rule. The same buildings could change use depending on the rulers. It was funny that during Communist rule, there was a large red star above the Parliament building. People at the time thought the star was made of ruby. When it came down in 1989, citizens discovered it was cheap, red glass.

There was an intact, Roman church from ancient times with the same roof from that era. It was converted to a mosque during Ottoman rule then returned afterwards to the Church of St. George as it currently stands. I could walk inside and admire the interior of the still-active church. Constantine used the church and built brick apartments just next to it for himself and his guests. There were thermal baths and springs which offered hot water running underneath the floors as a basic heating system.

There was a king that survived an assassination attempt. The plotters knew he was well guarded, so they killed his top general knowing the king would be more vulnerable at the general's funeral. They paid the priest to load the church basement with dynamite and exploded the building after people had entered. The king survived, because he wasn't even there. He was running late as he had gone to another funeral just prior to that one.

There was a mosque in the city that locals wanted to remove. While they couldn't plunder it legally, they came up with a clever plan. It was a rule that if the minaret tower of the mosque fell, people would no longer pray there. They loaded the minaret with dynamite and waited for a large thunderstorm to mask the sound of the explosion. The building became a museum. It seemed people were proud of their religious tolerance due to a city square bordered by a synagogue, a church, and a mosque. I walked along some smaller roads between sightseeing, and it felt as if I could have been in a small, American town, because the buildings, roads, and parking zones looked so familiar. The only difference was that signs were in Bulgarian.

The tour guide emphasized that every statue in the city had some errors. People were so proud of lions being their national emblem that they put three lions onto their coat of arms. One lion statue was made and on its way to Plovdiv, Bulgaria, when someone decided it looked too skinny and weak, so they plopped it in the city in isolation by the large church. The architect for the city's grand theater built a magnificent structure and painted gold on the statues over the entrance. He happened to paint the groin-area of a baby boy in gold, so he lost his job after that. The guide laughed that it was named the "Little Boy with the Golden Penis." Nobody ever removed the gold. Two giant lion statues stood in front of another building within the city. The sculptor realized after he finished the first statue that the lion was walking with both right legs together instead of naturally alternating with the left side. His discovery stopped him from making the same mistake on the second statue, but the first one remained much to the entertainment of its viewers.

There was also a yellow brick road that ran through the center of the city. The government paid large sums of money to import the beautiful stone from abroad. Unfortunately, the stone was very slippery when wet, so people were outraged their government wasted money on it. The government told people it was a gift instead of a purchase to appease them.

After my nap, I went with a South Korean, also from "The Night Train From Belgrade," to meet our German friends for drinks and conversations. We stopped by a candlelit bar and an apartment fully converted into several lounges in different rooms. Every room was full of unique decorations, music, and atmosphere. Because it was a home, every room had an atmosphere of ease and comfort even if it was empty. I returned at 3am and relaxed the next day to write and clear my head of the ideas that filled it as I thought and listened to others.

02/15/15: Plovdiv was extremely characteristic. I first heard of the city last year when it was nominated for "European Cultural Capital 2019" from an article about travel destinations. My hostel was in the center of the old town in a cute, old lodge and a three-minute walk to an ancient Roman colosseum. Plovdiv was called the "City of Seven Hills," but there were only six as the seventh was blown up to make cobble for the roads. The roads were entirely cobblestone of different sizes and shapes. Graffiti sadly ran across many rocks on the hills, but I came to see it as a way for disgruntled people to express themselves. This was a different feeling for me than seeing carvings into old, Indian sandstone temples and being angry at defacing such historical structures. I also saw a wall painted with "Love Your Mom."

I spent one full day venturing up two hills and out of the city center to visit the suburbs before taking a tour of the old town and ancient ruins. In the city center were the Roman ruins of an elongated arena, and the inhabitants built a medieval wall centuries later to define the city's border. Both lay in the middle of a much larger, modern city. People today still use a nearby large and mostly intact Roman theater for theater and weddings.

A statue sitting along the main walkway was of Crazy Milo, a famous local who could always be seen on the streets making jokes and playing with children in the 1950s. He had meningitis as a child which led him with a wild personality. One hand was on his ear, because it was said he was deaf. The other was in his pocket to represent his other indulgences. A patron of the city made a statue of him post-mortem, because he felt local unique citizens should be recognized as well as military heroes.

After the city tour, I went to a patisserie with two German women and one Japanese man. I ordered a Belgian hot chocolate, two scoops of gelato, toast with cheese, spinach and egg on top, and a coke float for six euros. It was exquisite and amazingly cheap. Location, location, location. Afterwards, I went to dinner where the two Germans and I shared the most delicious Bulgarian food from salad and local, feta-like cheese to fried and stuffed mushrooms. I bought a local beer, a glass of ouzo, and a glass of local liquor to taste. I again paid six euros for everything. The next morning, I woke up feeling I had seen most of the city, so I departed to the next city.

02/16/15: My impression was that I had never seen such a small and cute city with a historic old town. It was also a city of stray cats everywhere. In the old town, people bought houses and rebuilt the second floor wider than the first floor to gain property space without paying for greater land use. For Europeans, this translates to the first floor being wider than the ground floor. I learned the story of a wealthy man and his beautiful daughter who lived in one beautiful house. Bachelors wanted to court the daughter, but her father sent her to study in Romania where she found a lover. Upon returning, a lightning bolt struck the young couple and killed them both. The heartbroken father then donated the house to the city which became a museum and he moved away. In the perimeter wall of one courtyard was a small room built for women to gossip during Ottoman rule when women were not allowed to meet and talk openly in the streets. I left thinking very highly of the beautiful country with gracious people and charming, affordable housing.

Istanbul, Turkey

While I could have taken a night train with my train pass, I decided that morning to hop onto a bus leaving immediately towards Istanbul, Turkey, for 20 euros. The border crossing was delightful as I was singled out as the one non-Turk and non-Bulgarian. I was instructed to meet with a border guard who was relaying my passport information over the phone to someone. I was questioned on where I was going, what I was doing in Turkey, if I had friends there, if I was Muslim, what my job was, what my exit plans were, my phone numbers, and if I wanted to go to Syria. He was not satisfied I was traveling alone with no return flight reservation or accommodation reservation or friends in Turkey. After asking if I was Muslim and wanting to go to Syria, I realized what was happening as many Europeans were traveling to fight for ISIS. I only understood the name "Syria" after the fourth repetition, because I never thought of it as a plausible destination. It was an odd situation, but I felt grateful such checks were in place at a critical point of entry. I volunteered to open my bag at which point I pulled out dirty clothes and a bottle of liquor I had just bought with the last Bulgarian lev in my wallet. I remember the look of surprise on the two border guards' faces when I pulled out the bottle.

They asked me if I drank alcohol, and I said, "Of course."

After volunteering to show my travel blog as well as my contact with my cousin who would be visiting Florence, he let me go after even more discussion and relayed information over the phone.

I arrived at the hostel in Istanbul to a very courteous receptionist who smirked as he placed me in a room with an Argentinian lady and two German girls. After introducing ourselves, we gathered outside with a few Turks, two Brazilians, a Russian, and a Gazan. I introduced them to the social game "Never Have I Ever." Soon, everyone was falling over laughing at the stories that arose during the game.

Istanbul was a lot more modern than I expected with European-style streets, buildings, and shops with salesmen inside and outside. I was expecting something less modern, but it looked like any other big city. The only Turkish elements I could see were the people and signs in Turkish. I had the same feeling in Sofia when I could have been in an American suburb.

I explored the city and mosques with the two German girls and Argentinian lady. We even took a 20-minute ferry to the Asian side of the city for a few hours to grab 70 cm long kebabs. The views with seafronts and minarets that pierced the skyline were stupendous. The mosques were definitely the highlight of the city, namely Suleyminya, Blue Mosque, New Mosque, and Hagia Sophia.

02/18/15: I walked into some of the larger mosques of the city. I removed my shoes, put them in a plastic bag that I carried in with me into the enormous and elegantly adorned stone structures. There were faucets and seats outside to wash before prayer, and the marble had been worn out by water over centuries of use.

I appreciated the efforts taken at multiple mosques to educate people about the basics of Islam. I thought it was unique to see Islam as a way to repair the faith's identity from public scrutiny, but I was reminded later it was not unique to explain one's faith as I passed a Bible stand in the street. There was a sign in the mosque for those interested in understanding Islam that they should "Please contact our specialist in the Islamic Information Center."

One minute from the hostel was a restaurant sitting over a glass floor with views down to an excavated palace. It was a night to remember full of laughter and magic tricks with two Brazilians, two

Germans, and an Argentinian. We spoke English, German, Portuguese, and Spanish all at one table. This was a normal dinner conversation for me. We had two hookahs with apple and lemon throughout the night with coals that were replaced as many times as we wanted since the tobacco never ran out.

We spent another night at a bar across the street from the hostel where I met a Lithuanian couple. They were so helpful to the Gazan engineer who could not find work anywhere. They were adamant that helping him in Lithuania would help themselves as they called Lithuania a "tiny, boring country with nation-wide, fiber optics."

I found it intriguing how the young, 35-year-old Argentinian had her love affair go awry with an immature, 28-year-old Turk who ignored her completely after a friend told him she had hooked up with his friend unknowingly a year prior. I couldn't help but think he was conflicted between Western and Turkish values. I could tell he cared since he called her back to talk while we were walking to the bar. I kept walking and pushed the German girls onwards so the two could have some privacy in the street. I could tell it did not go well as she soon entered the bar crying and silently tearing away all night. The Lithuanian wife was so nice as she sat by her and talked about how immature boys were and such. It was fascinating to see an Argentinian and Lithuanian talk together in a mutual, second language.

The Gazan told me about how he had been robbed in another country, I forgot which one. He had 1500 of the local currency in his back pocket. He showed his empty front pockets to two teenagers holding him up, and upon being pressed to empty the back ones, conceded to take his robbers to an ATM. He withdrew 200 and gave it to them. On the way to the ATM, he befriended them by talking about their lives and school. After giving them the money, they parted ways in a friendly manner. On the way out, another man began to approach him, but the two teenagers told him this was their guy and to let him go freely. The Gazan could see the rest of the gang standing nearby, so it was good he did not try to resist, and he kept his 1500 in the end.

My favorite food in Istanbul was kumpir, a baked potato mixed with butter and cheese and filled with different pickled vegetables and sauce on top. It was very affordable, yummy, and very filling. I also really liked the yogurt drinks which were surprisingly easy to make and I think I will try back home. The Turkish coffee was so strong and so good! A sign of a good coffee was half of the cup being coffee grounds.

02/20/15: There was a snowstorm on my last day in Istanbul. I visited the Hagia Sophia and Blue Mosque, and then I went shopping in the local Egyptian market. It was just outside of the Grand Bazaar, and prices were about half to a third of what they were inside the tourist market. Tourist stores sold tea glasses for 10 lira each, but I bought a set of six glasses for 7 lira at a local store. The snowstorm made it difficult to walk around, but everything was really picturesque under the snow, especially the mosques. I enjoyed walking through small streets to find store owners making snowballs and throwing them at each other. A few high-speed pursuits flew by me with snowballs overhead.

I noticed two odd things: I passed by people selling fake money on the street with stacks of cash in multiple currencies that looked real to me. I even found a 100-euro bill in the middle of a crowded street, but my friend told me it was fake. I couldn't tell, so I just tossed it back on the ground for others to find it. The second odd thing was the poverty. I never saw so many families or mothers with babies before that always slept on the street. I passed by multiple children no older than five years old crouching on the sidewalk, specifically one little girl. It was very cold, and I was just warm enough with a sweater, heavy jacket, wool socks, and winter boots. She was sitting on the sidewalk with nothing more than a thin sweater, shivering, in front of a piece of cardboard for people passing by. As tragic as this seemed at first glance, what was more tragic was the story I heard on more than one occasion from other people at the hostel. Instead of offering children money which may go into someone's pocket, they offered the children food. The children refused the food and asked for money instead. I realized later that these children, if they wanted to, could easily find warmer places to be.

Similar to India, it wouldn't surprise me if these mothers and children were exploited for business and that getting money from passersby would probably be a reason to keep the children in the cold rather than helping them.

I spoke with a Kurd and a Syrian who had escaped his country months earlier. He was somber since he found out a friend had been killed that same morning. The hostel cook was either a Syrian or Iranian refugee. She had skills she could not use in Turkey, so she could only find work as a cook. The Kurd was incredibly bright and aware of social issues. He told me he knew people were good, and people only become so by being treated nicely. He said ISIS was not Muslim or human or even animals. I suggested ISIS looked like it came from the Middle Ages more than 500 years ago. He retorted they were living 5,000 years in the past. He continued that nobody kills each other in such a sick and disgusting manner. The rest of the night was spent watching him hitting on these two, new Argentinian girls over and over again. He was not subtle about it at all.

P.S. A Turk and Kurd each translated, "I love you," in their respective languages. The phonetics I understood, which they verified, were as follows: Turkish: "Sunny serviole." Kurdish: "Ass ash dot com."

I returned to the hostel lobby as I had a 3am airport shuttle to catch and later a noon flight to Rome. Earlier that night, I was in the same lobby. One of the Argentinian girls went up to get two cups of free coffee from the breakfast coffee machine upstairs. A hostel employee asked where she got the coffee at this time of night and that she should order and pay for it if came from the hostel. She said she had little packets they made it from. I sat on the couch watching the whole encounter. He tried to make it clear he knew she did not make it by stating they had cameras. As she spoke broken English, he asked me to help explain his view to her, but I knew she knew what she was doing. She admitted to taking it from the hostel finally, and he walked off angrily. She then scraped some change together with her friend to pay for the coffees. He later asked me how people could be like that. I had no answer. She was a college graduate and could not accept responsibility to pay for a coffee. I was embarrassed to be friends with such a person afterwards. If she was adamantly lying for a quarter-hour about something as trivial as a coffee, what trust could I place in her?

Italy

02/21/15: I arrived in Rome, took the metro into the city, and walked to the apartment of Daniela, a friend that my driver and I had given a ride to in Northern India. She was still at work, but her sister came out and brought me inside. She made me two sandwiches with a delicious unknown cheese, tomato, and a mystery, deliciously pickled vegetable followed by an espresso. Soon after, we left to pick up her daughter from school. Upon returning, we left with her other daughter who had an upcoming volleyball game. We dropped off her daughter and drove towards Basilica of San Clement which had three stories. At street level was a modern church. Below that was the Roman church whose columns were extended upwards to form those of the modern church. Even further underground below the Roman church was that of the tribal people before the Romans. The same columns extended through all layers to share a common architecture. After that, we visited the cloister and St. Paul's church, the biggest I had ever seen. I commented on its enormous size, and she said St. Peter's basilica was even larger. The cloister had a calming aura about it. I had never stood in one and felt so much at peace. It was impossible to describe the feeling found just by being inside that small courtyard.

It was time for her daughter's volleyball game of nine- to eleven-year-olds, and it was so much fun to watch. Some girls watched the ball go by while others shied away from it or hit it with their shoulders or faces by accident. I had just as much fun watching the Italian coach who was extremely Italian, to say the least, with lots of hand and body gestures.

I returned to Daniela's apartment after the heated match to meet her for the first time since Orchha, India. I settled in and talked with her before heading to dinner. She treated me to a delicious cheese plate, extremely flavorful, boiled artichoke, fantastic Italian pasta, and pleasant house wine. We ate the appetizers for thirty minutes before our pasta plates came out when I was already quite full and content. We took most of our entrees back as leftovers. I fell asleep as soon as my head touched the pillow.

The next day, I took Daniela's bicycle a few kilometers to St. Peter's basilica. In the main plaza, a man tried selling fast-pass tickets to skip the line for a higher price. After speaking to him for a little bit out of curiosity, he asked me what language. I said French, and he handed me a French guide. I was not quite sure how I should accept that he didn't believe English was my first language. Inside the basilica, my jaw dropped at the sheer size of the statues and paintings. I walked outside and paid a few euros to walk up to the dome and cupola atop the basilica where I had a birds-eye view of the plaza and city. The line I had stood in to enter the basilica was even longer now and snaked through the plaza. I was getting hungry, so I took out my leftover pasta and bread and had lunch sitting on the brick roof of the basilica. It was a hot and sunny day at noon, and I basked in the view of the dome as I ate my yummy Italian pasta.

I soaked up the view one last time then descended to the square and headed towards the Sistine Chapel and Vatican museums. After the Hermitage in St. Petersburg, I was a little bit museum'ed-out, so I was much more selective in what I stopped to see. I did find my most favorite painting and stayed there in the room for a long time. My favorite painting, "School of Athens" by Raphael, covered an entire wall. I couldn't believe I was standing in front of the original piece. The Sistine Chapel was packed full, and we had to be silent and no photos were allowed. Of course, I saw some people within the crowd trying to take pictures from waist level straight up. It was stunning to see the walls covered in frescos and the fingertip touch between Adam and God. Ceilings in every room were drenched in masterpieces. At ground level, marble statues flawlessly captured the waves of cloth robes.

In the contemporary section of the Vatican Museum, I saw a single branch coming out of the wall. I thought I must take a picture of it. I took a photo of the branch as a young woman stood next to me and also took a photo. I looked at her with a smile and a shocked look of what we just did. She returned the same look and smile, and then we parted ways. We did not exchange any words, but I'm pretty sure we both understood each other. I will definitely remember the encounter.

After the two sites, I took my bike and wandered the city, adding Trevi Fountain to my itinerary after someone told me to see it over a dinner of fresh pizza. I returned back to the apartment around 8pm to find my friend had just returned from work. We finished off the cheese plate from the night before, and with some pesto pasta she made, we had a great dinner in the apartment full of good music and laughs. She was a very high-spirited person, and it was entertaining to see how much I reflected that when I was with her. For dessert, we walked to a gelato place where I had the best gelato I could imagine. I had a scoop each of pistachio-pesto, dark chocolate, milk chocolate, and lemon custard.

The next morning, I quickly visited the Colosseum and Roman forum. I was speechless at the ruins I saw in Bulgaria, but Rome had many more. At a viewpoint overlooking the Colosseum, a girl asked me to take her photo. She showed me a photo she must have taken two seconds prior, saying that's what she wanted in the background. I agreed but was confused as the Colosseum was the only background available.

While walking through the forum, I passed by a couple who made sounds of "er, umm, excuse me" and pointed fingers in front of me. In one second, I stared at them confused, heard a beeping, turned around, saw a camera perched on a ledge, then purposely ran foolishly off scene. I heard laughing as I went, and I feel like I helped them have a great smile for their photo. Finally, I took the bike back to the apartment, packed, and headed off to the train station for Florence. For a two-day stay in Rome, I think I harnessed the expert tourist skills that I developed to absorb as much of the city as possible in so little time.

I noticed the difference between French and Italian languages. French was difficult to learn, because many letters were silent. Italian was difficult to learn, because what I thought were one syllable words suddenly increased in syllable count. For example, "hospital" in French is "hôpital" with a silent "h", but in Italian is "ospedale" with a vocalized last letter "e."

I had not seen so many selfie sticks since Japan. It didn't help I must have passed 50 salesmen on sidewalks selling selfie sticks and selfie tripods. Or were they just called tripods at this point?

I was more scared to cross the street in Rome than in any developing country. Oddly enough, I think it was because people expected surprise crossings in developing countries and were always cautious, but in developed countries, rules dictated right of way. I feared someone could misunderstand his or her right of way without thinking. It was a little irrational and also ironic that I felt safer crossing the road in busy traffic in Thailand than in Rome.

02/25/15: I stayed the last four days in Florence at a youth hostel. They had a pool that changed colors, a Turkish steam bath, and a sauna which I took advantage of. The pool reminded me of the changing showerhead within the old lodge-hostel in Plovdiv. It was so entertaining that I turned off the lights and showered under red, blue, green, and violet lights. Otherwise, I didn't spend any time at the hostel. I planned my arrival to Florence to match with my cousins and aunt who were visiting from France. The first day involved seeing Galleria del Academia and Galleria degli Uffizi. I saw the statue of David which was located at the end of a hallway. My jaw dropped when I turned the corner to see it, and it did not close until I left the room. I felt sorry for the statues between the hallway entrance and David as I imagined they received little attention. Its size and details were astounding as I could see veins and muscles that were so distinctly profound. Raphael, Michelangelo, and Caravaggio paintings I saw later did less to impress me in spite of how impressive they were.

Some paintings made me sit down and stare. Some made me smile as I couldn't help but respond in my head to the facial expressions I saw. Some drew me into the painting with them. Others made me stop in shock. The quality of work, be it painting or carving, astounded me every time. My companions found my doppleganger in a 400-year-old painting called "Orfeo" by Gerrit van Honthorst, and even I felt it was like looking in a mirror.

I enjoyed looking at art in museum at times, because it was like watching television. I could pick and choose paintings I liked as if I was picking channels. I skipped over commercials and spent more time with the shows I preferred. I particularly liked a painting of a room with many other paintings as if it was created just for the pleasure of the people centuries ago.

The second day involved visiting Pitti palace where I saw the bathroom Napoleon had constructed just for himself. My relatives and I visited Ponte Vecchio. The third day, we rented a car and drove to Siena and Pisa quickly. I heard a motorbike behind me in Siena, and I instinctively turned around to see where it was so I knew which side of the sidewalk to move to. I developed the habit of thinking motorbikes could ride on sidewalks from my time in Asia. Pisa was a nightmare to navigate as road signs were either missing where they should have been, hidden behind trees, or just wrong if they pointed in the wrong direction. Evenings were spent dining on pizza, paninis, pasta, soup, and lots of gelato. I averaged about a cup or cone per day. I was so happy to be with my cousins and catch up with them as I hadn't seen them in years, and one of them replaced me at home in California during Christmas while I was in India.

Walking through Rome and Florence helped me realize history books and pictures could not compete with the beauty of seeing the real thing.

I arrived yesterday in Milan earlier than expected without a map or WiFi available. I stopped in a coffee shop for two cappuccinos and pizza to write some things down before meeting my friend Alice. I had met her and her family at my homestay in Jodhpur, India. We rendezvous'ed after I reached her through a stranger's phone. She cooked a homemade, pesto pasta and made me a coffee which was in reality an awakening espresso shot. For breakfast the following morning, we had homemade cappuccinos which made me think Italian blood is half coffee with freshly squeezed orange juice and toast with butter and jam. I forgot how vibrant fresh orange juice smells in comparison to the bottled product. We went out into the city by Vespa, of course, to see the cathedral, medieval castle, park, Arch of Peace, and an expo I was interested to see on the Charlie Hebdo killings of satirical cartoonists. I found many of the drawings and magazines extremely clever and surprising that many of the same issues they drew satire against forty years ago were the same issues as today. Within the magnificent cathedral was a storybook of painted windows and one of my newly, favorite statues of a skinned man in which the muscles and blood vessels were visible. We finished sightseeing with a gelato.

Walking through Florence and Milan streets was like walking through a fashion magazine as everyone was so well dressed. Alice was studying fashion and reported that people in the streets were "fashion victims," a term she thought was common, but I had never heard before. It meant they lived for buying high-end clothing.

In each city in Italy thus far, I saw many Africans selling fake purses, electronics, or selfie sticks.

In Florence, my cousins and I saw an African enter the plaza shouting, "Alpha, alpha, alpha!"

Suddenly, the other Africans picked up their goods and began walking away. I looked behind them to see a policeman strolling along. While I was standing by another seller waiting for my cousins to leave a store 15 minutes later, he suddenly picked up his things and walked away. I started walking in the opposite direction when I saw a police car easing through the pedestrian traffic. Our safari jeep in North India used the same tactic to find the tiger. We saw deer running away, so we looked in the direction they came from to find the tiger walking through the trees like a fashion model on a catwalk.

One thing I wish Americans who have never left the U.S. could do would be to walk on a cobblestone street between old, stone buildings. It was a simple act that carried tremendous pleasure and appreciation for the history that built the city or town. Disneyland cobblestones do not count.

Thun, Switzerland

02/27/15: Stefan, a friend I met in Vienna, lived here. He met me at the train station and showed me the beautiful town of 15,000 people sitting at the tip of a lake. I was extremely lucky to have warm weather with clear blue skies which made it possible to see the Alps that looked like backdrops in paintings. We sat by the lake during the day and then at sunset by the castle atop a hill overlooking the town. The only sound was a highway buzz from a few kilometers away. We returned to his home to have raclette, one of my favorite dishes made of melted, Swiss raclette cheese eaten with steamed potatoes and accompanied by Rivella, a sweet, clear drink made from milk serum. It was only made in Switzerland and tasted nothing like milk as all fat was removed. The two of us had two blocks of raclette melted on a grill designed for raclette. We ate everything and afterwards had Swiss chocolate. After dinner, we watched *Lord of War*, the first movie to surprise me every two minutes with its witty dialogue and real-world relevance. I put it in the same category as *Blood Diamond* and *City of God*. We played video games until 4am as a great ending to a grand day in a marvelous area.

I would add three observations that surprised me. First, the supermarket offered hand-held, self-scanning machines while shopping, so one could rapidly pay when exiting. Second, the supermarket sold boiled eggs identified with colors like Easter eggs. Stefan was incredulous when I said scientists recently learned how to unboil an egg. Third, Switzerland has half-a-dozen subdivisions of organic in comparison to the single, broad category of organic in the U.S. which allows for mild levels of pesticides.

Germany

03/02/15: I met with Sabrina, the volunteer from Nepal, in Freiburg. After spending the evening with her and her boyfriend, we went to her village, Ewattingen, of 800 people. There was one store and one restaurant in the village. It was located in the Black Forest, and never before have I seen a landscape like that. The hills were long and vast with snow that blended into the horizons. Trees littered the valleys and German-style houses were either scattered across the hillsides or grouped together to form a small village or bigger town. I really enjoyed walking around the snowy village.

We had kebabs with her family for dinner. For dessert, we had a creamy, layered, homemade, Black Forest cake. Her father offered me a 12-year-old whisky and I returned the favor to his delight with my Bulgarian, pear schnapps. The following morning, I joined Sabrina for breakfast with four of her friends at an American-themed breakfast restaurant. It was not truly American, because there was a large variety of fruits, vegetables, cheeses, breads, and dips with the breakfast buffet.

When I arrived at her home in Germany, her mother offered to wash any dirty laundry I had. As I had a small amount piling up, I gladly accepted. Afterwards, it dawned on me that I was using a washing machine to wash my clothes for the first time since September. I had been washing my clothes almost every day by hand since I started my trip.

After spending a few days with Sabrina in her village, Max, another volunteer from Nepal, came to meet us. The three of us chatted over more Black Forest cake which is locally called "schwarzwalderkirschtorte." Max drove me back to his village an hour away called Gorwihl. My stay there was fueled by a delicious array of homemade, German-Austrian foods of cheesy bread balls, sauerkraut, and bread and jam covered in vanilla cream.

03/04/15: Max, his father, and I went hiking down the hill along a ravine which reminded me of hiking through northern California among pine trees except there was snow. The first night, we lounged on his brother's huge bed and watched a film using a projector with surround sound which turned the room into a small movie theater. The second night, we linked computers in the house to play a car racing game together with his neighbor. Yesterday, we went skiing in Feldberg which has the tallest hill, or smallest mountain, in the Black Forest. The bright, blue sky met the snowy hills on the horizon just like a painting.

I bought my last five flights for my return home. I was really shocked how inexpensive it was even by purchasing them a month before trans-Atlantic and northeast U.S. travel. Rather than using any flight-compare website I knew, I searched for "Flight from X to Y," and the search engine compared all airlines, not only those associated with flight-compare sites. The result was finding prices for one-way tickets at half of what I found with different websites with different airlines.

I woke up my last morning in Germany to catch a train from Switzerland to arrive in France. My voyage had finally taken me to a familiar country, language, and culture where I could relax in the nostalgia of seeing old friends and family.

Dijon, France

03/05/15: Geoffrey was a friend from my study abroad a year prior in Montreal, Canada. We spent the day following arrows placed within city center streets that guided us to churches, plazas, free museums, crypts, cafes, and bars. We went into a crypt below a church that was originally built in the 2nd century AD. To my delight, there were several gargoyles on the church. It was a night of good laughs and reminiscing over our Montreal experience together. Dijon was about as French a city as they come. We found a fromagerie next to a boulangerie next to a winery. There was also a moutarderie to sell mustard since it was Dijon. We bought nonettes, a type of spiced bread with caramel inside.

Similar Differences

Belgium

03/07/15: I met with another friend Antoine from Montreal in Brussels. He was very intelligent and easy to talk to. I didn't need to try socializing at all with him, because even spaces of silence with him were pleasant.

We walked around the city and talked across five bars where we had a single, Belgian beer at each. For dinner, I had notorious Belgian fries and a cheese soufflé. Brussels seemed like a typical European city to me. What made it unique to me was the Grand Place, a large plaza surrounded by the Town Hall and other eloquently designed buildings.

I woke up the next morning and decided to go to Bruges. I jumped onto the next train. Walking through Bruges reinforced my first impression of the streets and homes: Bruges is too dang cute to be a city. I managed to get my fill in this morning within two hours. I returned to eat veggie, gourmet burgers with Antoine in Brussels. My trip with him started and ended with a café on his back terrace in a quiet, large backyard. All we could hear in the middle of the city were birds chirping.

Similar Differences

Amsterdam, Holland

03/10/15: It was quite a city. The center screamed pure tourist. As I had seen from pictures before traveling to Bruges and Amsterdam, my gut feeling was right. Amsterdam was simply a larger, more touristy version of Bruges, far removed from the calm and simplicity of a small town. My visit was shorter than anticipated due to my lack of train schedule knowledge, but it still offered me the experience I wanted to have.

I stayed with Taliah, a friend I had met in Vienna. We joined a potluck her friends organized where I had the most delicious gravy with lentil cakes I had ever tasted. A group of us biked into the city center at night to walk around and sing karaoke. Taliah took me around the city by bicycle and through small streets on foot. The country was flat and the city was designed for bicycling. All in all, Amsterdam was a beautiful city with canals and paved roads but a bit too touristy for my liking even in the off-season. It was puzzling to see a red-lit window with its respective lady adjacent to a preschool on a Saturday afternoon.

We did stumble upon a student-occupied building where an intriguing speech was being given about the privatization of education. The one thing that stayed with me was how the term "university" 30 years ago was synonymous with "faculty," and today it means "administration".

Similar Differences

France

03/12/15: After a memorable time in Amsterdam, I took a train to Lyon. It was a long day with different trains from Amsterdam to Brussels, Brussels to Paris, and then Paris to Lyon. My friend Coraline picked me up at the train station in the evening. It was so great to see her since our last meeting was at the Safari Park in Thailand. Most of our time together in Lyon was spent tasting local food, delicious cheeses, and pastries.

The first night involved a magnificent dinner of pasta with a homemade pasta sauce. And don't think we didn't grate a huge chunk of cheese to put on top. She showed me high resolution video of us walking a young tiger and playing with the leopards as they jumped on us and played with the branch we teased them with.

The following day, we met for lunch in the Plaza Bellecour, one of the largest open plazas in Europe. The blue skies and sun made our lunch on the plaza even more enjoyable. I had a delicious croque-monsieur with a "caviar d'aubergine." It was beyond phenomenal for my palate. She went back to work while I walked up the hill to the basilica overlooking the city. The scent inside the church sent me back to my childhood when I strolled through a church in southern France. Similarly, the smell when I entered the house Antoine was renting in Brussels reminded me exactly of my grandparent's home in Southern France. For a brief moment, I was in another time and place.

Coraline and I met at her apartment in the evening for a meal of delicious snacking on macarons, cheese, jams, honey, and some Turkish delights I brought from Istanbul. I even added the big, American marshmallows courtesy of my friend's German father who wanted to give me a touch of home in my hot chocolate. We just stuffed ourselves and talked over the movie *The Secret Life of Walter Mitty*. Seeing the landscape in Greenland and Iceland ironically made me want to travel more.

For my last morning in Lyon, I took a stroll through the enormous Parc de La Tête d'Or, or Park of the Golden Head. The name came from a legend that a treasure with Christ's head could be found in the park somewhere. It was a beautiful and warm morning for a quiet reclusion to clear my head. At one point, I oddly heard some roaring. I continued walking to find what looked like the back of an amphitheater, so I thought someone was preparing for a show. It sounded like a dinosaur trying to clear its throat. I kept walking a few more seconds before I saw the source of the sound. There was a fully-grown lion roaring in the middle of the park behind a fence. He had a full mane and was truly a majestic and wild beast living in the middle of a civilized world. I returned to my friend's place to retrieve my bags before heading to the train station for an hour-long trip South.

I felt a peaceful energy when I walked on small roads in Lyon, but it was still unique from what I felt walking in any other old town or city. Each place had its own atmosphere. No pictures can do justice to the feeling of being there.

03/13/15: I left Lyon to arrive in Valence where my cousin Loic picked me up. We drove to his parent's house where my aunt had been cooking vegetarian dishes for me all day. She was clear that it was vegetarian, but I had to jokingly confirm. When I was younger, she tried to feed me ham quiche once, but she couldn't deny it once I discovered the small, pink pieces of ham. While eating dinner, I made the naïve mistake of filling myself on the first plate. She had made a quiche, and my family had one slice. I was hungry, so I had three slices. Once I was fully fed, she brought out the next two dishes: cauliflower au gratin and quenelles with mushrooms in a tomato sauce. I had forgotten that multiple-course meals are served in

France, and I was already full! I realized the gravity of my mistake. I was talking and absentmindedly filling my plate, but it was too late. The damage had been done. Needless to say, I was unable to finish my food.

I was happy to learn that both my aunt, uncle, and my grandparents had seen my blog. While my aunt could read some English, my uncle was sad there was no English-French translation. Alas, there were pictures. It was so nice to see my family again and even better that I could communicate without any difficulty with them and pick up right where we left off years ago.

03/19/15: Loic and I drove to Chambery to see his sister, Stephanie, and her husband and daughter, Florian and Lina. Lina was more articulate, intelligent, and cleverly creative from what I had in mind for a three-year-old. Saturday morning, we went to the outdoor market and then on Sunday to the boulangerie for a baguette. It was truly enjoyable to simply enjoy each other's company for the first time in years. It took the adults, along with the little one and the golden Lab, over an hour to walk to a nearby boulangerie and a good two hours spent at the open street market where Lina wanted to buy bright, red radishes even though she neither liked nor ate them.

I returned to Valence to eat pizza and watch a Marseille-Lyon football match with Monique and Alain. The next morning, I took a bus to Aubenas and was walking on my way to my grandparents' home when my father pulled up unexpectedly in his rental car. It had just been over six months since I had seen him, and the hug was long and far warmer and significant than any before. He had just flown in to meet me and see his parents. When we video-called my mother later that evening, I was shocked to realize that the time lapse since I last saw her made me see her more like any other person I had met on my trip. It had been such a long time since I had seen her face, and so many other people had crowded my mind since then. I was not the only one having trouble with faces though. My aging grandmother confessed she did not recognize me at first and wasn't sure if I was a woman or man. I could give her credit though as my hair had grown long. In discussing the health and stubbornness of my grandparents, the French doctor noted the post-world war mentality of my grandparents as "Shut up and continue to live no matter what." Unnecessary change was a threat to the satisfactory status quo.

Parking garages had always been tight squeezes, but in Europe where cars were smaller than in the U.S., it was even tighter. My father was trying to drive us out of a parking garage, and the passages were as wide as a sidewalk, making it feel like we were playing mini-golf with a car in order to exit.

In Japan, I came across a multitude of devices to help people function on a daily basis such as vending machines for meals among others. I had never thought of these devices before, but they made life so much easier. In Europe, I also came across devices that served beneficial purposes in everyday life, so I wrote some of them down. First, individual-use honey packets that crack across the middle, similar to how a stick will break away if both ends were pushed towards one another. This provided for a finger-clean, efficient, and more hygienic package to eat honey. Second, window shutters; they were everywhere. These were metal gratings that could descend automatically or manually like a garage door to cover a window for complete darkness. I had to sleep six months in an apartment in San Diego with poor-quality blinds and high-quality street lamps just outside my window. I didn't realize how poorly I slept there until how well I slept in a pitch-black room here. Third, a three-hole binder with a lever to open the rings. I had so many accidents pinching fingers or damaging rings as a child by manually pulling open the rings only to have them snap shut like a snake striking its prey. I would have gladly enjoyed a safer system when I was younger that would have also increased the lifetime of my school binders. Four, as I was leaving the park in Lyon, I saw a runner brush his shoes on a piece of blue turf to scrape off any mud. Why not? Five, only in France could someone receive a free bottle of wine with a purchase of three pizzas. I suppose it could improve daily life and maybe health if it was red wine in moderate amounts. Six, a TV homepage that showed all channels simultaneously on screen. The audio played for whichever channel was highlighted.

03/20/15: It was a bit odd to be walking alone through the streets of Pau. An eerie sense of déjà vu passed through me as I recognized streets and cafes from when I was here as a child and young teenager. The city was quiet with few people walking in the streets or sitting at café tables on the sidewalks. I walked through the city with a completely different purpose and experience. My cousin Lea had her apartment in the heart of the city by the chateau and church. Every 15 minutes, bells rang twice and even more on the hour. I enjoy visiting my family tremendously. This was a different kind of traveling. This was not a different culture or a different environment. This was not visiting old friends and visiting the cities they inhabited. This was making memories for times that never occurred in my childhood and strengthening bonds that would last my lifetime. It was humbling to realize all of the work my grandparents put in raising my aunts and uncles who in turn raised my cousins before I could relate to them and build these bonds many years later.

I went to see my grandmother Mamie Pinon. I talked with Mamie a lot and played with my first, second-degree little cousin, Jules. I could see the beauty of life on both ends of life as Mamie's face lit up at the sight of Jules. I learned a lot about my aunt's character and how deeply she understood her own two daughters. As I grew up so far away from my French family, I was extremely happy to spend quality time with each member. I even caught up with Jean-Philippe, my friend from St. Petersburg. We ended up at The Garage, a nostalgic bar I had visited four years earlier.

I left my family in Southwest France feeling extremely lucky. They spoiled me the entire time I was there with some of my favorite home-cooked food, warm, comfortable beds to sleep in, transportation from one place to another, and not letting me pay for my food or anything when going out. They were so well-mannered and considerate that I, as someone who has been described as very polite before, felt like a slob sometimes. I was grateful to have family like this and people in my life to show me different ways I could better myself.

My father and uncle equally defended me on separate occasions in front of my grandparents. "He just traveled around the world. He can make himself a cup of coffee without assistance."

03/26/15: It was an early morning wake-up call at 6:45am. After a full breakfast of toast and hot chocolate, I took a 7:20am train from Pau to Bayonne. Nico met me at the station. While my other cousin Elise was busy working that day, her boyfriend, Nico, took me on a tour of Bayonne along the Atlantic Coast by the France-Spain border while describing the historic and architectural beauty of the Pays-Basque. There had been an intense conflict for independence in the past decades, but the region now accepted being part of France. There were still proud radicals who wanted to separate, but they had relatively less power nowadays. Still, it was an extremely beautiful city that filled with tourists in the summer months as it lies on the coast. We stopped by Elise's apartment for a coffee before driving to Biarritz.

Biarritz was a smaller, coastal city and reminded me greatly of the cove in La Jolla, California, except I was looking out to the U.S. East Coast in the distance instead of Japan. It was cloudy, so we could not see too much of the coastline and mountains that extended into Spain. Biarritz was nicknamed "Little California," because Americans brought surfing to the area which became very popular among locals. It was also a popular tourist spot in general for Americans.

The city was fairly wealthy due to its location and desirability. I saw an elderly lady with her little dog, and I connected the sight to those I had seen many times in the U.S. My past experience was evidence for my toying hypothesis that the richer the city, the smaller the dogs.

I spent the rest of the evening in Pau talking with my grandmother. After she went to sleep, I stayed up and watched the movie *In Bruges* on TV. I was happy I could watch it in French and understand easily.

I had a slow morning as I woke up late. My uncle came over and bought lunch for one last meal with my grandmother before I left. We waited until Lea and her boyfriend, Louis, could come for an hour between classes to eat together and for me to say goodbye. After we dined, cleaned, and rested a little, I said my farewells to my family. My uncle drove me to the Toulouse Airport.

I slept in the same airport in Paris I did four years ago when I was also returning from a solo, short trip I did between Bordeaux, France, Athens, Greece, and Venice, Italy. The only difference was that I now had a big backpack instead of a suitcase.

Montreal, Canada

03/27/15: After six and a half months in Asia and Europe, I reached the third and last continent of my voyage. To this, I dedicate a paraphrased conversation I overheard between two young Americans at the airport in Toulouse. I could tell they were American by their heavy American accents

Male 1: Do you want to listen to X's latest album on the plane? I heard it's really f****** good.

Male 2: Have you listened to it?

Male 1: No, but everyone has been talking about it. I keep telling everybody I'll listen to it on the way to Paris. I'm gonna listen to it on the plane.

Male 2: Why not just listen to it in Paris? Then you can say you listened to it in Paris.

Me nearby: …

03/28/15: I used to add sugar and cream to coffee. In Saint Petersburg, I had a double Americano. It was the darkest, most bitter cup of coffee I ever drank, but also the most delicious. Ever since that one cup, I began to drink coffee straight. It is odd to say, but that one cup changed how I viewed the whole product. It also helped when I went through Europe where people drank espressos frequently.

The entire stay in Montreal was nothing short of pure relaxation. I stayed with Yassemine, a pole vaulter I practiced with while

I was here a year ago, and her brother. They spoiled me with food, a big bedroom, and transportation to the city and back.

One morning, Yassemine went to a boxing class, and I biked to a nearby shopping center to write in my journal for a bit. I had the pleasant company of Carlos from Trinidad and a Marcile from Barbados at the next table. They gave me their newspaper which was the Black Caribbean contact newsletter in Montreal. Reading it opened me up to an entire local community as the articles described the efforts and projects of local Blacks. I was impressed with the life stories I read. One was about a young girl with Vitiligo, the skin pigment-changing disease which first came to the public spotlight with Michael Jackson. For a young girl, it can be disastrous to her self-esteem, but with the support of friends and family, she became a spokesperson to raise awareness and support for those that share the affliction. Simply remarkable. A gentleman wrote an opinion piece on the radicalization of youth. With perpetual attacks from public media on their core religious or racial identity, young people could end up lacking a strong and respected identity, making them vulnerable to become disillusioned about using violence to regain respect. Nobody can be slandered that much without objecting somehow, and young people without guidance can easily become radical in their response.

Walking through the shopping mall was extremely disturbing. Yes, I was going through a bit of the cliché reverse-culture shock as I was now in an Americanized landscape with familiarly sized cars, roads, and restaurants. I could see material consumption on a scale which was almost nonexistent in Nepal. Some of the wealthier individuals in Nepal could afford many material goods, but I felt the average Nepali understood more than the average American that their material consumption didn't necessarily lead to more happiness, although we in the West believe it would. Just as people say some crime results from a lack of knowledge or availability of better means for success, I felt that some of the material consumption at the giant mall in Montreal resulted from a lack of knowledge or awareness of alternative means for happiness. The consumption I witnessed was insatiable, and I learned in Nepal that the happiness found among friends and family is much more fulfilling than any material goods.

03/30/15: I had the opportunity to spend a few hours wandering along the paths I traveled daily during my study abroad here. Here I was, having just crossed the Atlantic Ocean and taking a stroll through the city of Montreal. The whole experience of changing countries was about as eventful as going to the grocery store at this point. What mattered more to me was the people, friends, and family I met.

I sat on a bench in Mont Royal park besides McGill University. After all the miles crossed, I was extremely happy to simply sit on a park bench under the blue sky for a little while and find myself thinking of nothing at all. The seat was dry, but my legs lay flat on top of snow at the same height as the bench seat. That was a sense of pure bliss in that moment which I very rarely found but very much enjoyed. Serene was the word I would use to describe it, and I seldom use the word. Atop the mountain viewpoint, a single guitarist and singer brought speakers and beautifully played popular songs. His singing voice was great, but his French-Canadian accent sounded completely foreign to my ears. I had just spent three weeks in France speaking and listening to "French French," so the French-Canadian accent and different expressions were really difficult to listen to. I caught up with Yassemine that evening to watch her play a 2v2 soccer game inside a squash court. A true recycling of space, there were small goals on both sides, and players could use the walls to score.

My friend and her brother went to work and school early in the morning, so I hitched a ride with them into the city. I took the metro and bus to the apartment of my landlady's friend, Duska, who took care of me while I was here last. She was here with a British man she had met on her travels in Spain a year earlier. Coincidentally, he flew into Montreal four hours before I did from Paris via London. In his 60s, he had a lot of good critiques and broad perspectives of both the UK and U.S. that came from life experience instead of a college textbook. While they both had a mentality of their generation which clashed with mine a little, I was astounded at how their framework of life and people was still very forward thinking. They were both very interesting people worth listening to, so that's what I did while having a boisterous discussion to defend my viewpoints. I left them with hugs and handshakes to catch a bus and metro back to the school.

I met up with the mentor, Kristiana, I volunteered with at the Montreal Neurological Institute while I was here. Her father helped coach pole vault at the university. The work she does with patients undergoing immensely powerful and drastic journeys of body and mind due to ALS earns the utmost respect, and I was grateful to have had a glimpse into that field. I met her for lunch which turned into dinner. I had many great conversations on my trip about every topic imaginable, but nothing brought back the joy of talking with someone that knew biology on a similar level and was up-to-date with the science and politics of said science. For example, euthanasia had just been legalized in Quebec with heavy regulation. This was in contrast to the U.S. state of Utah that had just continued to uphold the firing squad for the death penalty.

I took a metro and bus to the shopping mall by the house. I missed the next bus by a few minutes and rather than wait a long time for the next one, I decided to walk home 2 km at 10:45pm. The moon was out and the air was comfortably chilled. I took many great walks in multiple cities, and each one was treasured as a calm way to straighten out my thoughts. It was a beneficial tool I never knew before, and I treasured the time alone in tranquility. On their way to work and school again the next morning, my friend and her brother dropped me off at the airport. Off to the USA!

USA

03/31/15: Airport bathrooms were always clean. I admired the vending machines inside them too. For two dollars, I could purchase a set of ear plugs, headache medication, toothbrush and toothpaste, razor, or condoms. Selling single condoms made me wonder. Either, the vendors were encouraging people to join the mile-high club or they were encouraging people to join the mile-high club safely. The mile-high club is a slang term used for those who engage in coital activities aboard a flight.

I never felt real power until I turned off airplane mode and turned on cellular data for the first time after seven months. I could feel golden energy coursing through my veins as I was free from the limits of WiFi!

Now that I was back to using American airlines, I could expect to not receive complimentary drinks, meals, or in-flight entertainment. Cutting services like human check-in and in-flight services does save money. I thought there was a minor tint of humor about in-flight services. While serving me an orange juice on my flight, I asked the steward if I could have some peanuts. He told me they only sell snacks! How can there be a flight without any peanuts? I thought I knew the lowest standard of in-flight services of any airline in the world, and they dropped below it.

145

04/03/15: I stayed with my brother Mat and his girlfriend, Chelsea, in their new home in Virginia. Housing there was very typical of traditional American homes. Everything was perfectly maintained. A short bike ride through the local park was a paradise.

I went with him to his work and finished a lot of writing I needed to do. I also enjoyed all of the free food and drinks that come with working at tech companies. After the first day of work, my brother and I met up with his coworker at the gun range. He let us shoot his 1911 and 9mm pistols, a custom-built AR-15, a Banelli shotgun, and afterwards, we rented a short-barrel AK on our own. The man at the range was helping to explain how to use the gun.

He was clear about how easy it was to use: "If eight-year-olds in Africa can figure it out, so can you."

It was a dark joke to say at a gun range to say the least. We had our best accuracy with the AK. His buddy later told us it is extremely easy to be accurate with such a rifle at 50 feet, but I was happy nonetheless. It was my first time shooting a gun, and I couldn't deny the power I felt using it and also the uneasiness about how easy it was to fire them. This was a new part of the country for me, so what better way than to learn about its local culture than to participate in it.

Mat, Chelsea, and I drove down to Raleigh, North Carolina, last night to celebrate Easter weekend the Southern way. I was excited. On the road leaving Virginia, I asked if the distance on road signs was in km and not miles. I had actually forgotten. Moving around in the U.S. made me realize even more so how different living was compared to the parts of Asia I visited.

I kept saying, "I have not done this in 6 months," or, "This is the first time in 6 months I've eaten this."

I really had forgotten about the conveniences and commodities that are part of daily life in the developed world. Each experience back in the U.S. was as if I was living it for the first time, except it was enhanced by the nostalgic effect of remembering how things used to be or taste when I lived in California seven months prior. I would say I was annoying myself, because I heard myself express my astonishment every single time I did something simple.

04/05/15: I spent Easter weekend with Chelsea's family. They did their best to introduce me to Southern culture and mentality. I was spoiled as we ate at fancy restaurants with buffets nearly every meal. I visited two different Easter Sunday services. One was a more traditional service with an older audience which included a choir, organs, Bible passages, and a bell choir. The second, more contemporary service was essentially a rock concert whose powerful music gave me incredible chills. The audience at the latter was mostly a younger crowd. After service, Mat, Chelsea, and I left to play corn hole before I flew out to Chicago.

I saw some bizarre things that could only be seen in the U.S. There was a stand of American flags in the store. Of course, the flag had to be made in America for national pride, but the pole and bracket did not and were, in fact, made in China. This reminded me of visiting the gift shop at Hoover Dam a year prior where one little shelf said proudly, "Made in USA," meaning the rest of the merchandise in the store was probably made in other countries. At home, my brother asked for an empty, cardboard box to ship something out, and it arrived inside another cardboard box. It seemed wasteful.

The South carries a very different culture from California. In the words of someone living in North Carolina, "Physical education, college, and healthy eating just aren't the typical things done out here."

One night, we went out with Chelsea's friends to celebrate her friend's birthday. At one time, they began what I thought to be a thoughtful conversation on racial issues. Chelsea asked if I was surprised and expecting to have an intelligent conversation in the South. The discussion lasted two minutes. I asked, as racism was socially accepted as normal in the South, if racism becomes an issue only when it conflicts with businesses or law? I was speaking in reference to the Indiana Religious Freedom bill in which businesses can deny services due to religious differences and the Uber driver who kicked customers out of his car for being gay. The response I received was what I would call simple rhetoric of how whites do not experience racism as a daily experience, which was true but did not entirely address my question. I had just as much enjoyment, if not more so due to novelty, talking to farmers in Nepal who barely spoke English. I couldn't deny I was extremely dissuaded about discussing more serious topics with Americans as I found it impossible to maintain and engage in a debate like I had in Europe and developing countries. Other conversation topics always seemed to arise to interrupt.

While I saw ingenious devices around the world that served unique purposes, I only began to see devices and rules whose purpose I really questioned here. At the airport, children could keep shoes on and reduced-risk smaller containers and printer cartridges were allowed. I told the Transportation Security Administration agent that many of the rules did not make sense to me, and he admitted many did not make sense to him either, but the rules came from Washington, DC.

I could have a free check-in bag if I paid for another service. After having been through dozens of airports in different countries, it struck me that basic, free services which are standard everywhere else in the world had been taken away as the new norm in the U.S. Then, airlines could charge to return those very services. Many airlines were proud to be adding WiFi and in-flight entertainment when many foreign airlines already had those services. One lady's water bottle didn't even fit into the slot on the back of the seat in front of her. WiFi was supposed to make my life more convenient, but the service required I install an app to manage the service myself. It made my life more complicated as I began reading through instruction screens and avoiding any traps to install additional tracking or advertising software that was defaulted to install when connecting to WiFi. In this case, WiFi was actually a service whose main purpose was to sell more things or collect more data from me. I gave up and opened my book instead.

04/06/15: I sat on the train after flying into Chicago to meet my other brother Jon. I offered a man on the metro who was dressed in a dark hat and sweater and snuggled into a corner some Easter candy, but he smiled and refused. Caution towards accepting candies from strangers apparently applied to adults too.

I was thinking about how in the last month of travel, I had not unpacked my bag like I did earlier in the trip. It was filled with clothes and gifts nicely packed away. I simply cycled back and forth between two sets of clothes that I kept on the top, so I never had to dig deeply through it. I was thinking of some other things when a man stepped onto the train across from me. He took off a shoe and sock and began massaging his bare foot. That was fine by me. He probably had an ache he wanted to soothe. Then he began scratching the skin and flaking away chunks of dead skin onto the metro floor. My only reaction was of slight discomfort as I gazed away. My stop was arriving.

I stepped off the train to have a group of teenagers yell a cuss word at me for no reason, and then I stepped over a white rag that was contrasted heavily with blood. The train experience competed for oddity with the one I had on "The Night Train from Belgrade."

04/07/15: There were certain Gotham-esque feelings to the city with its tall buildings and underpasses. Lights in Chicago at night were as numerous and arranged as letters on a page of a book. Street art was magnificent and unlike any public art I saw before.

The University of Chicago was an extremely picturesque American university. It had that prestigious, Ivy-League feel to it with its stone exteriors, wooden interiors, and libraries that look like they popped out of the 1950s. There was a beautifully simple and gothic church on campus that Jon told me serves as a multi-purpose room for all faiths.

I stopped by the large hospital nearby to sit inside the lobby and sense the ambiance. From my mentor's hobby of combining neuroscience with architecture in La Jolla, California, I developed an appreciation for relationship between structure and mood of one's own body. I sat in the hospital lobby and felt uncomfortable as very little seemed smoothly organized, and there were too many corners and pathways of foot traffic crisscrossing one another. I compared it to other hospitals I had been inside where the layout was much more uniform. It was impossible to become lost due to clear signs directing people where they needed to go, and I was not stressed with claustrophobia or fluorescent lighting when walking inside.

Later that evening, Jon and I went downtown and shared a deep dish, Chicago-style pizza. It was extremely delicious and not overly filling with white bread as was typical of most fast-food pizzas.

04/09/15: I walked around Chicago to explore the city and develop a sense of what life was like there. Compared to San Francisco, it was a much larger city but nonetheless less stressful to be in. Things seemed to move a little slower with less honking and things going on. It was a foggy day, but I was so happy to be in this new city. I started from Soldier Field and walked past museums along the water and through Millennium and Grant Parks up towards Navy Pier. I sat on the railing facing outwards to the water to absorb the fresh air. I walked back to the metro and went to Lincoln Park and the open zoo. I headed back into downtown to meet with two, old teammates from San Diego. We went up to the lounge at the top of Hancock Tower. It was dark outside and with the heavy fog, we unfortunately had no view of the streets below. Still, it was pleasant to catch up and see familiar faces.

I sat in on my brother's graduate-level lecture on mixed models for continuous data. While the minor details eluded me, I understood the overall approach and logical flaws to analysis. The professor, one of the founding minds in the field of meta-data analysis, described paradoxes and analytical mistakes that could only be caught if the analyst had a deep understanding and common sense about the data. He described how data could be presented in skewed or biased forms, often accidentally, that disguise true causes and may mislead any actions based off of the data. Data was always presented in single sets, meaning it took an educated observer to learn what the data actually said and its implications. It reminded me of a news channel that zoomed in on a bar graph between integers 35 and 36 to highlight the difference between group A and group B. The difference looked enormous, but an educated observer would realize the scaling was inaccurate as the difference between 35.00 and 35.99 was minimal on the scale of 1-100. The data was presented in a skewed way to elicit a particular response from the viewer.

The professor stressed the value in understanding context to understand the data in order to better structure the analysis. He also discussed the importance of breaking down data to individual components, a process called stratification, to better understand how data worked together. Otherwise, lack of context can induce a "misapplication of statistical methods." He described two studies which

traced the suicide rates of veterans, and each produced vastly different results. Interestingly, one study followed veterans a long time
after a war, and the other was completed immediately following a
war.

Proper data analysis was very important especially since it
could lead to political and economic policies that affect lives in very
real ways. The professor offered the comparison of effectiveness of
talk therapy versus drug therapy. When the data showed little distinction, many lawsuits arose targeting insurance companies for not
reimbursing both treatments equally. Also, patients who were very
sick would not have been found in randomized clinical trials, thus
biasing the variable group to a range of lower illness severity. Personal judgments about how patients' health improved or degraded
affected ratings. The timing of data presentation also had an impact
on how data was perceived. Just as a student absorbs information
differently when prepared for class, an observer can distinguish between data and prior personal bias to understand how data could be
interpreted by other people. Becoming an educated observer can
help anyone, because everyone will be faced with statistics and information from friends or news sources during their lifetime. People
need to break down topics into their components like people are
broken into the data points collected on them.

04/10/15: My father picked me up at the San Jose airport
and brought me home after a long day of delayed and canceled flights
out of Chicago. I remember distinctly when we got to the front door
of the house. I could not process where I finally was. This door and
house was my home, but it did not feel like it in that moment. I took
one step into the doorway. All at once, all of the hostels and hotels
in Thailand, India, Europe, and other countries began rushing into
my mind. I traveled through seven months in seven seconds. The
journey that had enveloped my entire reality for seven months, a lifetime of experience, had finally come to a braking halt when I stepped
through the front door. I could not accept where I was and what I
saw: familiar food, familiar furniture, and my mother. I had met so
many people that my home references and landmarks were a bit di-
luted, and my mother's face got a bit lost in all these memories.
Without realizing it, I had matured and experienced a lot and my

own family was not the only reference it used to be. The trip was a revolutionary stage in my life, and it gave me more skills and resources to be a better person with both a global and individual understanding I could not even imagine when I began.

The people I met and the hospitality offered to me astounded me; I will never forget, and the experiences will always affect me. I can only express a deep gratitude for each and every person I met and new friends I made.

One benefit of traveling through Asia before Europe was that I met many Europeans and Aussies who were also traveling through Asia. Consequently, I made fantastic friends whom I could graciously visit on the second portion of my trip in Europe in addition to the friends I already knew.

In Japan, I stayed with a friend from high school.

In Singapore, I stayed with a friend from high school.

In Vietnam, I stayed with a childhood friend.

In Prague, I stayed with a friend I met in Thailand.

In Budapest, the son of a volunteer I met and helped in Nepal took me out to lunch.

In Rome, I stayed with a friend I met in India.

In Milan, I stayed with a friend I met in India.

In Switzerland, I stayed with a friend I met in Vienna.

In Germany, I stayed with two different friends that volunteered like me in Nepal. I unfortunately missed seeing a third one.

In Dijon, I stayed with a friend I met studying abroad in Montreal.

In Brussels, I stayed with a friend I met studying abroad in Montreal.

In Amsterdam, I stayed with a friend I met in Vienna.

In Lyon, I stayed with a friend I met in Thailand.

In Valence, Aubenas, Pau, Bayonne, and Casteide-Candau, I stayed with family.

In Montreal, I stayed with a pole-vaulting teammate from there.

In Washington, DC, and Chicago, I stayed with my brothers.

In San Jose, California, I stayed with two of my greatest supporters: my parents.

I am incredibly grateful to all those I met and let me stay at their homes for a short time. It gave me a glimpse into different cultures and ways of living I could not gather from a hostel or an article. A coffee in Italy was not the same as a coffee in Switzerland nor was a tea from Nepal the same as a tea in Germany. The world is truly not such a large and scary place. I tried to say thank you in person, but that doesn't do justice to the fact that a day in each of their homes was a lifetime of memory and priceless lessons for me.

Similar Differences

Replica of a traditional
pharmacy in Osaka, Japan

Buddhist temple in Nara, Japan

Okonomiyaki dish in Osaka, Japan

Arayashima Bamboo Grove,
Kyoto, Japan

Preparing for the morning parade
during the Vegetarian Festival, Phuket,
Thailand

Feeding 7-week-old leopards with Coraline while volunteering at the Safari Park in Kanchanaburi, Thailand

Deepak in front of the pharmacy in Amarapuri, Nepal

Nepali brothers and sisters left to right: Asthmita, Shila, Sadikshya, Asok, Pratikshya, Adhitya

Daily Nepali meal of dal bhat with cooked spinach, other vegetables and sometimes curd, with fresh milk and water

On Poon Hill with a view of Annapurna Mountains, left to right: Sabrina, Anna, Benjamin, Yubaraj, Max, Nele, "Ma-Nose"

Pashupatinath Temple, a Hindu temple in Kathmandu, Nepal

The room I stayed in with my Nepali brother Asok in Amarapuri, Nepal

Farewell ceremony from Amar English Higher Secondary Boarding School

Guy, a fellow traveler I rode with to visit different Indian beaches

Jahangir Mahal citadel in Orchha, India

Boat ride through backwaters in Alleppey, India

Russian Orthodox believers celebrating Epiphany, the baptism of Jesus Christ on January 19th

Standing outside the Burj Khalifa in Dubai, UAE as it ascended into the sky

Walking by Catherine Palace in Pushkin, Russia with Jean-Phillippe and Elvira

A remarkable view of Raphael Loggias with biblical scenes within the Hermitage Museum in St. Petersburg, Russia

In one view, the modern street lies above the medieval church which stands above the ancient street level in Sofia, Bulgaria

Hagia Sofia museum in Istanbul, Turkey

Enjoying a delicious dinner at home with Daniela in Rome, Italy

Sitting with Stefan overlooking the lake and Alps from Thun, Switzerland

Off to ski with Max in Feldberg, Germany

Looking over the beautiful, snowy landscape and village of Ewattingen, Germany

Grandfather Lucien,
father Gerard, and son
Benjamin

Easter brunch buffet in
Raleigh, North Carolina

My travel belongings
fitting in one backpack

A familiar but forgotten sight of a typical
American street in North Carolina

Landing in Washington
D.C., USA

Landing in Kathmandu,
Nepal

Part II: Person to Person

Travel

International travel involves a spontaneous and involuntary opening of one's mentality. New cultures present new customs, languages, and ways of life.

First, a traveler sees everything as foreign. Second, a traveler tries to make sense about what he or she sees by relating it to what is known from living in the home country. Third, some sort of consensus is made that makes sense of the new and the old, thus forming a new awareness that is a combination of both foreign and home cultures. If done enough, a traveler can end up with a vastly different mentality and cumulative understanding than the one they had before traveling. Being exposed to different cultures expanded my ethical and moral standards which allowed me to grow into a better person.

In the United States, young adults, including myself, find a greater sense of independence after they move out of their parents' home for college or work. While I learned how to survive by living on my own during college, I learned how to live fully while traveling alone.

As far as I can remember, I've eaten fairly delicious foods in the United States, but I have never had a dish that made me close my eyes, put my fork down, and breathe in appreciation and awe of such a mouth-watering food. I can now say I experienced this sensation multiple times, and they were all during my travels. I look back on the strong, Americano coffee in St. Petersburg, Russia, that was so good that I proceeded to only drink coffee black. I had a plate of mushrooms wrapped in truffles in the capital of Vietnam that left me wanting only that for dinner. I couldn't speak after trying a salted, caramel dessert in Lyon, France. I had to stop walking on the sidewalk and close my eyes after I bit into a macaroon in Amsterdam, Netherlands. My palate will never be satisfied without international foods like this again.

My sense of the kind of world I live in changed. The world is as large or as small as I view it. From the moment I landed in Rome, Italy, to the end of my travels, I stayed with family and friends whom I had made previously on my travels that both housed and fed me. The experience graced me with the opportunity to witness many examples of the deepest hospitality I could imagine amidst Western culture. In summary, food can be microwaved at home, but I never would have known how much better it tasted when it comes directly from nature, either made by someone else or when eaten with my hands.

Travel is more valuable than saving money for something else, because the experience gained teaches invaluable lessons impossible to find in any textbook or documentary. There is no substitute to what one feels when in a completely foreign environment. I am now a strong believer that it is only when one is pushed to the limit that one is empowered and strengthened. Physical strength expands when facing new challenges in sports much like mental strength expands when facing, for example, new experiences during international travel.

Value and Culture

Values are the different parts of life people give importance to. We have social values for how to treat other individuals, ethical and moral values about what rights we have as individuals, and material values about how important, for example, a car is. Values do not stand alone though. They are grounded within a culture we see and experience daily. Different social, moral, ethical, and material values provide the basis upon which we first develop a culture. In the United States, moral and ethical values were originally described in legal documents which formed the culture of this country.

The values we define for ourselves create the dominant culture we share. As our values change, so does our culture. Slavery in its early form was valued under the culture of the United States' early years, but it is not valued anymore and is thus not included in today's culture. Women's right to vote was not valued until the 1920's, and now women's equality is growing within our culture. Civil rights hardly existed in the culture prior to the 1960s, but it is deeply engrained in our values today. LGBT rights were not valued until recent decades, and the discussion of how to incorporate these rights into present culture is currently underway. Our values do change, and our culture follows.

These broad examples within the United States operate on a societal level, but I found individual examples while I traveled through different countries and cultures. Different cultures gave hints to the values the locals shared. For example, as I walked through the Colosseum in Rome, I was intrigued by how we romanticize gladiators today. They were fierce, highly respected killers in their time but would not hold the same respect if they existed today. Rather, they would likely be labeled as brutal murderers even within a game. Different values are held at different times in history.

Bargaining was a new experience for me and an example of how values can conflict. A friend in Vietnam defined bargaining as an aspect of informal markets. Prices were determined by mutual agreement rather than the formal, economic markets with standardized, fixed prices with which I was familiar with in the United States. As a result of traveling to developing countries, my Western value towards money became out of place. The value I adopted towards bargaining, on one hand, was not to think twice about spending on necessities regardless of price. On the other hand, I would think twice about luxurious spending, be it 10 cents or 10 dollars. In reality, the value I held towards luxurious spending did not matter in developing countries since very little money could purchase more in a poor economy.

I had to change the value I had towards strict pricing, so I could be flexible and negotiate. I questioned the differences between paying a local price versus an inflated price versus a cheap price. A local price was what locals paid. An inflated price was a local price adjusted for wealthier tourists. A cheap price was an objective price of a product in the global market. For example, I wanted to buy a small padlock in Nepal. The street peddler asked an inflated price of 90 cents for it, but I paid a local price of 50 cents. Objectively, even 90 cents was a cheap price, but I wanted to pay what I subjectively felt to be the right price. Sometimes, it was not worth the time to haggle over matters of forty cents. Other times, it kept local prices low for the locals, and I felt good about paying what I felt to be right price. It may be cheap, but I would feel cheated by paying a higher price than I had to. Still, sometimes I paid closer to an inflated price, so the bargaining could end sooner. I still bargained over a dollar for sandals when in reality, my time and inconvenience of not having sandals was not worth the money saved by bargaining.

Many tourists paid the inflated price, because it was still a cheap price, and they felt they were helping the locals. One study I read suggested these inflated local prices damage local economies. Nonetheless, I lived two months with a Nepali family, and as I lived their culture, I picked up their value towards money and desired to pay as close to local prices as I could. It also helped as I was on a tight budget.

Call me an academic, but I tried to think of the societal consequences of bargaining from the individual upwards. Singapore established strong rules, fares, and checks on employee-customer honesty. My taxi driver in the small country told me if I tried to cheat him by leaving without paying, he could call the police and have me arrested. Likewise, if I felt he tried to cheat me with the meter, I could call his company and have him fired. This mutual understanding and promotion of honesty made me feel safer and less anxious about being cheated. If greater honesty and fairness arose from fixing prices so that any tourist or ensuing foreigner paid the same price as locals, it seemed bargaining between the vendor and customer would then become a remnant of developing cultures. Still, bargaining should not be stressful for the traveler. It should be seen as an opportunity to calmly and respectfully pay what is desired.

I also looked for the principles in spending, and I had many examples of this in a village in Nepal. For a good cause I trust, I will gladly spend ten dollars. There was a village concert fundraising to provide care for two boys who had developed Hepatitis B. I donated $10 and received great recognition and appreciation from the village as I was the first foreigner, certainly an American, to ever donate in such a small village.

When I was at the health clinic with my Nepali colleagues, a beggar with no tongue came and asked for money. The man with no tongue had a card from the government describing his situation in both Nepali and English and offering karma for helping him and curses for not. I offered him some money, but he refused, showing his accounting booklet that showed even higher donations. I was speechless and confused when he refused, thereby allowing my Nepali colleagues time to collect a small additional amount and give it to him. He targeted me for being a foreigner and was discontent with the money my peers and I offered. I felt cheated and victimized after I gave him a dollar, because I thought he did not respect anything about me other than my wallet. I discovered shortly afterwards he continued to chew tobacco which was why he lost his tongue in the first place and made the donation seem more futile and more similar to thievery than aid.

A mad man in the village beat his forehead with a small rock to drink the blood that dripped down. He appeared poor with his shaggy clothes and lack of shoes, yet I was told he had over two million rupees to his name. He gestured for food, so my friend pointed him towards the restaurant.

Begging often involved guilt-tripping, and I despised guilt-tripping as a weapon to abuse the trust of others. I was fortunate I did not have to beg in my life, but many people here lived in a poor country and work hard, sometimes failing and falling to desperate measures. Whatever lessons I learned while traveling, I always found an exception. The 70-year-old blind man who was eventually convinced I was American and sang for me did not ask for money. He only wanted to share a smile with someone.

In France, during commercials for foods or other products, there would be Public Service Announcements (PSAs) at the bottom of the screen for the entire commercial. I translated them and, having been habituated to American television commercials, was quite shocked they even existed. Some of these PSAs were as follows: For your health, do not consume too much fat, sugar, or salt. Do not snack too much between meals. Regular physical activity and playing is good for a child's health.

The culture of how citizens view health and consumerism in France is vastly different than in the United States and is a simple example of cultural differences as such PSAs would never be seen on American television. This can be demonstrated in the following analogy. Americans value their cars. They take great care of them to ensure they look pristine as long as possible. Europeans take this same value of increased function and longevity towards their health. It shows in the French and European value of healthy foods, exercise, and restraint of unhealthy habits. Some Americans do not seem to value health the same way, and the culture surrounding health is different as seen by the diet, lifestyle, and healthcare system. The U.S. values the business of food which is different than French values of the social nature and health of food.

It does cost more to buy a new car than to provide upkeep through preventative maintenance. If one values the thrill of speed over a car's longevity, the owner will wait until the very last minute when the car is breaking down to seek a mechanic. Ironically, Europeans care less about their actual cars' appearance as seen by bumping other cars in order to parallel park into spaces smaller than the size of their cars. Perceived value of health can be seen in the disparity in health spending between the high costs of the United States with extensive care after things break down for lack of continuing care and many European countries which emphasize more preventative care.

I grew up bicultural having grown up in the United States with French parents. Already accustomed to cultural differences, I was naively surprised to encounter several unexpected attempts to compare different cultural values during my travel as I met other travelers and locals in developing and developed countries. I met an American girl studying in Milan who stated Italy was so different from America. I explained I found Western European culture similar to that of the U.S. in terms of housing, shopping, and driving, and she elaborated what surprised her was the difference in mentality between Italians and Americans. What I found obvious from years of observation growing up was new for her. For everything that was to be experienced and seen, it would always be new to someone somewhere, and I could not patronize her for being less exposed to foreign cultures as I would not want similar treatment from those more traveled than I.

Outside of the health clinic I volunteered at in Nepal, the village priest called me an untouchable. He was a Brahmin, the elite social caste, and an untouchable was of the lowest social caste. He expressed himself mostly through hand gestures that he would not eat food if I prepared it. He continued that while he, a Brahmin, came from the head of the creator, I came from the foot. I was speechless at first as to what to make of the encounter. I later found out from my Nepali brother that the exchange had been very rude.

However, to me, it was a harmless, social interaction as he was expressing his thoughts, and it helped me understand what kind of man he was and the surrounding culture he lived and breathed on a daily basis.

In the U.S., I did not need to ignore vendors, because it was not in the culture for merchants to heavily push products on clients. Without excessive demanding from vendors, a culture of politeness flourished. However, when people were trying to make ends meet, they could not afford not to be demanding. In developing countries, I had to draw strict boundaries to protect my own time and money from vendors.

The culture I found in different countries often surprised me. One sign the world was really a small place was that I heard American music in every village or city, no matter how remote. American culture is truly a global culture, and Europeans assimilate it slowly over five to ten years. It reaches developing countries even more slowly as I saw many 1990's haircut styles in Nepal. My perception of the Latvian, Max, I met in St. Petersburg changed dramatically as I spent more time with him. He had developed his own philosophy. He ate many vegetables and loved vegetarian cuisine, because he knew he had to balance meat with vegetables. He showed me a vegetarian restaurant near the youth hostel that offered delicious foods. I did not know what the Russian foods were called, so I ended up eating two, cold Russian salads, because that was what I accidentally ordered.

While we were eating, I noticed a flyer for yoga on the table. Max refused the yoga idea as "it is too much peaceful and relaxed."

He continued, "There is a duality between aggression and peacefulness. Money is power and aggression. Yoga people become extremely peaceful and lack the necessary aggression to obtain what they need in the world."

Meat was power, so he balanced it with vegetarian meals. I found there to be some truth to his idea, although any black and white duality ignores a potential, third voice that perhaps some people need more aggression or peacefulness than others. As we walked around the city together, I enjoyed hearing him talk about travel as a way to feel new emotions. Every corner we turned was a new experience. Every mistake was a new emotion to feel. These are the same emotions that we find as we turn the corners of life on the streets we choose to walk down.

I reflected back on being a vegetarian on my travels. I tried not to bring it up, but I often had to ask if there was meat when I encountered an unknown food in a new country. New friends I met would ask if I was vegetarian, and that would be it. Sometimes, they would ask why, and I could give an answer they would accept. The conversation moved on. Across all of the countries in Asia and Europe, nobody harassed me for being vegetarian. Something struck me as wrong when I returned to the United States, and the conversations I had for over a decade growing up restarted; Some Americans were shocked I was vegetarian and, even after asking why, would continue to promote eating meat and encourage me to do the same. I will not labor long on this point, but it is worth addressing once. I have never told people they should stop consuming meat, but I have been told I should consume meat hundreds of times. Just as I wouldn't eat the wooden table I am sitting at, I wouldn't eat any animal flesh. I could believe meat tasted delicious, but just as I was sure bungee jumping was exhilarating, I still had no personal desire to do so. The common trend I noticed was for others to take my personal reasons for my behavior as an argument for all vegetarianism, so then the conversation became a soapbox for the other person to explain why everyone should eat meat. The conversations were harmless, but the trend was too coincidental and identical to be happenstance. One reason people become defensive is if there is a personal unease or criticism with eating meat. In other words, the strong, meat culture in the United States was under attack for being unhealthy, and the unease dissipated out unintentionally against me. The alternative explanation was that heavy meat eaters had little understanding of the vegetarian lifestyle, and there is always an initial resistance to the unknown. My brother once told me I received criticism for being vegetarian, because I made myself a target when I constantly announced it. I disagreed. There was something to be addressed when everyone I met around the world responded in a neutral way and only Americans responded differently, and that was exactly what happened.

Traveling to so many countries forced me to change cultures like I would my clothes. I also noticed cultural differences meant that no culture was any better than any other culture just as different people wore different clothes. My experience taught me to pay attention to popular culture as an indication for the strongest values of the people at that specific time.

Congratulations for reading this far! Maybe I should share a fun lesson indicating how values and perceptions can change. One morning in Nepal, I had eggs, bread, and jam for breakfast. The jam was neon-red and tasted equally artificial. I looked inside the jar and saw ants either dead or swimming, so I just picked the non-graveyard portion of jam and ate that. Halfway through my meal, I turned over some toast and found a toasted ant wedged in the bread, so I just picked out that section of bread and ate the rest. I didn't care anymore, but three months ago, I would have tossed the jam and bread and lost my appetite.

Without a doubt, we are human beings and social cooperation has allowed mankind to develop to its status today. Amid the many societal differences between Nepal and the U.S., Nepali culture fosters a strong sense of community. In calling everyone "brother" and "sister", everyone is family. Strangers called me "brother," and I called strangers the same in return. In the U.S., families are on their own to survive. Overall, the United States are a place of development and cleanliness with a higher standard of living than in Nepal, but I see the fight for survival is the same. People are the same; they are only wearing different clothes.

Language

Language is a way to communicate in daily interaction. It can also be used in rhetoric to shape mentalities and as triggers to induce defenses. There are strong emotions and reactions to words like immigrants, abortion, gay marriage, socialism, terrorism, and feminism.

I strove to have honest discussions with people wherever I traveled, and through these discussions, I learned how to listen carefully for what they had to share and the words they chose to share it. Similarly, I discovered the words I used to convey my opinions were indicative of the culture I came from and my understanding of the topic. While I was in Istanbul, Turkey, I introduced the Gazan engineer Omar to something I believe in: the law of attraction as well as quantum physics. He had escaped Gaza with his life and had difficulty finding a job anywhere due to his controversial, political background as a Palestinian. While he argued and disagreed with me about the law of attraction in the beginning, he agreed with me once I had figured out the right wording to describe it. Namely, having good thoughts brings more good thoughts, although he had initial difficulty grasping that thoughts are connected to physical reality and serve to produce tangible results. This is why most people pray; they desire a physical return.

Language is also dependent on the culture one comes from. As bad as Americans swear the c-word is, it has culturally-dependent usages. I first came across its use in Goa, India, when an Australian used the c-word and f-word repeatedly to discuss his country's political leadership. In Prague, I met an English girl who used it repeatedly, and I unfortunately picked up the habit. I surprised myself with a propensity for picking up habits from people I spend a lot of time with, such as a Scottish accent when I was with a Scot in Phuket, Thailand, or the laugh of a close friend from San Diego, California. I let slip the c-word towards Andrew in Vienna, Austria. I later apologized for the vulgar term as I knew it was crude, but he said I was justified in using the word as he fit the term in the moment. It would seem its meaning, while abhorrent in the U.S., is widely used in the UK varying only in its quantity and quality of use. The English often cuss each other out as friends without much serious impact, but its rare usage by Americans makes it more powerful and drastic. I imagine confusion arises when the same word has different meanings to different people. Even words are products of their time, sculpted like statues to tell a story comprehensible only to those who know their speaker.

Another example of language are musical instruments, forged by their use throughout history. Instruments created in medieval Japan or Nepal were created with local tools and materials. I could not find a Japanese, bamboo flute in Nepal. That is why listening to different music is like listening to different people at various times in history.

The words we use give way to how we feel, and only after learning how to detect key words in conversation does one fully understand the values and emotions a speaker holds. I visited North Carolina with my brother, his girlfriend, and her family. In comparison to constant travel, I found an extremely sedentary life. I spent days on the couch watching movies and eating. I was isolated to the house as I did not have a car in suburbia, and everyone else was running errands.

When I was describing people in the South, my brother pointed out how I used the words, "lack of college education," which implied something was missing. I had to think about why I used such language as I truly meant no disrespect. During a bike ride the day prior, I was told college, physical education, and healthy diets in the South were not a huge part of the southern culture. I was also told that verbal racism was common. Coming from an athlete in the middle of her exercising combined with my personal experience and observations in Nepal about the value of education, I experienced a cultural clash that led to this misunderstanding. I also performed introspection to see my own, personal culture from the San Francisco Bay Area where attending college is the norm and there are constant fights for equal opportunity for higher education across racial divides. Clearly, my understanding of the words I heard were filtered through my beliefs based on my background. Once I explained my reasons, my brother clarified how I should be careful about the words I choose.

Personally, it is none of my business if someone is happy with a different culture than mine. The conversation with my brother forced me to analyze my own culture from California and compare it to the culture in the South. I learned to be understanding without accidentally patronizing. A shallow understanding of a topic offers humor and prejudice as I demonstrated. A deeper understanding of how and why something exists replaces misunderstanding and the offenses that follow.

The manner in which people discussed any topic was just as important as the content of the discussion. I tried to engage in as many discussions as possible with as many people from almost as many countries. The result was that I talked with people from different countries almost daily for seven months, and I found a common theme that superseded any cultural or language differences. The theme was the difference between making a discussion personal versus impersonal, and this relied heavily on the frame of mind of those involved.

For example, in terms of debate, an argument is a single piece of evidence or belief, and it is not necessarily an entire debate in itself. A discussion can become impossible when a person channels personal feelings in order to pass judgment. In return, the listener responds by justifying his or her arguments, and the discussion quickly turns into a battle filled with personal attacks and defensive walls that obscure any cognitive, mutual understanding in preference for self-defense.

The best discussions I had were not in terms of content but rather in the fluidity and efficacy of discussion. These occurred when arguments and ideas were presented objectively, so that speakers explained an argument without sounding personal. In those discussions, I found people were less offended when a controversial idea was presented with its corresponding source of information. The person responding could then choose to address either the controversial idea or the source rather than feeling attacked and the need to become defensive.

Due to the possibility of people avoiding controversial topics, I sometimes presented my own idea as, "Someone I know said…," just so the person I was addressing would not feel that whatever followed was a personal judgment coming from me. I never passed on personal judgment, but I had to choose my words carefully to ensure the listener's frame of mind did not misinterpret my statements. One's frame of mind was incredibly important to gauge how a discussion would continue. If I presented the same idea to two people, the person with a frame of mind strongly attached to a certain mindset was much less likely to be receptive to new ideas in comparison to someone who was more flexible and aware of his or her own knowledge. Like in the novel *The Giver* by Lois Lowry, "starving" and "hungry" were noted to have different meanings although they were often used interchangeably. Words could be innocent and fun for puns and jokes, but they could also be used for influential rhetoric and propaganda. Only with an open frame of mind that was aware of both categories could an individual differentiate between the two.

Language has a context which can either be expansive or limiting. I learned conversational Nepali in a month and surprised locals when I spoke it which greatly enhanced my experience there. I also enjoyed picking up local words and trying them in most countries I visited.

My Swiss friend, Stefan, told me of a punk German he had met who repeated rhetoric that "NATO is bad." When asked why, he responded, "Because it is NATO." Circular logic was a flaw in the thinking process, and it can be detected by language. I saw the same logic in the American, self-proclaimed anarchist I met in Bulgaria in his opinion towards government. At one time, I read an article about how "just 10 new cases" of Ebola had been found in Sierra Leone following the Ebola epidemic. "Just 10 new cases" made the epidemic sound like it was declining. When the epidemic was starting, I doubt the headlines read, "Just 10 new cases." The same event of "10 new cases" was portrayed and received quite differently depending on the context.

Language is about how something is said. I can "steal" something or "permanently borrow" it. Short people can be "vertically challenged," so could it be that overweight people are instead "horizontally challenged?" Language is a key tool to promote, disguise, or change the truth.

Across Asia and Europe, I discussed and debated controversial topics without any serious confrontation except perhaps with the anarchist who had a unique frame of mind. As soon as I returned to the United States, I realized the intensity of discussion I experienced for months could no longer be maintained. From the Thai hotel owner who took me to a cultural fair and explained local customs to the Indian hotel worker about my age who knew as much of the American social and political systems as I did, I became accustomed to conversations that started at the superficial level and delved into analysis for a greater mutual understanding. I tried to have conversations with Americans about the same topics and in the same manner as I did with Europeans, but I suddenly became perceived as offensive. Americans perceived my questions as personal attacks, and I came upon a realization; to disagree with someone or inquire about logical flaws was to offend them. Instead of the two-way discussion I had become accustomed to outside the U.S., I found myself in heated arguments with strangers simply to hear repeated the same rhetoric I had heard from their politicians. To explain this phenomenon, I believe the bipartisan culture of a two-party system separated the society into only friends or enemies, with friends not criticizing or questioning friends and enemies avoiding talking to each other. Suddenly, my sincere curiosity in peoples' beliefs became an offense. I quickly learned to stop asking questions about people's cultures and beliefs and talk only about general topics such as television shows and food.

How people handle situations can also depend on affordability. I relate affordability to a tank of gas. People have more patience when they feel they have the fuel to listen and more compassion when they are not desperate for their own survival. There is a reason refugee workers are not as desperate as the refugees they provide aid to. Established refugee workers are not in need of basic supplies and are more willing to share the aid than starving refugees would. Affordability is not only a question of what someone can afford but also what someone wants to afford. Hospitality and kindness are free and noted to be more universally understood by the poor than the rich. I imagine hospitality and kindness may change through a lens of wealth. This is not to say all poor are gracious and rich are not, but the mentality can change as having more of something can cause someone to feel like there is more to lose if it is shared. I have examples of two gracious host families in Nepal in comparison to the wealthy owner of the volunteer organization who was difficult to communicate openly with, because his awareness had focused around the personal distribution of his wealth. Awareness of what he could offer the world and of what he could afford to give changed as his experience changed while his wealth increased. In a world with many financially poor people, my awareness, if I stood in their shoes, would extend to my own survival needs instead of promoting sharing and compassion with my neighbors.

The environment we live in creates a context that greatly dictates the words we know, choose, and use. Words in language have a meaning that can be altered by the context in which they are shared. Similarly, words represent the context in which they arise and act as ambassadors for the meaning they carry and the beliefs supporting them. It is for these reasons that language is an incredibly powerful tool that can be wielded, depending on the speaker's intent, for clarity, confusion, empowerment, or oppression.

Education

In the village of Amarapuri where I volunteered, nearly all youth were in a private, boarding school. I taught middle-schoolers on gender inequality from their textbook as education was the primary focus for reducing family size and reducing the age at which couples started having children. The same was true for Rashmi's family in Beldiya, the lower-income village next to Amarapuri. The only difference was income and education, but education led to better jobs and income and also inspired development. Restricting education could be used for gender oppression, ethnic oppression, or societal oppression depending on who was being restricted.

I visited the village of my Nepali rafting guides which was a five-minute hike straight up the hillside from the two-lane highway. The homes were the size of the bedroom I was staying in with my Nepali brother in Amarapuri. The homes were small, but the hillside was beautiful amid terraces growing cabbage, spinach, corn, squash, and other local vegetables. Smells of smoke and fecal matter from chickens, goats and cows filled the air. Dirt paths wide enough for two feet weaved from home to home up the hillside. Two dirt roads passed through the village center. I enjoyed walking through the village by the electric tower that generated power for the homes. Wires ran from home to home in the same layout as children throwing an unraveling ball of yarn from child to child. It struck me that education was much less influential here. Here, the guide's three-year-old son would soon go to a government school where the quality of education, including English, was much lower. I stood in a rural village where people and education were poor, yet they were the same, hardworking, kind, honest, and sincere people I met anywhere else in the world if not kinder.

I recall two conversations. The first was with my whitewater rafting guides. I spent a lot of time with them over the three days I was there. They showed me their rural village during the day, and we talked by the campfire at night. I inquired about their marriages to better understand their life stories. Santosh had a love marriage at 20 years old, but he now believed it was better to marry later in his 20s. Oddly, he had two girlfriends for "passing the time" with talking and kissing. He said more than kissing may come after several months of dating. He had five years of marriage without any such girlfriend. He admitted monogamy was better. I asked if his behavior seemed normal, and he admitted it was normal for husbands to have girlfriends which only became a problem if the wife found out. I inquired if the opposite was true, and he retorted it was not normal for a wife to have boyfriends as "that is very bad." His 3-year old son will attend a government school. Nepali who spoke English well usually attended private schools. I explained to Santosh the discrepancy in male versus female behavior as perhaps a form of gender discrimination, but he could not understand the meaning as his behavior was the social norm in the area. Coincidentally, the material was fresh in my mind since I had lectured on gender discrimination from the textbook at the private school a week prior.

The second conversation was with another Nepali who had worked in Japan as a rafting guide for the last 15 years. He married a Japanese woman and had a child there, but she divorced him. He said she was a "bad wife." He returned to Nepal and now had a Nepali wife, a "good wife," because she will never divorce him. He fathered children in Nepal, because he was happier with his Nepali family. I assumed his ex-wife was educated and had a job to survive financially without depending on her husband. In Nepal where education was less accessible and possibly of lower quality, the wife was dependent on the husband and unable to divorce. Divorce rates were lower. Divorces did happen, but not publicly. It was common for husbands to live elsewhere for work, so the couple just lived apart and no one else knew.

Retraction: I talked to my Nepali friends in Kathmandu who were more socially aware, and they said having girlfriends while married was not okay or normal. The rafting guide from the village where I understood education was less prevalent had an isolated understanding of marriage. It was a small yet good lesson for me not to overgeneralize what I heard from the population. It also reinforced the importance of education and having positive role models, a situation that seemed harder to find in rural areas.

In Nepal, I met the most kind, sincere, and considerate people in the middle to low income status. It was unfortunate to see their education as the biggest hindrance to a better job as they all worked harder than most people I knew and for much less money. If anything, the rudest people I met came from those running businesses who were the most desperate to cut corners to make more money.

It appeared education lessened gender discrimination as it empowered women. After comparing developing and developed countries, education was really the fastest and best way to develop a country, improve social rights, and boost the economy. On the other end, restricting education was a form of oppression to limit such development. Education could be limited to a particular ethnic group, gender, or society. For example, I saw the most educated people in Nepal making the most money. If income rose with education, limiting education was an oppression of the uneducated and poor. The logic followed that increasing education usually erases poverty.

A Ghanan I met on a bus in Dubai told me how a lack of education in his country really slows growth and limits the options people have to resolve conflicts, typically leaving them to resort to violence. He said education helps people learn how to use the courts to resolve many issues. Unfortunately, many people are in dire need of immediate income by working at an early age and cannot invest in their education. As the highly educated find work abroad, few role models are left behind to inspire younger generations to stay in school.

While most children attended school in Nepal, some parents could not afford it for their children. My first, largely naïve thought was that the parents should not have children if they could not provide for them, but I learned about the culture, the preference for boys, gender discrimination, and many parents being uneducated about family planning. Still, a child was not responsible for who his or her parents were. The distinction between developing and developed countries had become very clear to me. Education was the number one source for stable, future development. Many educated individuals left Nepal for better work and money abroad which robbed the country of benefitting from its investment in education. Unfortunately, this behavior highlighted the lack of access to quality education in the U.S. As government funding declined, the burden of college tuition shifted to families which crippled everyone but the rich, and that is how a country shoots itself in the foot for future economic and social growth. I met two Americans on my trek, and they were concerned about the U.S. lacking funding for its infrastructure such as railways, social services, and education while public spending was mostly directed to the military and large corporations. It was good for the country's image but maybe not so much "For the People".

Some might wonder if education for everybody is charity. When it comes to health, people want doctors to treat everyone equally regardless of race or income. The goal of a doctor is to improve the quality of life. It seems the same would apply for education. Additionally, not everyone in society needs or wants a college education. Rather, some need artistic and vocational training. It is crucial to teach children that differences are okay, and the hierarchy of high-paying jobs does not have any bearing on the value of people themselves. The capacity of thinking and reasoning is the strongest potential weapon of humanity. If used properly with the knowledge of one's own goals, strengths, weaknesses, and tools to master them, a person could accomplish anything. Entire empires began with just a thought.

Formal education sometimes does not guarantee that social skills will follow academic ones. I met extremely educated individuals who must have been great at their job, but they had difficulty talking about anything outside their fields of expertise. Nonetheless, formal education is what is valued in society. Individuals remain competitive by taking a variety of courses to increase experience and knowledge.

A most curious thought crossed my mind. What if I did not think at all or problem-solve with self-analysis and external analysis? What if I completely lacked the skills I learned in school and from my mentors? I would see the world as a playground for survival to get what I needed regardless of the means, thus contributing to the disorder in society. A world of critical thinking pushes me beyond immediate gratification to see the world as full of choices to make about what makes me happy on an inner level. An education provides many opportunities to live a good life, and while some people without formal education do quite well, the grand majority of them benefits greatly from having an education.

From what I saw in developing countries, an educated society vastly helps in making the country grow stronger and faster. Education benefits individuals and the community. Without a greater understanding that comes with higher levels of thinking, whether attained through an education or through life experience, people may misunderstand their roles as citizens in society. Living in a society with other people and businesses means there is a lot of information to process. There are news, advertisements, politicians, national celebrities, and local role models that each present their own opinions or facts. A joke about the latest health craze that struck the United States is a person at the grocery store asking for grass-fed chicken when it is cows, not chicken, that consume grass. Ideas are plentiful as there are 7 billion people and each one has good ideas and bad ideas. I believe sorting through the wealth of material found among different people and cultures to avoid manipulation requires solid analytical skills. In most countries, military personnel are highly revered for their service to their country. Likewise, I would say citizens should serve their country by obtaining an education to better help their own community and country.

Similar Differences

Marriage

There are love marriages in which a couple falls in love or confuses lust with love, and they choose to be together. Other times arranged marriages occur when a third party helps bring a couple together. I discussed arranged and love marriages greatly in Nepal and India, and I found more similarities between the two types than I anticipated.

After Ekadashi festival, Asok, his friend who went by "Punks Not Dead," and I ended the night by the river. We each had one beer, and they smoked cigarettes in secret. My Nepali brother started smoking after a break-up. Love marriages are what the Western world values with its culture of "true love" and "love at first sight." Here in Nepal, there are no Disney movies spewing fairytales of a Princess and Prince Charming; only real life that dictates financial support, procreation, and hard work. Perhaps the developing nature of Nepal reduces the image of couples to its bare roots for survival whereas young couples in the U.S. more often have the luxury to marry for love. Nonetheless, families, either stemming from love or arranged marriages, appear to share the same, cheerful qualities and bonds. I did ask my Nepali brothers and sisters whether they would prefer love or arranged marriages. The overwhelming answer was that everyone wants a love marriage, but if they do not find one, they know they can ask their parents to arrange one for them.

Arranged marriage is culturally looked down in the West as a repressive feature of developing cultures, and in some cases it is. In other cases, it is not if both parties voluntarily choose it. I recall one study that showed in the first five years of marriage, love marriage couples are happier, but that reverses after five years. My perception is that arranged couples must communicate and work together even more to sustain their marriage from the very beginning and thus have a greater chance of sorting out their differences and making the marriage work. In contrast, I observe couples in love marriages may lose faith once feelings of love dissipate a little or a lot, and they interpret the loss of feeling as a sign to move on to the next love marriage rather than solve the conflicting issues at hand. Marriage comes from the belief that a person can spend the rest of his or her life with the same person in happiness. Beliefs in love might initially be stronger and more passionate than beliefs in an arrangement, but those beliefs can change and lead to separation if love is seen as a right rather than something to work for. As love marriages make the two parties feel more freedom to follow their passion, couples often develop a stronger love through time. Ironically, as much as arranged marriages are looked down on in the West, online dating serves as a hybrid of the two types of marriage to match people. Instead of parents or village priests playing matchmaker, candidates put their beliefs into scientific methods to match compatibility and personality to create the best possible love match.

To prepare for a later discussion, I would add that initial attraction relies on one-dimensional slices. These slices are brief impressions or conversations that register well with one's personal beliefs and motivations. The longer a relationship lasts, the more dimensions are integrated into the couple's understanding of one another. In contrast, a marriage or relationship that begins with too few dimensions of simple physical attraction and fails to add new dimensions of communication, compassion, and patience will have trouble enduring hard times.

Children

Usually, parents care for their children as they are not legally independent adults before 18 years old. Adults care more about children, because children are more susceptible than adults to physical and psychological abuse. There are more resources available to protect children from such traumas as well. What would it look like if we did not protect them? We can, at the very least, see the importance of providing a nurturing environment to encourage our children to grow into healthy adults who hopefully respect one another instead of harboring deep hatreds and resorting to destructive ways of communication.

I observed a spectrum of children in both developing and developed countries. I watched some wear dirty, torn clothing, because they had nothing else and some freeze in sub-zero temperatures as adults walked by in heavy coats. Other children begged for anything better than garbage. Those children were treated slightly higher than garbage on the pot-holed and trashed streets. I watched other children who were loved, washed daily, well fed, hair combed, dressed in brand clothing, housed in their own bedroom, and held by their parents every day. The only difference between the children I saw was in which country or which part of their country they were born and how much their parents could support and love them. I could find no responsibility to the child for the circumstances in which he or she was raised by the parents. My privilege in being cared for as a child has shaped my thinking, and while I do not presume my upbringing would work for everyone, I do feel a childhood free from the stresses of adulthood is beneficial and liberating for a child's mind and growth. It seemed ideal for children to be free from concern about money, clothes, food, and fear for his or her life. To do anything less is allowing to raise a fear-oriented individual who sees differences as a problem rather than an opportunity in a globalized world.

We, as adults, cannot do everything we desire to protect and hide children from the dark evils of this world, but we should not be doing nothing to provide the greatest lights of love and education for them. Without the latter, we become bystanders to the children discovering darkness without the wisdom of our personal experience and mistakes. Adults hold more responsibility and authority over their own lives than children, meaning children cave easily to external influences. The question that arises is what do we do to ensure one generation of susceptible children does not turn into the next generation of susceptible adults? Does it make sense to care more about children than adults?

Every person I meet is given trust and a smile until he or she gives me a reason to remove one or the other. For children, I see their behavior as a product of their education, parents, and community influences. I wonder about teaching children and who should be responsible for their education. I also wonder as to what kind of parents would bring a child into this world without the ability to offer affectionate, parental support or possibly choose to abandon their child. Most parents care for their children. How can an adult say one child deserves more than any other? The amount of attention and parenting depends on many factors: the parents' own childhood experiences, level of education, life experiences, presence or absence of role models, and financial means among others. Some parents can and want to encourage their children to take piano lessons, join soccer teams, and go to summer camp. Other parents cannot or do not want to offer such things for their children. Nonetheless, every child regardless of country of birth deserves a basic education to provide basic opportunities beyond starvation. Children should not be punished for the mistakes of their parents. Nobody should be handed opportunities, but opportunities should exist for those who desire them.

In the United States, protecting youth has been at the heart of many debates for decades. Sexual education is the perfect example of such a debate. Some parents want to protect their children from learning about such information until a time they personally see fit while other parents knowing teenagers are frequently sexually active want to prepare and protect their children from sexually transmitted diseases and teen pregnancy. Statistics show actively teaching sexual safety leads to fewer cases of STDs and teen pregnancy, but education must still be balanced with the right of parents to influence their own children. Child vaccination is a more recent controversial topic between some parents wanting to protect their own children and legally guarantee other children are protected from diseases while other parents want to protect their own children from potential, harmful vaccine side effects ranging from mild to severe. The topic is emotionally-charged and highly controversial, because parents universally feel the need to protect their children, but there are clearly debatable methods to accomplish the task. A single standard will never work for everyone, meaning there must be a discussion to balance scientific knowledge and how it is privy to parental concern.

Similar Differences

Happiness

Happiness is a universal emotion we all strive for. We want it as much as possible, and we do our best to provide it for those we love most. There is no standard means to attain it, because happiness is different to different people. Consumerism is the comforts and things money can buy, but the highly-valued habit of capitalism does not always lead to happiness.

A celebrity once said that he wished everybody could have all the money they wanted to realize their dream, but this is not the path to happiness. I befriended some of the happiest people who had no material possessions, yet some of the wealthiest people felt empty and in need of more.

Happiness is universal, but it does take cultural forms. It was eerie to observe the scale of consumption within a large shopping mall in Montreal, Canada. I realized my phone and other goods could not compete with the happiness found in the bonds formed through the shared experiences with friends and family.

After seven months of travel, I look back on the places I've been, and the sightseeing only fulfills a fraction of what made my trip valuable to me. As the countries tallied up, I found myself focusing more on my relationships with the people around me. The friendships and family ties will outlast any photo or sightseeing escapade I did on my own. My greatest memories are my most honest conversations with locals and other travelers, the comfortable silence

I could share with a friend, and the laughter shared with the most unexpected of people.

Happiness may seem complicated to attain, but it is surprisingly simple. Two movies I saw highlight this idea. *The 100-Year Old Man Who Climbed Out The Window* and *Forrest Gump* follow the lives of two men who are open to any and every new experience, and as a result happen to find themselves in every major historical event during the 20th century. These films mirror what I discovered. As long as I had a smile on my face and respectfully greeted someone, I could engage in a friendly conversation with anyone from any culture. Respectfully greeting someone is culturally dependent yet not difficult.

Children often fight with siblings over toys. Parents teach sharing among siblings to reduce jealously and conflict. When the same children become adults, they are taught pride by not sharing and defending their honor frequently through violent means either individually or as a country. There is nothing naïve or hidden about life; it is all a social construction of what we need, want, and can afford. Money pays for external happiness and additional wealth, yet the poor in developing countries know how to live life happily. The simple truth is that it is the only life they can live. If they were poor and homeless in developed countries, they would not be as happy, because they would constantly be reminded of the wealth they would require to be happy and function rather than through happy relationships between friends and family. Seeing a movie with others is better than watching it alone. It is the environment that manufactures a people, not the people themselves. To reverse the words "environment" and "people" in the previous statement requires a deeper understanding of what happiness is.

An individual without an education knows kindness and happiness on a different level than someone with an education. The assumed hierarchy of education and "good" is invalid, but it is undoubtedly true that an education gives perspective to understand, see, and value happiness differently. There is a simplicity and joy to life that is not found supernaturally in God or in gadgets like tablets and smartphones. Those are additional dimensions of happiness that do add a collective value to one's life, but I can say my happiness first comes from within and then is followed by a shared, tangible joy between myself and another human being. Joy from within is distinct from tangible joy found in games, books and friends. Tangible joy is a step to inner joy, yet tangible joy no matter its quantity may never lead to inner joy without an understanding of inner joy and how it arises from tangible joy.

Lastly, living in a third world country teaches the same lesson of humility as when we are told "no" as children. Beyond necessity, wealth is only a tool for happiness, but it does not define happiness. I am at my happiest when I have my necessities, encouraged intellectually, and I feel safe and respected.

Similar Differences

Silence

Stefan told me the story of how he and some of his friends watched a beautiful sunset over a mountain in silence. One of the friends he noted was an American who had to fill in the silence by commenting on the sunset, and his peers criticized him for ruining the moment.

Silence is a time to reflect internally. In my daily routine, silence refreshes me when spent reflecting retrospectively on my experiences. If I instead spend the silence worrying how I will plan the upcoming hours in my day, I cannot relax and be happy in the moment.

Nowadays, noise is everywhere. Some people feel they must constantly talk or express ideas to be validated by others. Simply being present with others without talking is sometimes seen as strange.

When people do not have the time to be silent or lack the motivation to do so, it becomes very difficult to learn from their experiences. Just as the brain subconsciously learns from the day's experiences during sleep, a conscious and quiet introspection allows the individual to actively learn and adapt. One reason I enjoyed my friend's company in Brussels, Belgium, so much is that we could walk together in silence to compose our thoughts during a conversation without any discomfort.

Similar Differences

Loss

I lost my Nepali shawl while leaving the ski resort in Semmering, Austria. I was devastated for a few days due to my attachment to it. It had reminded me of my time in Nepal with my friends and the experiences I had there. I wore it around my neck in -17 degrees Celsius in St. Petersburg, Russia. Just like whip cream twirls around on top of ice cream, the shawl wrapped around my neck and left my head as the cherry on top. I had already pictured it on my table once I returned home. Nobody could understand the sentimental loss completely if I only said, "I lost my scarf." I felt the same way to a lesser degree when I left in Amsterdam the pen I had purchased in Nepal.

The feeling of loss can be small or large, but it is difficult for an observer to discern the two. My cousin's apartment in France had a television which was reporting the loss of three French Olympic athletes who had died in a helicopter accident and the mourning from their friends and family.

During an interview, a friend of those lost said, "We lost people and role models," which was true as friends and fans looked up to the athletes for their success.

I was struck by how similarly people grieved over the deaths of their friends in France. Despite a different language and culture, seeing people grieve with an equal degree of pain was a simple but effective lesson that even if we are not always looking where pain exists, it does not imply that the pain does not exist. People like those I see in any local community can be found everywhere around the world and will grieve their losses just as we do at home. It seems childish to say, but it seems understated today: Understand that everyone feels loss but likely anger if the loss was at the hands of or benefited someone else.

I had mixed feelings about the anonymity that traveling to unknown places allowed me to act any way I desired, because nobody would see me again. It offered freedom to act beyond what a person might be shy of doing normally which was surely a positive thing, but it also allowed those same people to behave rudely without consequence. The Macedonians I met in Belgrade, Serbia, offered that I join them to see Skopje, Macedonia. Besides their crazed antics, I finally wrapped my head around the idea of joining them as a potentially fun experience. The next day, I awoke and waited for them to start the day only to find out they had left before I even woke up. Yes, I put it behind me the next day, but it was still disconcerting to be left behind. Whether the loss of an object, life, or experience, each loss is uniquely personal to the individual. Just as others would not understand the loss as I felt it, I imagined I could not understand the losses others felt. The best response I received and could offer in return to any loss was to be understanding and offer to help alleviate the pain.

Internal and External Beliefs

I stayed a week on the beaches of Goa, India, with Guy as we ventured 90 km away on the back of his rented Royal Enfield motorcycle. Every moment with him was a delight as we conversed on topics ranging from our past experiences with people we had met to current events around the world. We sat in the dining area of the hotel on Om beach. I could see the ocean over the fence, and a different cow passed in front of the door every few minutes. I had just finished walking along the soft sand and swimming in the tropical water. My heels dug into the sand as I leaned back in my chair and sipped a cold drink. I grabbed my journal from my bag and began writing some ideas that came to me while swimming.

Guy walked in sometime later and sat beside me, and we started talking. He proposed the notion of internal beliefs and external beliefs. External beliefs, as I understood, are conscious thoughts about our own reality, and they are easily recognizable by others. They range from visible labels of political affiliation and religious belief to well-understood ideas about the dangers of drinking and driving and the benefits of knowing basic arithmetic. Internal beliefs are less well known even to oneself, but they often fuel our external beliefs beyond our conscious awareness. They extend to how one feels about people of different ethnicities or genders, our personal sentiments about our own identity, and how we identify ourselves in relation to others. They even extend into deep insecurities and emotional baggage that can make our actions unpredictable and difficult to understand. Internal beliefs are hard to spot and can create biases unknown to the beholder.

Racism is no longer popularly viewed as an acceptable external belief, but it remains an internal one for many people. In times of stress, we resort to our internal beliefs that supply our gut instinct. As a result, the police have shown to make split-second decisions based on their subjective gut instinct and were discovered to hold internal beliefs of racism that sparked riots and calls against police brutality and racial profiling. Their decision to fire was a complicated symptom of the underlying belief.

An audiobook I listened to while traveling titled *Blink*[2] by Malcolm Gladwell provided more examples of internal beliefs in action. In 1999, an innocent African American male in Brooklyn was shot 41 times for running away from four, street-clothed policemen. While pulling out his wallet for fear of being robbed by four men approaching him at night, policemen shot him in response to seeing a weapon being drawn. Their internal beliefs were that an African American male standing outside his home at night in the Bronx must have been up to no good. Racial profiling is an internal belief. It clouded their objective judgment of the situation and led them to believe he was dangerous before there was proof. When one policeman drew and began shooting, his colleagues supported their colleague and drew their arms as well to fire. The result was an unarmed victim shot 41 times. The policemen were tried for second-degree murder and acquitted.

Another example was a female trombonist who won a screened audition. Before screened auditions came about, a musician would sit facing the judges who based their decision on the quality of music produced. The judges thought themselves trained ears for music and certainly not as sexist, musical experts. When accusations of gender bias came to light, they offered to hold screened auditions in which the judges had no information about the musician other than what they could hear. If candidates gave any information to the judges about their gender by accidentally clicking heels or coughing, they were shuffled back into the lineup. A female trombonist astounded the judges with her skill, and she shocked them even more when they saw her face. They could not believe a woman could play a trombone, a thunderous, booming instrument with equal power as a man, but she did. It was clear the supposedly unbiased, unscreened audition process turned out to be full of bias and personal judgment both unconscious and irrelevant to the sound of music produced. Once the audition process became screened, women began to enter orchestras. Orchestra management fought for 13 years to evict her from the orchestra, but her determination and talent protected her reputation and job from their slander.

There is a saying that first impressions are the most important. In the United States, a business interview requires proper attire, eye contact, and a firm handshake. In Nepal, a courteous introduction requires smiling, eye contact and pressing one's palms together in front of one's chest before saying "Namaste." One may even bow slightly when doing so. First impressions are judgments that will set the tone for future encounters. A business interview will not go well if the interviewee constantly stares at the ground, and strangers in Nepal will be taken aback and possibly offended if hugged at the first meeting. This is not because hugs are not appreciated, but there are social customs to adhere to. I did not hug my Nepali sisters or mother goodbye after seeing them nearly every day for two months. I simply waved goodbye. The emotional connection and sentiment of missing them was just as strong for anyone I've said goodbye to, but a physical embrace would not have been culturally appropriate.

First impressions and even last impressions are judgments. In terms of evolution, snap judgments are vital. A hunter who ponders whether a nearby, roaring lion is hungry or scared may not live to repeat the experience. A first sighting of a lion in the wild immediately initiates fear and the desire to escape danger. Today, most of us do not live in constant fear for our lives. The survival instinct is not dictated by wild animals but rather by long-term economic and familial survival and success in a society in which everyone else is instinctively behaving the same way.

Most of our everyday lives in the United States are free from violence. First impressions are still necessary to function daily and determine whether we high five someone after a business interview or our eyes widen when we see someone of a different ethnicity. The latter is explicitly visible in a melting pot where people of different nationalities and faiths live together. Whereas external beliefs explain the fear when someone sees another person carrying a weapon, internal beliefs are responsible for when an assumption is made about another person possibly carrying a weapon. External beliefs are the signals and signs taught to law enforcement and security personnel to identify dangerous people in a crowd. Internal beliefs can be assumptions criticized in society for fueling racial stereotyping and biased profiling based on subjective feelings that associate danger with a racial identity instead of objective feelings that associate danger with a visible sign. Internal beliefs can fuel employment bias when candidates show equal qualification except regarding their race or gender. Internal beliefs of a company's culture can encourage a glass ceiling impenetrable for women even when lower qualified male peers are promoted. Internal beliefs can be circular in logic: the beliefs used to justify assumptions about someone may be the same pre-conceived assumptions. Such bias is no longer approved of in societies promoting equality and freedom of opportunity. Businesses need to be entirely discrimination-free and public figures must retain a good image. Homophobic CEOs have induced company boycotts and racist NBA team owners have lost their careers because of their internal beliefs which when identified were exposed against general external beliefs.

Each of us move about our daily lives as if we are cars on a highway. We each have our own car and abide by certain traffic rules to reduce the amount of possible conflict and promote safety. Assuming the road is intact and there are no detours, our beliefs support the decisions that guide our path. People sometimes disobey the rules and cause damage to others, but by and large the roads of our daily lives should be safe. Rarely, a national security threat may rain heavily and threaten everyone's safety. It is important to distinguish true threats that pose an immediate danger from perceived threats that manifest more from internal and external beliefs than reality. Perceived threats that are exaggerated forms of true threats may send us in the wrong direction.

Guy explained racism as a belief, and beliefs are changed via experience. Giving people new experiences by interacting with different cultures can change their beliefs, including tasting food, meeting people with different cultural backgrounds, or attending new cultural festivals. Indeed, racism is both localized and a cultural phenomenon. I doubt the people of two warring, central African states learned to despise all blacks since both are black. Travel is an easy tool to attain completely new experiences and change external and even obscure internal beliefs. In contrast, those that do not travel or have a variety of experiences can easily find themselves settling into a world comforted by external and internal beliefs that are never challenged or questioned for their accuracy and validity.

There is always an initial shock of seeing something new. Oddly enough, I experienced so much on my travels that I could relate to new experiences and eliminate the shock effect which might negatively affect my first impression and judgment. It is important to distinguish between believing in something and acting on it. Freedom of belief is an essential component to the Western world, meaning anyone has the right to be either full of hate or love for any group. For example, I respect someone's right to be a bigot, but I will not stand by passively and watch beliefs unfold into discriminatory acts, and neither should a society advertising freedom and equality. We are all legally protected from hate speech, but not socially protected as those around us continue to develop their own opinions in response to those legal barriers. Consequently, we see individuals express controversial ideas. It is more difficult for individuals representing a company or school, because the institution has the responsibility to suppress any external belief that may lead to harmful situations.

Societies project fairness as good and ideal. Opposition to fairness, like sexism and racism, is unacceptable. In the global court of public opinion, a tyrannical bigot is isolated and socially despised. To attain such fairness, we must distinguish between inherent, first impressions that make a judgment based on experience and our internal beliefs that make a judgment before the experience. First impressions in society are not as simple as confronting a hungry lion. They are often influenced by deeper internal beliefs. How do people react when they learn someone is rich? Poor? Republican? Democrat? Gay? Mexican? Muslim? Quite often, we make snap judgments undeserving their target. When a first impression is accurate, its consequence is complete and positive. When a first impression is inaccurate, its consequence is incomplete and negative. Stereotypes, biases, racism, sexism, homophobia, and most phobias typically fuel inaccurate first impressions. Fairness tries to eliminate these behaviors. The Civil Rights movement in the United States strongly fought for fairness in the 1960s, and now we see Feminist movements and Gay Pride movements fighting for similar fairness and respect.

In the city of Alleppey, India, boats are a way of life. The roads between rural homes and commerce are waterways. Ferries become city buses as they sputter along from dock to dock along the large canals. Two men quickly lay down wooden platforms between the boat deck and dock. Commuters step on and off simultaneously before the men pull up the platforms and tie a rope to block further passage. The driver atop the ferry engages the motor, and the boat sputters quickly towards the next stop.

The highlight of my aquatic experience in Alleppey was the all-day canoe ride pushed by bamboo rod instead of fuel. It was smaller than the ferry and houseboats, so it could pass under tiny, cement bridges and through tiny canals covered in water lilies. The canals were quiet, so we could hear the birds chirp as they flew overhead, fish splash when they came to surface, and people walking and working nearby. There is a natural serenity on these waters unfound to me anywhere else in the world. Still, loud motors from larger boats distorted the peace for the sake of performing daily duties. I was someone who believed it would be difficult to inhabit a world where the natural environment can no longer support the diversity of life we see today.

Upon seeing and hearing the motorboat, my first thought was that environmentalists could try to prohibit motor boats as they pollute natural waterways. I had seen it done in lakes near my home in California. My internal belief held that the environment needed human protection to avoid human destruction. It fueled an external belief that we should protect the beauty of Alleppey by removing fuel-powered boats. Surely, many environmentalists would agree of the harm being done. My second thought then rationalized the first: it would be invasive for me to come in and assume I knew what was best for this community that had been functioning long before I arrived. Was motor pollution a problem now? The waterways were not overcrowded, so was it at risk of being a problem in the future? How much did people rely on motorboats to work? A relatively simple, harmless thought suddenly became more personally subjective than objective. The boats suddenly disturbed me. I valued the health of the water over the lifestyles of the local people. I had no information about the extent if any of water pollution and was making judgments without basis in fact. This simple, two-minute debate that occurred in my head while on the canoe in Alleppey served yet another lesson in humility and respect. A scientist can only build a hypothesis from concrete ideas, and a human being today should only judge what is factually evident. To do so is to reduce potential conflict when a wrong assumption turns into a problematic action.

In Rome, Daniela stated, "Recognizing limits is not to say that we can't go beyond a certain point, but that we don't know how to improve or make room for improvement."   Her   words tied back to internal beliefs about ourselves, such as insecurities and self-doubts, and the level of awareness necessary to grow into mature individuals. I then wondered that if learning is about always trying to understand the unknown, why do people naturally fear the unknown even within an ever-changing external reality? Our worlds have constantly changed as the current decade is vastly different than the 1990s and more so than the 1950s and before. Change is a scary thing as its definition entails taking a step away from a status quo that exists, because the status quo is comfortable and does not require constant adaptation effort. However, only change remains constant over time. If learning the unknown is mandatory for personal growth, and we also fear the unknown, we open a Pandora's Box in which ignorance is bliss, but we must learn what is unknown to become aware of our ignorance. To not understand what is unknown is to be free of fear of the unknown, yet it requires active learning of what is unknown so that we finally get to know what we don't know. This tongue twister is irrelevant in a world where we make no efforts to learn and understand ourselves, but alas that is not the world we live in.

Individuality

We all know we are each different from every person we see. Biologically, our genes are unique, and we are each the first human being with our set of genes in history. Socially, we meet different people growing up, have different parents, and have different role models. Geographically, our location on this planet greatly affects the ideas our elders teach us, the relationship we have with our government, neighbors, and environment, and how we perceive each other. Historically, my place in society would have mostly been influenced by my country of origin and my ethnic appearance with little opportunity of change. Our internal and external beliefs are different from those of our ancestors; they are also different from those our neighbors hold today, and they will certainly be different from what our children will hold tomorrow.

Traveling through so many countries within a short time offered me the transformative opportunity to meet new people from around the world that differed greatly in mentality, beliefs, social behavior, poverty, wealth, and in their ideas about how they perceived the world they live in.

One older gentleman I met in North Carolina had a vast collection of John Deere tractor models in their original boxes. It would never have occurred to me to have such a collection unless I had a similar childhood as he did on farms with tractors. The culture of my childhood in California distanced me from tractors and placed me in front of a computer. It would be arrogant and naïve to rank one's collection of childhood experiences above the other as he became extremely successful, and I strive to emulate some of his better qualities.

A self-described anarchist in my shared room in Sofia, Bulgaria, was anti-government and anti-establishment. I talked with him for an hour and tried to understand his views on many issues. Every question I asked was cause for another story that dragged me further away from my original question. His train of thought was the most erratic and unjustified I had ever heard which probably reflected his anarchist mentality. The arguments were sporadic facts rather than critiques. He went anywhere from police should be privatized, so they may compete to solve crimes in the quickest way possible to everything the government says is a lie and propaganda.

He had an interesting metaphor that, "Taxes are violent, because you get a gun pointed at you and thrown in jail if you stop paying taxes."

Being thrown in jail for not paying taxes was the justification that taxes are violent? My favorite idea of his was about climate change. He said it was just another way to impose more laws. I asked laws about what. He had no answer, so I pitched in my two cents about reducing the human impact we have on the planet and environment which is radically changing weather and causing a rapid extinction of many species called the "biodiversity crisis." I didn't share that last term with him. The laws would be increasing fuel efficiency and reducing our reliability on oil by looking at alternative energy. His retort was that his Honda from the 90s had great gas mileage, but here is my absolute, favorite part. He asked what my take on climate change was, and I explained to the best of my knowledge after taking a college course on the matter that irrefutably showed its existence that our industry has vastly affected the natural cycle of climate that occurs over hundreds of thousands of years. He thought it was crazy that we were trying to "stop the weather" by stopping climate change altogether, not the human influence. His credibility deteriorated a little by his loud volume and extensive use of profanity which made him sound more angry than rational. He was eating alone at dinner, so I invited him to join me and a South

Korean from the train ride to Sofia. The conversation was casual about what he was reading or watching and what our travels were like. He never left the hostel and just read or watched videos all day and night. Then things became political without my intention, and it became a soapbox for his ramblings. I tuned out after 30 minutes when it turned from a semi-discussion to a ranting, anarchist monologue.

Over breakfast the next day, I was talking to two Belgians, and I realized afterwards I went on my own ramble. One of them was a journalist going to visit refugee camps in the North, and I voiced a concern a German law student told me a few days prior about the hypocrisy in accepting refugees because of a moral obligation to aid fellow people in need but discriminating against them in society when it comes to work or education. I added a little about my conundrum in which it seemed that human life had a different value under different political or wartime conflicts. My anarchist friend was sitting at another table and felt motivated to pitch in his two cents. In his loud voice that echoed through the whole common area where hostel guests were eating breakfast, he told me in a vulgar manner that I was lying as I had told him the day earlier that an American life was worth more than a Bulgarian life. I neither remember such a thing nor would I say it as I don't believe it. I explained that I must've been playing devil's advocate which I sometimes do to have people explain their points further. He repeated that either I was lying now by saying lives are equal or I lied to him earlier before storming off. I couldn't help but smile at the bizarre nature of it all, and I looked at the Belgians who had shocked looks on their face.

When the anarchist had told me that the police should be privatized, it seemed like a plausible solution. Maybe competition would create better results. I went to my German friends and the Belgians and suggested the concept of privatizing the police to improve efficiency. Both laughed and said that was an outrageous idea, and the Belgian pointed out it would work for those who could afford it but what about those that couldn't? I didn't get to mention this reply to my acquaintance as I had nothing to say to him after the breakfast encounter.

These are just a few examples of the types of people I met. Each person is a unique accumulation of his or her past experience and exposure which shapes that person's understanding of other people in the world. Appreciating these two facts helped reduce my own stress when I tried to understand someone with different beliefs. Any discussion that addressed the experiences that helped shape an opinion in addition to the opinion itself was exponentially more beneficial to both parties than simply arguing about the rhetoric of an opinion. It requires substantial effort to separate a belief from the sources of that belief especially when each individual is comprised of hundreds of such beliefs developed over years of countless experiences. Nonetheless, collaborative progress develops even when two opposing people can appreciate the uniqueness of the other's situation and see both how far the other is willing to compromise as well as how far oneself can. If both people can attempt to understand the inherent individuality of each other, a lot of unnecessary stress dissolves and the focus shifts from annoyance to identifying a common ground for peaceful resolution.

Life

In India, I mostly posted about architecture and sightseeing, and I left out the cultural and experiences with people I talked about. At the time, I was not quite sure what to make of it. I talked to other tourists and Indians who spoke good English to make sense of what I experienced. The facts are that in Northern India nearly every business and social encounter left me feeling disrespected, cheated, and mocked. I became very frustrated with the whole situation. Everybody with experience traveling or living in India told me that it was just the way things were; businessmen were aggressive and I had to be an equally tough customer to get what I wanted. After two months in Nepal, I encountered perhaps three people total during that time who were dishonest or made me feel suspicious and with whom I had dealt with in buses, villages, cities, and schools. It reversed in Northern India where I only met a handful of good, kind people among the businessmen and employees in the cities and hotels. I knew poverty wasn't the root of this behavior, because I had just come from a developing country where essentially everyone was incredibly nice and friendly and was now in another developing country where I felt severely uncomfortable. I admit I fell miserably sick for several days upon arriving in India due to my own arrogance in thinking I could easily digest local water after living in Nepal, but I tried not to let that affect my judgment of what I was experiencing. Indians in both North and South India universally gave the same

211

explanation that overpopulation made competition extremely fierce. In addition, not a single Indian denied many North Indians were cheaters and would answer one day to God. Some Indians who worked closely with foreigners understood the aggression and scheming tactics were beginning to fail as tourists talked to each other and learned to avoid certain areas altogether. If tourists were not happy, tourism declined.

Indians expressed high hopes that the new Prime Minister Narendra Modi would rapidly develop the country within the next five years and people would change as well, but it remains to be seen. Some may say my feelings towards North India were an overreaction and this was just India, but after removing my Western standards of behavior and expectation in Nepal, I still felt disrespected in North India on a basic human level. People were pleasant and friendly in Goa and kind in Kerala, yet North India was a huge shock after Nepal despite many cultural and Hindu lifestyle similarities. The overpopulation and lack of development of Northern India pushed people to be creative to survive, albeit in ways Westerners and Southern Indians disapprove of.

The largest shock upon visiting Northern India was the altered value of human life. I felt that when there were so many human beings, death became a regular reality. Dogs and puppies were hit by cars all the time. Road safety laws were non-existent or not enforced. I found this in contrast to the #BlackLivesMatter campaign halfway around the world in the United States, a campaign dedicated to reducing statistically high rates of racial killings by police and supporting equal treatment across racial differences. It raised questions as to whether some parts of the world really valued one life more than another based on economics, race, or nationality. It was an odd feeling when someone told me if any natural disaster occurred in a developing country, my government would pick me up first. Or if Americans became infected with Ebola, those specific citizens received extradition and more treatment than any other patient. Or if 3,000 lives are lost on one day on September 11, 2001, hundreds of thousands of lives of men, women, and children are justly lost in the retaliating Iraq War.

What is the value of human life? Doctors are supposed to see each one the same. Many people truly do, but even more do not. Government policies that speak for equality and act towards equality are two entirely different things. "All men are created equal" is written into the U.S. Constitution, but few would agree with it given the nation's history.

Differing values of a single life can easily be portrayed with animals. Nearly all dogs I saw in India ran free, and the females had so many litters that their bellies looked like cow udders hanging just above the ground. Dogs in the U.S. seem to have more accessible healthcare per capita than people with their own doctor visits, vaccines, and complete daily meals. I couldn't imagine people thinking twice if a dog died on the streets in India, but it was newsworthy in the U.S. If a dog was treated poorly in the U.S., it would attract great attention. Americans believe a dog feels pain and can suffer, and laws should protect against animal abuse. Simultaneously, a cow treated poorly and killed for meat does not raise an eyebrow. In India, if someone even touches a cow, the holy animal of Hinduism, and does any harm to it, that person will undergo great punishment. A road accident with any bovine would be the driver's fault, and I would not want to be responsible for harming a cow in India. Cute dogs receive attention and care while cows do not in the U.S.; the opposite was true in India.

Maybe the treatment and value of life is subjective to the local culture, geographic borders, and maybe other borders too, such as how cute we find the animal or how holy and protected the animal is. Perhaps not all lives are as equal while people sleep better thinking they are. Thinking of cows as food is clearly culturally dependent and good food for thought. People see animals performing complicated tricks or tasks as smart but do not extend that thought to others within the same species just because they do not pass the artificial tests. We choose perhaps unconsciously whom we stereotype, picking some animals as smart and not others based on our own criteria.

The value we attribute to losing a human life is also subjective. When I experienced a large loss like missing my flight out of India, I was more aware of the significance than when I lost a pen I had bought in Nepal. Similarly, a large, sudden loss of human life captures our attention more in comparison to people trickling to death with old age or repetitive killing over years in either war zones or society's systemic infrastructure. One does not have to look far to see several examples of U.S. law enforcement repetitively shooting citizens before any crime is committed in direct opposition to the law stating a person is innocent before proven guilty. In the film *Minority Report*, Tom Cruise's character imprisons people for pre-crime, citing suspects are equally guilty just before committing a crime as after having committed a crime. Doing so is the equivalent to shooting potential threats. People are frequently assumed guilty before innocent in the real world too. The most insightful commentary I heard about an African American teenager shot dead was how big a tragedy it was, because he was "such a good kid." The implicit message was that killing a "bad kid" would not warrant the same emotional reaction. In one case, we feel tragic loss. In the latter, we might feel apathy as it was only a matter of time, or even worse the victim deserved to die.

I walked through memorials and cemeteries in Europe, and the graves looked the same no matter which side of war or part of society the person died. People kill because someone decides to, but there are simple reasons why they kill just as there are reasons why people commit simple acts like eating donuts. There are upstream reasons that cause downstream harm. Political motivation can produce government coups and geopolitical strategies. Revenge from isolation or emasculation has been used to explain school shooters. These acts occur regardless if the victim is foreign- or domestic-born. Killing can be out of necessity for survival and basic resources, but with basic resources taken care of, killing is a choice with identifiable reasons to support it. It is as much a personal choice to obey an instruction given by Person A to Person B to kill Person C, and that choice is what separates us from remaining animalistic.

Nina in Belgrade, Serbia, told me of the most distressing story I've ever heard. It involved mental and emotional abuse from a parent, total abandonment, and forced abortion. I cannot imagine what it is like to lose a child as I have not experienced it. The most I can do is push my imagination to the limit in order to try to understand its magnitude. To empathize is to reflect an emotion, but I must mimic it in this case. This is not a sick manipulation of emotion, but rather I want to express my sympathy in the only way I possibly can. Perhaps this explains why in movies the villain always asks the hero if he or she has a child or a family just before committing a heinous act as if it explains or justifies emotions like anger and pain or a desperate action. I have not experienced the death of someone close, so I cannot empathize the same way as those who have. There is no right way to grieve a loss of life, but there is a wrong way to show it. The happiest part of Nina's story is how she manages to live a healthy and productive life after her childhood and young adulthood. It was beneficial for me to hear her story and learn how the medical and justice systems created to support victims can be manipulated to create victims. Her father made false police and medical reports to protect himself from retaliation for his abusive behavior.

I admire her notion that it is better to live life rather than just survive life. It is easy to indulge in drugs, sex, violence, junk foods, or entertainment yet hard to survive from paycheck to paycheck, so we learn self-discipline to control ourselves and find a balance between indulgence and practicality.

Guy described the balance by saying, "We all need some stupid, childish fun" sometimes to break up the monotony of our daily rituals.

Nina now dedicates her time to children with mental illness, because she knows what not to become. Her victimization as a young woman offered a new understanding of life which she converted into her strength. She suggested Americans are exceptionally open to new ideas, because they have rarely suffered or been a victim. September 11, 2011, and Pearl Harbor were the largest attacks on U.S. soil in over a century in comparison to the number of American battles fought on foreign soil which are less visible to the American public.

I sit in a coffee shop in Mumbai, India. I have another seven hours until my train to Goa. There are some things I want to write down. A major lesson on this trip of mine is that there are many kinds of people as I have already said. Desperate competition and poverty plague India whereas I feel Nepal faces only the latter. My friends in the West, a phrase I never thought I would use, face many luxuries.

People living a life of comfort free from the stresses of survival can easily forget how hard other people must work to live beyond survival. Developing countries with lower life expectancy see life less so in terms of haves and have-nots and more so as life to be supported and cared for. People trying to survive know how common losing life is to political, social, and natural disasters. After major disasters in the West, I frequently see people in developing countries determined to express their sympathy. They understand the pain associated with sudden losses of human life. I could feel the value of life more tangibly in smaller villages where I could interact with each person individually instead of larger cities where life becomes a constant sea of strangers. A simplified analogy is how I value gas in my car a little less after filling up the tank versus nearly empty when every drop counts. Each life is more visible and personal. No matter how bad the current state of affairs is in any location, people work hard to make their lives better and improve the value of life to the best of their ability.

Life is as good as could be right now while I sit on Kudle Beach, India, after swimming in the warm water. Still, life can be as good as my awareness allows it to be. As I have not met every single human being, my ignorance of other lives and their experience is not a reason to annul their existence. In an ideal world, each man, woman, and child inherently deserves to live life to the fullest. Their actions will determine how others treat them. Likewise, our actions determine how others treat us. My actions determine how others treat me. That is the beauty of life. My life is a life like any other, equally justified to exist in a world of other lives. "If it walks like a horse and sounds like a horse, it is most likely a horse." Mysteries of medicine are said to often have simple solutions rather than the most abstract diagnosis one can think of. Life, on the other hand, seems to have answers more complicated than they initially appear, and only upon honest analysis can one reflect back to learn from it. The world is a playground for thought and experience, and living is more than just breathing.

When I entered churches or temples, I crossed my heart and made a circle. I used to follow the gesture with the prayer reflecting that everyone in the world will find peace. I had entered dozens of places of worship that all shared the same energy to me, but I felt different when I entered a church in Belgrade. I had the feeling I would not passively watch people try to absorb peace as it does not enter their lives passively. This is when I decided that my life would be spent actively helping people find peace through my knowledge of medicine.

I really enjoy the discussion about life. It remains largely unanswered, but I would like to see it play out more in the future. Essentially, I am supposed to respect all life as a doctor. I include animal life in this field as I feel they experience pain and emotion just as much as we do. Either I respect all life or none of it. There is no middle ground to pick and choose which life I support. With animals, this means killing a cow is the same as killing a puppy. With people, this means a black is the same as a white and the value of a gay is equal to that of a straight. Politics may place a higher value of some lives over others. Nationality and skill set increase the value of life. A large number of people in any given area obscures the value of each life. Too many puppies on the road and no one cares if one gets crushed, because there are so many others. Does life matter or does it not? Either way, whether we really care or society tells us we should care, I do trust people to respect humanity. Having faith in humanity is to believe most people are good and a few are bad. Unfortunately, the bad receive the most attention, because their acts are the most shocking. A man and woman hugging in public receives no attention, but a man slapping a woman in public receives much more attention. The good is normal, and the differences are noticeable.

Similar Differences

Reflection

I first came across the idea of reflection two years ago after test-driving an electric car after work. The car additionally held a gas motor for driving beyond the battery's capacity. It was a luxury car, driving extremely smoothly and reacting immediately to acceleration as the battery instantly powered the wheels. The car cost $75,000 and with a small trunk was barely useful for carrying groceries. The company was trying to extend their clientele to a younger consumer base as they had the reputation for catering to older, affluent, Caucasian men. I honestly informed the assistant who rode alongside me that it did not make sense for a young individual as myself even with a possible yearly salary around the cost of the car itself to spend it entirely on a car. To my surprise, she said that some people would.

After parking the car, we continued to talk about the factors that influence someone's spending habits. The company's detailed analysis of their market required an understanding of the thinking behind their consumers in order to help consumers think they want the company's product. I mentioned I was also interested in people's behavioral habits and hoped to be a doctor to serve underserved populations. The assistant, an African American woman, told me I would be a great doctor, because I genuinely listened and conveyed mutual respect rather than patronizing people who are different such as herself. She informed me some doctors have difficulty communicating across cultural and ethnic divides and showing mutual respect eliminates such difficulties. I asked for her advice for how to be the best physician I could in an underserved community, and she said it was important to show respect to both adults and children.

What she said next has stuck with me ever since. Caucasian children see Caucasian adults as doctors, lawyers, police, judges, senators, teachers, and artists, and they are told repeatedly they can be successful in any one of a multitude of possible careers. African American children mostly see African American adults on television and in society as criminals, athletes, and as aggressive people with less education. They are rarely portrayed with careers as doctors, lawyers, police, judges, senators, teachers, and artists. In other words, Caucasian children see themselves reflected in successful role models, and African American children are less often shown their reflections in similar roles. Reflection is already a common idea. Bad employees are fired, because their actions reflect poorly on the company. Olympic athletes reflect their nation's pride. Movies capture the essence of reflection by making personal connections to viewers by portraying real emotions within 90 minutes. Childhood aspirations may aim lower than their potential if children cannot see themselves reflected in high positions of society after years of seeing themselves reflected poorly in society. In contrast, childhood aspirations can aim towards their full potential provided complete reflection across a variety of nurtured opportunities.

One of the Caucasian, Australian girls I met in Alleppey, India, went to a remote area, and a local man called her an angel. She later discovered the only images of Caucasians the man had seen were of angels in the Church. The local had never seen a Caucasian reflected back to him in a form other than an angel, so he thought she couldn't be anything but an angel. When we grow up, we see our lives reflected back to us in a variety of role models, and while reflections of productive citizens are arguably better than only seeing our reflections in criminals, a child cannot be penalized for learning from the surrounding environment. People believe what they hear over and over which often includes what they hear as children when it is harder to differentiate between positive and negative role models. A child looking up to a parent will be less resistant to parental opinions and radical ideas. An adult accustomed to analyzing differing opinions and critical thinking will be less susceptible to radical ideas. On an individual level, I am one who absorbed the exact messages I learned from my parents and my unique life experience. I am not particularly responsible for what my parents taught me during my childhood, but I can't deny what and how I think now is due in part to what they taught me as a child. I am neither particularly responsible for the community my parents chose to raise me in, but I cannot deny either I saw myself reflected in the adult family friends, teachers, neighbors, and television characters I observed. The first thing I can remember wanting to be when I grew up was a police officer, because I saw how they protected and helped people in need. I saw adults I wanted to be like and adults I did not want to be like. I saw reflections of what I could be. No one can blame me for being a product of the environment I grew up within, but I am responsible for the environment I leave behind me based on the current mentality and understanding of the world reality I currently have and how that environment will affect other children downstream.

Everyone experiences reflection as a child in the form of having a role model and eventually becoming a role model for young adults and their own children. For me, it was a shock when I learned younger people looked up to me even though I, in retrospect, unconsciously did it to those older than me. Unless we step in someone's shoes on all aspects of their life, we do not know what others experience and how they are being reflected or see themselves reflected in others. To see how someone is reflected in an environment and what the person chooses to reflect is to begin understanding why someone thinks and acts a particular way.

Similar Differences

Picking and choosing

Few actions universally lack room for debate such as abhorrent acts of rape and murder on a whim. Most other actions are debatable and depend on the culture and values a society shares. People like certain films, music, clothing, people, and ideas. For as many likings as we may have, we also have as many repulsions from different genres, styles, and behaviors we do not like.

It makes sense to most of us that if I do not like horror films, I will avoid watching them altogether. It also makes sense that if I care about the environment, I will not leave behind my garbage when camping in the forest out of respect for other campers and local wildlife. I would feel encouraged to ask others to do the same, so that I am not constantly stepping over trash in nature. Would it be confusing then, if not hypocritical in nature, for me to tell others to pick up their trash when camping, but for me to go ahead and drop my trash on the forest floor? I assume most would agree and be upset with me for being two-faced about the matter. What if I discovered a way to profit financially by throwing my trash into the forest? If I placed my value of making money higher than my value of caring for the environment to ensure its sustainability, I will try to make money at the cost the forest's cleanliness. I am now faced with a financial incentive to pollute, but polluting forests is heavily criticized publicly. I would surely lose respect of society and my friends if my actions were discovered. As long as the public does not discover my actions, I attain my goal to achieve profits. If my polluting is discovered, I would dissolve negative criticism by making a public statement apologizing for my actions and proceed to clean the discovered pollution. A consequent law may prohibit me from polluting the forest. I did not choose to pollute the forest until I could profit from it, but I would continue to advise others not to pollute because that would be the publicly favorable action. Picking and choosing values may lead to inconsistencies in thinking and action.

In this hypothetical scenario, money trumps ethical behavior. I can pay lobbyists and politicians to fight legislation from hindering my plans and thus protect my profitable line of work. The environmental issue came into question only when my two values of caring for the environment and profiting clashed. Profiting at the expense of being environmentally-friendly has been criticized heavily since Rachel Carson's book, *Silent Spring*, published in 1962. The current biodiversity crisis in which species are going extinct at an alarming and unprecedented rate has refocused public attention towards protecting nature by targeting shady practices of fracking, GMOs, overfishing, dolphin killing, shark fin soup, and unethical animal treatment. The point is that pumping black smoke out of factories and car engines was accepted 60 years ago, and it is no longer accepted today. People pick and choose how they feel about certain political, economic, and social issues based on both the time they grow up in and in terms of what is beneficial and to whom.

Language is an example of picking and choosing. People choose their words carefully to convey their messages. If tuned listeners can understand how words are used, they can analyze people's words to decode additional meaning and motives. In the U.S., school shooters are not called terrorists. A Muslim aggressor is immediately identified as a terrorist, but a Christian aggressor is never characterized as such. Describing someone as an "innocent, white girl" is to unite innocence with ethnicity, a dangerous identification to make, because of what it implies about other ethnicities. The fight for political correctness tries to eliminate inner beliefs from prejudicing external actions.

Language also describes the mentality behind the words. The anarchist from Sofia gave me insight into his mentality and perception of reality. He made up his mind that everything he heard was a lie. Thus, he could not accept anything he heard as true from that point forward. He was unjustly angry when he felt I had lied to him, and he had a profound hatred of others and authority. Ironically, he presented himself to me as a weaker authority on his opinions as his logic was flawed and inconsistent, his voice loudly arrogant and naïve, and his tone angry and hateful. I learned just as much from listening to how he used his words as I did from the words themselves.

In January 2015, two New York City policemen were killed during an anti-police movement about anger and retaliation for the killings of innocent youth. People felt more threatened than protected by those meant to protect and serve. NYC police felt little support from the city mayor afterwards. The following police strike led to a 66% to 94% drop in drug arrests, traffic citations, and court summons. The result was surprising as the city did not erupt in chaos as would be expected if the police had stopped doing their jobs. The strike showed an immense growth of awareness about human beings in that not all police were ruthless killers, and people were not as violent as we assumed them to be without police. Citizens and police want to be treated fairly equally with respect to their roles in society. Movements addressing preferential treatment of certain people over others target the human nature to pick and choose. Those movements try to create respectable boundaries, so that everyone may live fairly and safely.

We like to think our choices are conscious decisions we make independently, but there are many influences that can affect what we choose that we are not aware of. These influences can be the values we hold, past experiences that remind us of specific consequences, subliminal messaging in advertising, and chemical compounds in food and scents that target unconscious brain receptors.

Social media gave viral attention towards a photo showing a doctor crippled by the death of a 19-year-old patient. I would describe this as an example of opportunistic empathy. It initiated buzz and media, but it was a single image of emotion taken to capture people's attention for as long as they were interested. Doctors undergo such traumatic experiences almost daily, but the public rally around the image offered an experience they could relate to as one human being to another. The reaction was overwhelming, because we chose for a week or so before the viral buzz dissipated to sympathize more. On one hand, we can relate to doctors living in our cities and empathize with them. On the other hand, we tune out people in certain parts of the world who die en masse daily. We cannot normally relate to them, so we cease to sympathize until an event elicits an actual response to end mass deaths elsewhere. We place our emotions selectively on what we can see and relate to.

Many other aspects of our behavior rely on unconscious choices. We like comedians, because they will talk about any uncomfortable, taboo elephant in the room. Humor touches a world unattached from societal rules and expectation. Comedians make fun of equality where there is none and joke about unfairness where there should be equality. Some critics target humor for perpetuating inappropriate attitudes and mentalities. However, there are critics who support humor for directly addressing uncomfortable issues. Commentators classically argue against violent video games and song lyrics, because they perpetuate real-world violence. As a result, video games and song lyrics came under heavy scrutiny as a result. Those commentators picked video games and songs to target while ignoring violent movies. American film culture is classically defined by characters who achieve goals via violence, be it *Rocky*, *Terminator*, *Die Hard*, *Mission Impossible*, or *James Bond*. Violence became acceptable as long as the hero looked suave and classy when doing so, but the heroes in video games and songs typically did not. Why didn't people attack violent movies for inducing violence? Maybe the people criticizing the violence liked the movies but neither liked nor engaged with the violence in the video games and song lyrics. While that may be true, it does vindicate one form of creative expression over any other.

At a cultural festival, people can present their heritage by adorning their historical garments. At a college party with an ethnic theme, people can mock and degrade a particular heritage to elementary, inaccurate stereotypes. When is an ethnic dress viewed as traditional attire to admire or a mocking caricature? What is the difference between the two scenarios? A costume based on an ethnic heritage at a cultural festival holds a more complete and thorough understanding of the heritage versus a shallow, single impression of an entire people for a quick laugh. It is the difference between an accurate, inoffensive, multidimensional representation and a hurtful, one-dimensional stereotype. I remember the visceral, ill feeling when I discovered a friend hosting a French-themed party. Being of French descent, I felt the theme touched at my heart and identity, and for a slight moment, I suddenly felt I was in a place of prejudice. I envisioned one-dimensional caricatures of French culture that would have constantly been reflected back towards me in a way that would make it difficult to distinguish good-hearted jokes from actual mockery.

People have picked and chosen what they like and do not like since people have been around. With recent globalization, mass migrations are at an all-time high as people from around the world are mixing. Technology increases communication between people who have been separated for centuries. Because of these efforts, the picking and choosing by individuals in political power no longer hold true. Unjust policies that keep the powerless without political, economic, and social powers are questioned. The mixing of different people together encourages civil rights movements to grow and, through perseverance and determination, universal tolerance and acceptance to foster not choosing some people over others.

The centuries of picking and choosing one cultural or national attribute over another now appear as double standards, creating an endless list of hypocrisies in which the powerful preach equality but practice favoring specific people over others. By attacking these double standards, we enhance credibility and accountability. As lawyers discount witnesses by attacking their credibility and showing inconsistent behavior, international bodies increase accountability and hold individuals and societies responsible for their actions when they act inconsistently. Unfortunately, it is difficult to apply when world powers disagree. It is the thought that counts, but actions speak louder than words. People are both speaking louder and becoming more active against double standards.

Similar Differences

Dimensions

Perhaps the most important lesson I learned from my voyage was the notion of dimensions. Dimensions are defined as levels of understanding about someone or something. Understandings can consist of single dimensions or multi-dimensions, and there are proper and improper uses of both. For example, a one-dimensional understanding of someone can be a first impression. A multidimensional understanding of someone can arise from knowing them on many levels of past experiences, heritage, role models, culture, values, goals, and preferences.

Having one-dimensional opinions about others seems to be the natural evolution for how everybody thinks and wants to live. One-dimensional viewpoints are critical to survival and to judging immediate situations. The author of *Blink*[2] used the phrase "thin slicing" to describe the act of making snap judgment. Seeing a lion in the wild demands an immediate reaction without pausing to think about how cute the nearby cubs must be. Car salesmen rely on one-dimensional viewpoints of both the customer and their own appearance. They present themselves in a confident, reassuring light to cater their sales pitch to a customer's attitude and desire.

Many people around the world, as I witnessed in Florence, speak poorly of vegans. Most people have one-dimensional views of a vegan diet from their observations of people around them that try the meat-free and dairy-free diet. Sometimes, vegans fail to remain healthy and even become ill if the diet is not properly managed. In fact, many elite athletes are vegans, because they know it is the least toxic form of energy and nutrients for the body, free of added chemicals, hormones, or pesticides that require additional energy to process and excrete from the body lest they negatively alter the tissues. Without hearing examples of individuals who successfully manage vegan diets, people only observe those that become sick and rightly associate a vegan diet to be unhealthy.

Another example of the one-dimensional view is the inherent bias in journalism. Headlines and short articles attempt to describe often complex social and political issues through the understanding of the journalist. Good journalism dissolves as much bias as it can through selection of a broad base of information in order to present a comprehensive, multidimensional portrayal of the described events. Poor journalism accentuates bias by carefully selecting words and single dimensional viewpoints that will influence a reader to believe a specific opinion.

I sat at Margao train station in Goa before boarding a train to Alleppey. My taxi driver who left me there gave me a good lesson in one-dimensional thinking during the 30-minute drive from my hotel. At first, he, a Hindu, started criticizing Muslims for bringing drugs into his country and having too many children while Muslim politicians wanted to make his country entirely Muslim. My natural response to hearing his broad generalizations was to think of him as prejudiced and closed-minded. In response, I suggested how all political parties share the same faults. He laughed when I described how Nepali blame Indians for their country's problems, and Indians blame Nepali for the same reasons in their own country. These blames were based on one-dimensional views. Nepali saw only poor Indian laborers and beggars and believed Indians to be cheaters and thieves. Indians saw mostly Nepali migrant workers as drinkers and partiers. It was not a surprise that each nationality thought poorly of the other. His understanding of what I said showed he did not believe that all Muslims and Nepali were bad. His impression of both groups was based on his personal, incomplete experience as it did not include my impressions and understandings of Muslims and Nepali.

People are inherently multidimensional. No one can accurately describe someone in one sentence and also capture the entire person's past life experience, present work, and future potential. In addition, dimensions of understanding describe a perception of the external environment and the external environment itself. On one hand, people become inherently multidimensional after experiencing a different culture or people exhibiting different values through travel or other means of education. On the other hand, people can become increasingly one-dimensional by the reverse process of becoming multidimensional. After living in a single culture lacking broad diversity in culture, values, and behavior, people develop a structured, simple impression which makes it more difficult to adapt to change and understand differences. A simple example of this is food; a person who only eats one ethnic food may likely find after many years a strong resistance to trying a different ethnic food. The key to understanding people as the multidimensional beings they are is to see them through as many windows as possible. One window is one dimension. If it had not been for speaking and spending time with people in their homes and stores in different countries, I would have developed very different, one-dimensional understandings of those different from me.

Is multidimensional thinking good or bad? For certain tasks, it is dangerous to be multidisciplinary, because many tasks are best accomplished by someone with a one-dimensional understanding. Efficient military command occurs when subordinates do as they are told without interpreting the multidimensional strategy assumed by the commander. Conversely, an efficient commander cannot be too focused on specific tasks which can make it is difficult to see the larger picture. Ideally, a balanced individual knows when it is best to apply either a single or multidimensional approach to a problem. Snap judgments to solve immediate issues are often necessary, but the same snap judgments can have greater accuracy if one already has a strong multidimensional understanding.

Long-term collaboration requires multidimensional thinking instead of one-dimensional thinking for survival. An effective, interdisciplinary, and team-based approach to a problem requires a degree of humility to accept that one may not have all the solutions. Each discipline brings a unique solution to the table that, with enough single dimensional experts to offer their input, a multidimensional solution will arise. By tackling a major project with experts from a multitude of disciplines, all dimensions are addressed properly. In terms of fully and wholly evaluating a life experience, an individual is better off having as many dimensions of understanding as possible to find the best solution.

People cannot be defined by first impressions as people are constantly changing. I would not be happy if someone continued to hold onto their first impression of me if they met me when I was 10 years old. I like to think I have changed a lot for the better since then. To ignore how I have changed would be an injustice to me and an obstacle for them to see what I can offer. Using first impressions for long-term relationships leads to confusion and unsettled problems that develop into incorrect internal beliefs or larger issues. When my cousin's husband found a blue chair in a store for their living room, she did not like it. Upon bringing it home to see how it fit with the other furniture, she suddenly liked it. A thin slice of the blue chair in the store was unimpressive, but a contextual viewing of it in the living room helped it fit in well. Any long-term relationship requires nurturing and adaptation as it grows. To eliminate the possibility of a first impression hindering a new relationship, I decided everyone qualifies for respect at first for being a human being, and I give them two chances to lose it before reevaluating if the disrespect is worth the current relationship.

I discovered numerous examples of dimensions between people used well or used poorly to either create confusion in some scenarios or push social, economic, and political agendas in others. One American I met in Budapest worked in Silicon Valley, a concentrated area with many technology companies in California. I showed him an article I had read just days before about the glass ceiling for women to advance in the fields of technology and business. He thought sexism in Silicon Valley was "bull****" as the women he had worked with did not want to get their hands dirty enough to succeed.

"The glass ceiling is their own fault," he claimed.

I heard the same argument about rape too. I couldn't deny his logic and reasoning which was based on his experience with women in the work force. The women he knew were comfortable with the jobs they had. I had to point out that his coworkers may be women who do not strive to lift themselves higher, but there could be obstacles in place for women that aim high. Was he wrong? No. Was his argument incomplete? Yes. Telling him "he was wrong," instead of "his argument was incomplete," would be statement that would hinder any change of his understanding as he would have become defensive if I accused him of being ignorant and invalidated his past experience. By not calling him wrong, I could keep the dialogue and inform him of other cases in which his argument did not hold. In other words, he had a one-dimensional slice about the glass ceiling for women, and he was assuming that the women he observed represented all women. Similarly, to hear people say, "I have black friends, so…" or "I know women that…" is to assume that some social interactions with different people provide the same information as knowing the challenges relevant to their gender or ethnicity that they must overcome to succeed. An effective team member understands and respects what other members can offer in comparison to what he or she can offer. An effective individual is better prepared to evaluate arguments when he or she can identify if there are thorough multidimensional understandings instead of limited perspectives which may unnecessarily limit their resolution.

The American anarchist I met in Sofia didn't like Russian girls, because they were "all Russkies" also known as commies. Some American friends also mentioned they would not visit Russia, because they disagreed with the country's current politics. On the contrary, from my experience in Russia, I spent more money on museums and local businesses compared to the government, and I only met kind Russians who were equally enthusiastic to meet an American. In retrospect, many countries would be empty if their citizens left whenever they disagreed with the government. The people and the government are two different entities, and I would find it naïve to deny myself and locals the opportunity of learning from one another based on how I feel about their government.

one with laws or restriction

Learning new information about anything adds a greater context to the world I live in and how I place myself in it. Learning too little information can leave me inadequately prepared and vulnerable to oppression and miscalculation. Learning too much information can overwhelm the senses and lead to confusion and a lack of decision making, for any decision would have a negative consequence for someone else somewhere else. Between the two, the consequences of knowing too much do not begin to compare to knowing too little. It is better to know too much and decide what to select when making a decision than to know too little and make a decision with incomplete information. Worse than someone not knowing enough is someone not knowing what he or she does not know. The perception one has no more to learn can become a real obstacle to grow. Without accessible education and a self-motivated population, people will have greater difficulty fulfilling their potential for themselves and society.

Different time periods host different dimensions of understanding which encourage different values. We sometimes assume values are simply products of each generation but not always. Racism in the 21st century has proven time and time again to exist despite legal overturn with Jim Crow laws. Older people are even more shocked that racism still exists in young adults that grew up after the civil rights movement and institutionalized racism. A possible explanation is that there are subtle dimensions of American culture promoting racism that are not proudly admired and have remained out of the public spotlight for decades. Today, racial conflict is the conflict of different values leading to a different culture which in turn leads to different beliefs and dimensions of understanding of people. Arguments addressing different dimensions bring light to the topic, but they only scratch the surface. The culture cultivating racism is easily visible and targetable when people look for it, but it is a distraction from the real conflict. The real conflict is a battle of values. Racism as a value propagated due to the highly profitable economic institutions of early American history. Two hundred years later, racism as a value has been publicly executed. Still, the United States is a country where different values are protected. Indeed, the country was founded on the most important value to respects one's right to personal belief no matter how radical as the founding fathers did not want others to experience the religious persecution they left behind in England. Only oppressive countries jail and execute their citizens for having a different faith or political view. The United States will jail and possibly execute a citizen for committing crimes based on radical values, but it is one's right to harbor such values without fear of retribution. Vocal racists and their counterparts have both expressed how much better they feel society would be without the other, yet a society cannot simply eradicate one portion of their population without appearing criminal. Thankfully, intolerance as a belief is protected by law. U.S. Democrats and Republicans hardly tolerate the other in the current political climate, but both can exist independently. Sadly, intolerance as an action can occur before the law can stop it.

I caught myself being the subject of my own lessons. While talking to a Belgian journalist studying local refugee camps and his friend in Sofia, I tried to express some of my ideas about political refugees. I was so excited to share what I thought that I jumped through my train of thought too quickly for them to follow. I gave one example after another in rapid succession. Even if it clearly made sense in my head, I had to slow down and explain myself from multiple angles to offer them the space and evidence to understand my conclusion. A single explanation or example was like a single dimension of the point I was making. I had to put many dimensions together for my ideas to come across completely and accurately. I learned to be more patient and clear when communicating new ideas to other people.

Photos of my travels have trouble capturing the emotions I felt. Photos are like thin slices of what I experienced, hence the phrase, "You had to be there," to obtain a fully comprehensive understanding of the experience.

U.S. culture is engrained with the one truth that it is "The Greatest Nation in the World." Americans firmly hold the one-dimensional image that if the basics like gas in the car and bread on the table are satisfied, little change needs to occur. To regard the status quo as anything less than the best can be seen as un-American and can make people very resistant to change.

Different dimensions of understanding are not always clear to the public. We the public like to think we live in a right-and-wrong, objective society established by rules that ensure safety and security, but justice is subjective to change over time. It is for this reason we have courts to decide on the gray areas, lawyers to argue different viewpoints of a single story, and people placing much emphasis on electing Supreme Court justices.

Everyone understands any lifestyle requires basic food and shelter. Heavy drugs and violence are alternative lifestyles, but it is fairly well agreed upon that it is a limited world for the consumer and usually not very positive. Exercise is another lifestyle and can be found to vary from using a thumb to click the TV remote to running a marathon before lunch. Still, any dimension of life can exist for all thoughts and ideas are equally valid. How people understand those thoughts and ideas is what matters. $2 + 2 = 4$ is a commonly agreed thought. $2 + 2 = 5$ is typically controversial as it leads to either creative innovation in terms of thinking out of the box or extremist radicalization depending on the time and place of reception. Judgments are always made from a reference frame of mind.

I met two older ladies when I studied in Montreal, one of whom I found to be a deeply jealous person. As her friend told me when I caught up with her in the city, she had divorced her first husband and chose to keep the house instead of custody over her two children with one being a two-year-old son. She sold the house and gave $50,000 to her two children and $750,000 towards an investment that turned sour. She lost her money, was bitter, and strove to be the hardest working person and "crush everybody." I could have been angry at her for treating people poorly, but after learning of what she had gone through, my anger turned to understanding and compassion.

There are good people in this world like the caretaker at the Safari Park who enthusiastically drove volunteers around and helped us learn Thai to make the gatekeeper laugh. There are also desperate people like the bicycle driver who wanted to charge me for a ride to the youth hostel I would soon discover was 50 meters away. He didn't know I had already walked a kilometer or that I knew the youth hostel was nearby. After I understood the sincere friendliness of the caretaker and the desperation for money of the bicycle driver, I saw both individuals equally in their very different interactions with me. They behaved the way they knew best, even to survive in the case of the bicycle driver. Similarly, I approached my experiences with the tools I had learned to use and the understandings I gained.

Understanding people for what makes them whom they are with a multidimensional perspective allows me to step much more into their shoes than before. The inevitable result is any anger I had towards them dissipates. Spur-of-the-moment anger can still ensue, but long-term hatred cannot endure with the empathy that arises through greater understanding. We praise the lone policeman who bought mattresses and food for starving, thieving citizens when the law states they should be imprisoned. The policeman did so, because he expanded his understanding of the citizens beyond the immediate act of theft to see the real problem was not from the theft of food but rather the desperation to survive. Our faith in humanity, or lack thereof, is reflected in how we see and understand ourselves.

Part III: Person to People

Groups

I think back to the discussion with one of my two German friends on the Night Train from Belgrade. He informed me that a country writes a constitution to establish values which are set and shared by people. The government in turn represents the laws that these people choose. For example, common values for equality aim to eliminate prejudice among similar groups, and a government will prosecute discrimination that attacks equality. The very act of a group of people agreeing on a set of values defined in a constitution is to inherently exclude those not inside the group. The exclusion is always by differing values and sometimes by geographic location. The government clearly understands who is included and excluded under its laws. There are historical examples when, for the sake of migrant labor to meet job demands, governments benefitted from offering freedom and equal rights to the excluded yet had no true motivation to follow through. After establishing a government in charge of protecting values for the included, a simultaneous conflict arises when the excluded living in the country desire to share in the benefits that the included receive, such as healthcare, security, education, and social services. Internationally agreed rules protect basic human rights and prevent abuse or killing of the excluded or to limit what governments can do.

It is even more complicated in a country, notably the United States, where all groups are included under the Constitution. There are more than just included and excluded people. There are groups divided by wealth, race, education, socioeconomic status, and values that are not defined in the Constitution. Overall, the included group of citizens is comprised of groups of people from all over the world that share the American Dream. While cultural differences occur, the basic needs of survival, food, shelter, and safety from discrimination are present for any included person. Economic competition can hasten hatred between groups even though all are legally protected from violent acts. Without a doubt, never in history has a group in power fought in their self-interest on a matter that wholly included the needs of the less powerful.

I return to the American individual with his ideas about discrimination in the technology industry. Everyone can pick their own group. Most often, people pick a group of people that reflects similar cultural preferences, ways of speaking, and beliefs. Even when selecting someone for an assignment should be an objective decision, recent history speaks differently. Job hiring or auditions can be chock full of personal biases stemming from internal beliefs. Employees can be chosen or ignored for their gender, religion, racial or ethnic identity, economic status, college name, or geographic location. Studies showed equally qualified applicants differing only in name were disproportionately chosen based on the names that commonly belong to specific ethnic groups. In the book $Blink^2$, the author described a case study in which men and women of equal education, professional attire, and a well-spoken nature visited a multitude of car vendors to bargain on car prices. The results astonished the organizers as women received higher prices than men and African American men and women were given higher prices than their Caucasian counterparts. After I graduated from university, career advisors recommended companies and medical schools that preferred college graduates from my university. I even discovered a company that only hired graduates from the same university as the boss' university. The American admitted he saw even backwards discrimination in which women would not hire other women. It is common to prefer one group over another due to perceptions of those in the group, but with enough training and awareness, it can be corrected unless we let unequal discrimination perpetuate.

Personal experience and knowledge often skew any decision-making process along individual or collective biases. The solution to remove bias is objective standardization, but it is difficult to create for multiple reasons. Identifying a bias in one's own thinking requires a level of humility and honest introspection. Objective standards like blind musical auditions or self-goals to treat potential car buyers equally requires breaking engrained habits over time. There must also be constant effort to learn from mistakes and refine the standards to produce as equal and discrimination-free a system as desired.

I have discovered a new method of discussing a topic. Rather than spew out my ideas while my interlocutor spews out his, I instead searched the hypocrisies and flaws in his thinking and then showed how my ideas filled in those holes. Indeed, I helped him analyze some fallacies he could not explain. There is an expression that defines two different things as comparing apples and oranges. Well, I could not defend apples to Mr. Orange, because he is strictly against apples. Rather, I could explain what the two fruits have in common, aka their similarities, to rationalize their differences. He hated excuses, or reasons for why people would not get off welfare, but all he had were reasons, or excuses, for why the status quo existed. To him, women do not want to get their hands dirty and additionally, African Americans have a culture of drugs and no education. This American sounded both liberal and conservative at the same time.

His stereotypes were based on his personal experience and founded by exceptions. In other words, his exceptions became his norm and reasons for stereotyping a group. Schools target radical students because they negatively reflect on the school, and thus people may generalize the entire school to be unprofessional based on those few students. Companies do not want to hire a bigot, because it reflects poorly on their business image. A few radical Muslims do not indicate all Muslims are radical. A war against the Japanese in World War II did not mean all Japanese-Americans were spies. Stereotypes are based on exceptions to the whole group and should not be applied to every individual in the group. It is a simple idea but difficult to practice. Overcoming this harmful prejudice requires practice to change one's own mentality.

Racial bigots often justify their beliefs about African Americans for not valuing education and hard work. While there are examples of people that provide a basis for these beliefs to arise, the beliefs are prejudiced against everyone in the group and thus unfair and an injustice to society for ignoring the potential of the people striving to grow. After looking at how education can offer new perspectives, I would suggest new values of hard work and responsibility can be learned with available opportunities for education. Without equal opportunities for growth, racial bigotry will continue to exist as there will always be a disadvantaged group.

I just started watching the opening to a rugby game in southern France when the French sang their national anthem. I noticed when I felt proud to share in this identity that being part of a larger group is beneficial for camaraderie and uniting different people for a common goal. Schools and companies want their students and employees to feel part of their family and pride for being a part of their group. They often exemplify their group pride with names and merchandise, and they always have a mission statement which clearly defines the group's values. In a different context, a group can be manipulated to negatively view another group, the opposite of sportsmanship, and history provides many examples where individuals follow the group's mentality. Our voices eventually become those of our group if we forfeit individual thinking. The group's opinion can even differ from personal opinions as membership is more important. The idea of groups is strongly engrained in the social nature of human beings. Appreciation of group diversity is learned. Dislike of particular groups is also learned. This can occur at a societal level and even within a family unit as there are examples of parents pushing gay children out of their home and disowning dishonorable children.

Being part of a group is necessary. Groups offer a method for representation and a greater voice that extends beyond individual circumstances, but it is critical to ensure we define the groups, not the other way around. When I first arrived in Freiburg, Germany, I joined my German friend on a tram clearly full of Germans. I was so acutely aware these people were different than me as they spoke German and my mind instinctively tried to match their faces to other

Germans I had met or seen before in movies. I was clearly not with my group. Perhaps I was keenly aware of my surroundings, because 70% of the Germans I had seen in my life had been Nazis in WWII movies. I was re-registering information about Germans from what I was observing; mothers pushing baby strollers home, fathers returning from work, and children returning from school. This experience stood out to me so much, because in addition, my friend offered her seat to a standing, old man whom I had not seen standing right in front of me. I was too busy processing my environment in my head to notice him. Being surrounded by German culture was possibly one of the most noticeable and striking experiences. It is a culture I had largely seen in movies in time periods from as far back as seventy years ago, and it was refreshing to see firsthand how similar living in Germany now compares to living in California.

The United States is a country composed of diverse groups, and the nation values protecting the rights of everyone over the rights of specific groups in the name of national security. An unfortunate result of national security is the government can jeopardize the very rights of those citizens it was founded to protect. Hence, we see the illegal internment of Japanese-Americans during World War II and the illegal testing of mustard gas and other toxins on African-American and Japanese soldiers during the same period to help the war effort. The National Security Agency disregarded the First Amendment rights of American citizens during the 21st century and the Federal Government withheld basic human rights from prisoners interned at Guantanamo Bay to help the war on terror. Even more disheartening was the disregard of primary and mental health services from the Veterans Affairs health system for American soldiers upon their return from overseas conflicts. Soldiers, as a group, are possibly the most respected and recognized group of citizens in the United States, because they are needed for implementing U.S. foreign policy and risk the greatest sacrifice a person can make for their group. After they were no longer of service to the military, they were consequently under-served medically until public scrutiny criticized the government to offer better care for its own veterans. The U.S. is a group of groups, and its dislike for certain groups within its borders confuses many people. Immigrants from developing countries didn't cause problems as colonization kept them at bay, but extending rights to them now means extending the boundaries of the group to include more people. The normal reaction is a fear that sharing more resources with outsiders will put strain on the group.

Let me summarize the idea of groups with an analogy. Everyone drives their own car. People see what the car looks like and the group of cars on the road around it. People naturally group the car owner with others that would buy the same kind of car. It's simply a part of what makes us human. The decision to like or dislike someone else's car for reasons that apply to all other owners of the same kind of car is learned. It is up to society to manage to what extent those opinions affect people's lives.

Society

The day of competition among the most talented singers and dancers had arrived. I put on my single blue and white striped shirt and tucked it into my jeans. I walked to the village school across the highway to meet the Nepali dance teachers and their pupils. I had been invited to watch two young girls practice the traditional dance two days prior in their school uniform. Now, they were adorned in a red robe that twisted around their bodies with gold furnishings and jewelry around their necks and arms. Two older students wearing their school uniforms joined us to sing. We squeezed onto the local bus towards another school 20 minutes away. I banged my head upon entering the small bus and again on handle rails hanging from the ceiling when I reached the back of the bus. I later bumped my head against the doorway of the small, outdoor restroom much to the innocent amusement of the much smaller and younger students who walked in with room to spare above their heads. I spoke with the principal of the school, a remarkably well-spoken, young gentleman with dual master degrees and studying for a third. I do not recollect how the topic arose, but he was excited to share his knowledge and offered me an analogy of capitalism versus communism.

"Imagine there are ten thirsty people," he said, "each with their own empty glass. One person has a full glass of water. Communism would dictate the full glass of water be divided equally among ten glasses, so that each person has some water albeit not much. Capitalism would suggest the person with the water drink the full glass of water and leave nothing for the others." I proposed capitalism would find a way to make ten glasses of water and sell them.

Society quite simply is the mixture of different groups of people interacting and working together. Society is like driving. There are expected rules drivers must follow to negotiate the roadways efficiently without causing accidents which lead to further traffic congestion. Other drivers can be erratic, and it requires a proactive driver to responsibly maneuver through obstacles on the roads of society. Capitalism stresses the responsibility of the individual for securing his or her own future, and its society grows as a collection of individuals, each gaining one's own necessities and desires. Socialism encourages a collective mentality in which everyone gives a little, so that those who need greater social services like healthcare, education, and retirement wages are provided such and the society grows as one. Communism is the extreme of socialism where everyone gives everything to erase private property and create a much larger pool of resources for a central authority to fully supplement the entire population regardless of how hard any individual strives at their labor. Medieval monarchies relied on a single individual to rule on all social, economic, and military matters. Medieval societies, like ISIS in the Middle East, are the complete ideological opposite of a society as the rest of the world today defines it. Medieval societal growth occurred by reducing the diversity of its groups to create a single and simple mono-culture around an extreme understanding of faith and ethnicity. Their primary mode of expanding their society was through violence and messages of violence. Their culture, by nature, could not expand by including different cultures openly.

Today, developed societies in the West are ruled by elected representatives that work together to make laws. Legal issues often require advisory experts to accurately assess and refine laws to fit their practical application. Frustration arises these representatives start ruling on matters based on subjective beliefs and 3rd-party influence rather than rational, conflict-of-interest-free matters that best serve the interests of their constituents. Even more frustrating, if not disappointing, is to see laws passed that bar experts from advising politicians on issues related to their respective fields and politicians instead accept input solely from strictly corporate interests that seek short-term gains, far from the long-term development a country needs to propel itself forward safely without setbacks. One element of the greatest governments of the world is that a single individual does not predominate over all law. We spread our expertise among dedicated experts who have turned their fields of interest into careers. We thankfully as a nation do not yet assign nationalist haircuts or tell people what clothes to wear in public. However, some states are straining these principles with legislation pertaining to bathroom use or women's health issues. This is a reversal of the fundamental principles that separate us from our discriminatory past of religious persecution, and frustration will arise when we see a government ruling on matters extending into personal issues such as one's appearance or body.

Similar Differences

Diversity

What kind of people do you see when you walk down the street in the United States? Most likely, they come from different regions of the world, wear different clothes, and maybe speak another language. Everyone knows what diversity is, but our lack of understanding about diversity produces many conflicts. Some of these conflicts stem from something as simplistic as skin color to as challenging as job competition. For example, a few immigrants in a region often do not raise concern, but too many immigrants will be seen as a threat to the job market for local workers.

Yet, diversity is increasing. Global immigration and the number of refugees are increasing. The United States is seeing an internal increase of diversity with many minority groups growing in size, popularity, and power. To ensure a conflict-free increase in the recognition of different social groups, the education system has introduced ethnic and cultural courses to eliminate misunderstanding and prejudice. My very first introduction to this material was two summer courses at a local community college when I was 15 years old. They were called Intercultural Communication and Race and Ethnicity Theories where we defined the perceptions of different peoples, their histories in the United States, and each group's respective customs. Fast-forward three years to my first year in college. Everyone in my college was required to take one year of Dimensions of Culture. It was split up into three sections called Diversity, Justice, and Imagination. The first section involved studying the discrimination many ethnic groups faced in early American history predominately by wealthy, Caucasian males who wielded complete political power. Instead of feeling personally guilty for belonging to the privileged group of Caucasian males which I reflected, I was more interested in how one group could dominate entirely over all other groups. There was a lot of discontent expressed by students for the course claiming it was teaching a skewed version of history in which Caucasian males were repeatedly portrayed as unjust and biasing laws to favor themselves while degrading others. Indeed, it was not pleasant to discover one's own government had placed selected citizens in internment camps while it was fighting to dismantle concentration camps abroad. Most of my classmates were of Asian descent, but they were not the ones expressing discontent. Rather, they showed gratitude for learning about a side of history never taught to them prior to college. I surveyed my peers and found all the discontented ones were Caucasian students who must have felt personally attacked. In my opinion, here was a social group that had been reflected for their entire lives in all positions of power and opportunity, and it was disheartening to discover their power and opportunity was likely the result of centuries of discriminatory justice. In other words, it became difficult to sleep soundly in a dirty bed.

Teaching a diverse community about tolerating diversity is no easy task. There is resistance to learning about forms of discrimination, because it becomes inconvenient to the learner's understanding of how to properly treat people. People already have their own personal dimensions of understanding about other people, and they may filter and interpret diversity lessons to fit into prior structures of understanding. When the lessons cannot fit nicely into what they already know, the only option for those people is to complain about the injustice of being forced to reduce discrimination. This description is not to paint those individuals as intolerant of equal diversity in a negative light. Rather, it is to show how diversity as an inevitable trait of society today can be resisted, sometimes unknowingly. The resistance is the product of beliefs held, and beliefs are not easy to change.

In addition to resisting greater tolerance, there remains a misunderstanding of increased tolerance itself. Classes on diversity simply teach what diversity is, but not how to accept diversity within society. By overlooking the latter, a void is created and filled with personal interpretations of how society should function with increased diversity. The result is the general public talking about where the proper balance between tolerance and intolerance lies instead of our greater acceptance of diversity.

My favorite example of this is Feminism of the last decade. The general public seemed to support equal rights and pay for men and women. It was social suicide to admit men deserved more than women for the same work. Once the emotional charge of that recent movement dissipated, moderate feminists in support of gender equality tried to separate themselves from extreme feminists who fought to take down patriarchy and men entirely. Tolerance is the understanding that different groups must coexist and be granted equal rights. Until all groups understand and subscribe to this concept, complete freedom will not exist, especially in a country ostensibly based on freedom. "All men are created equal," is often quoted as an ironic statement in which history has shown little to match it. Having a multicultural society is not enough to label that society tolerant of diversity. Yes, people may tolerate neighbors or groups they hate, but it is not particularly healthy for society moving forward.

In Thun, my Swiss friend Stephan gave me some insight into his dwarf-like nation of gold miners and mountain-dwellers.

The Swiss officially speak French, Italian, and German, and while they love the languages, "They hate the people of their neighboring nations."

He did say the cities nearest the border are more tolerant than those more centrally located, because of more exposure to the actual people across the border; this was in comparison to the citizens situated further from the border who relate more to isolated myths passed from generation to generation. The same then must be true for St. Petersburg, Russia, as well considering locals told me those in Moscow are much more patriotic and pro-government than in the cultural capital.

Stephan also told me that being neutral is difficult for a country. Switzerland did well in WWII to wash Nazi bounty money to profit and avoid being attacked. Today, it sees what ISIS is doing but can make no military move, or else it would be considered a declaration of war. So, the country must close its eyes to ISIS, a difficult task for any nation at this time. He described the Swiss people as fearful of all their neighbors, because Switzerland is a small country. Logically, it invests heavily in defense. Fear stems from the country's history in which people defended their borders and preserved their national pride. I asked him whether being more multicultural makes one more or less tolerant of other given the example of the Swiss, but neither of us could answer the question at that time.

Diversity comes with the territory, and the Swiss, like the United States and many others, are having to come to terms with sharing power with different groups. So, while a multicultural society is inevitable and deporting or killing a different group on a whim is frowned upon, we are left with the only thing left; learn how to accept diversity in a way that reduces conflict rather than perpetuates it.

People are irrational and emotional. We say many things that indicate we accept this behavior as fact. For example, "This is India," when we observe disparate behavior in India, or "This is Africa," when we see corruption and the raising of an army of child soldiers. We also say, "Boys will be boys," when men do childish things and "People will be people," when they do anything to earn money to survive. Very few people would say a healthy, romantic relationship between two people can develop when either one or both carry heavy, emotional baggage which they ignore and hide away rather than face it. As a result, insecurities arise and cause explosive reactions to simple situations, and it becomes scary to face unpredictable behavior. A healthy relationship occurs when both people treat each other respectfully and acknowledge the other's needs and respond appropriately. Marriage counselors help with just that. Likewise, it is very difficult for someone to have a healthy relationship with local neighbors or a larger society with diverse groups when the person prefers to ignore their "baggage," such as hidden internal beliefs that continue to feed intolerance unintentionally. In addition, allowing desperation fuels more insecurity in people and makes it harder for them to develop a healthy relationship with their neighbors. Just as we can teach tolerance, we must be careful not to teach intolerance if we do not want to see the same conflicts repeated.

Similar Differences

Honor System

My interactions with people were fueled by how honest I sensed they were. Most were respectful and simply curious without malicious intent. Regardless, I knew these travels supported every ideal I held and were important to my self-development.

On my trip, I was surprised to find out how easy lying was in an attempt to escape responsibility. I narrowed my mind and ignored people in India on the streets to protect my time and money. I imagine people protect what they can't afford to lose. I could afford giving out a dollar to a beggar, but I couldn't afford the mental exhaustion that came from engaging every beggar that approached me, so I began to ignore people or make up excuses to get away.

Honesty is a luxury that few in this world can truly afford. People in desperate circumstances face a lot of risk in their daily life, more so than someone who lives comfortably with a clean home, a car, and a grocery store around the corner. A single risk increases the chances of either winning or losing one thing, but many risks threaten a person's physical and cognitive stability. Constant risk-takers are often on the verge of physical and cognitive affordability, because the stakes of winning or losing many things are so high. It makes sense they are more likely to try to wiggle out of a stressful situation, because there will be another risk soon afterwards. People are risk-takers by choice or forced into it by the local environment and life circumstances. In other words, if I took the same person out of a high-risk environment, that person could afford more patience, understanding, and better communication often exhibited by those in safer communities.

I was invited to lunch with a guy I named Mr. Lamborghini because of a shirt he always wore with the name on it. He was one of the only two people I grew not to trust in Nepal for the two months I was there. My distrust began the first day I met him at the clinic when he offered me free sex with Nepali girls. We sat down for lunch and started with chow mein and two large beers. I was not particularly willing to drink beer on a lunch break from the clinic, but he offered politely and repeatedly. In addition, drinking alcohol is a sign of poor character in Nepal, and I was not looking to dampen my alertness. Then he pressed to split a third bottle. Later, Prem, the owner of the clinic, and second man I grew to distrust joined us at the table. When he supported ordering a fourth large bottle of beer for myself and our mutual friend, I invited Prem to share the drink as well so that he would be equally guilty of drinking during the day. He firmly said, "No," stating it would reflect poorly on him if the head of the clinic was seen to be drinking, yet he had no qualms about pushing me to drink more. My instinct now went on alert, saying beware of those who buy you drinks after you've said enough. My thoughts returned to a previous experience on my voyage when alcohol was used as a weapon against my better judgement instead of as a beverage for enjoyment. To add to my caution, Mr. Lamborghini was prompting me repeatedly to join him at a local crocodile farm for free sightseeing an hour away. Prem reinforced the idea, further adding to my caution. I knew that once I hopped on the motorcycle with him, I had no say over where he took me. Still, my curiosity pushed me to stay at the table and wait to see what they wanted. I began to feel the alcohol slightly, but I was very careful not to let my guard down. The duo began sharing how honest Nepali people are which made me ask them if they thought I was afraid or thought them dishonest. They laughed it off. They questioned how much I had paid for my voluntourism package, stating they were offering something that was not included. They asked if I felt drunk. While I was not, I let them think I was more intoxicated than I was to see what they would ask next. There were never any indications of physical danger, so I thought, why not let them talk? Prem was keenly aware alcohol prompts honesty, and I also knew it to be true from social drinking. I was acutely aware of every word spoken and body language exhibited. Mr. Lamborghini paid for lunch, making me think he wanted to make me feel indebted. Prem soon asked if I had a credit card and how much I can pay per day with it, but he stopped asking after I ignored his questions. Unsure of both local culture and his persona, I answered that I had a credit card although I denied saying how much I could spend. When he took me to a local fair with his colleague on a different day, I also entertained his question about how much money I was carrying in my pockets. He explained to be wary of pickpockets, but I figured he just wanted to know how much I had on my person. Even though he invited me to the fair, he had me pay for most of the rides, a total sum of $7 by the end. I asked my Nepali brother if I was misunderstanding Prem's seemingly crafty behavior, but he made it clear Prem was bullying me and his behavior was disgraceful. I forgave Prem initially for his rudeness only to find future experiences with him equally disappointing. He was a bully without a doubt; he only spoke to test his boundaries without self-respect and honor.

I define the honor system as placing a large bowl of candy outside during Halloween trick-or-treating with a sign to take only one piece. Some children cannot say no to what looks like a pot of gold. I imagine adults are less tempted by a bowl of candy than children, and I would expect children would more frequently take more than one piece of candy than adults. Stealing more than just candy may often be caused by desperation. If people could eliminate financial or emotional desperation from their minds and lives, many crimes of desperation could be eliminated. A real-world example I learned was how Portugal tackled its heavy drug user problem. In Budapest, I met a Portuguese who shared with me that Portugal decided to shift funding and efforts from heavy incarceration of users towards treatment, rehabilitation, and decriminalization. By changing the stigma of a drug user's motives from a personality trait to a crime of desperation, the government could target the desperation and found drug use decreased by half after a decade.

An honor system is more likely to work in developed countries where people are more likely to afford entertaining morality rather than desperation. Personally, I found I would make rash decisions on my trip when I had little time or information to think about the best decision.

Honor will often lose to desperation when someone cannot afford, financially or emotionally, to take the high road in a stressful situation. Scams and choosing passive-aggression over active-assertion are examples in which desperation to win overpowers self-respect and honor. Developed countries offer more opportunities and regulations for safety and ethics to encourage honorable behavior than do developing countries. Medieval knights operated within their chaotic world by following rules of honor and chivalry. Today, Hollywood films about high-end mafia families show that in a world far from government authority and rules, honor is all that is left to establish rules of behavior such as loyalty. A snitch who rats out friends or family to the proper authorities is labeled as someone without honor and loyalty, and the snitch quickly becomes excommunicated from the community when discovered. People often become snitches when in desperate situations and they have no alternative options left. This does not mean developing countries are without honor, but increased poverty accompanied by desperation sets the stage for questionable behavior. Nepal is filled with poverty, but I did not see desperation.

I asked one Nepali if he felt there was anyone starving in Nepal, and he said, "Except for Indian beggars, no one was starving as rice and lentils are extremely cheap and greatly available."

I did not see starvation in Nepal, but it is certainly possible to exist in extremely rural areas where resources are scarce. Northern India, based on my experience and validated by Indian feedback, not only has extensive poverty but overcrowding as well. This overcrowding makes the few resources available even more valuable, so desperation was much higher. As a result, I unfortunately enjoyed very few interactions with Indians during my three weeks in Northern India as I could feel the desperation creeping into business encounters and simple social interactions. Southern India was much less crowded and people were extremely friendly. I will never forget walking through the roads of Alleppey, and seeing strangers pass by me on the road and say "Hello" and "Good morning" in good English and continue walking without the desire to trap me into buying something. A Ghanan I met on the train towards Amsterdam described the corruption within the Ghanan government in which ministers are paid to live extravagant lifestyles while working very little for the people. The people themselves may also charge $300 from one another for something that costs $150. There is no honor with cheaters. I told him I could imagine how a government official could wonder why he or she should help a bunch of cheaters.

He replied, "The government should help fix why people feel the need to cheat, give them steady jobs, and most people would be good. Not all, but most."

Courtesy of a Nepali who shared the many strategies of how one may enter the U.S. via questionable means: The first one I learned was to join a diplomat as part of his personal party or "security detail," travel with said diplomat to the U.S., and simply disappear when the time comes to leave. The second method is to marry an American and then divorce after emigrating. This can also be done for family as a brother in America can marry his sister, bring her over, and then divorce. Another method is to go on an Indian trading ship and simply jump ship when it arrives in the United States and swim ashore. A riskier method is to pay upwards of $30,000 to be smuggled across the sea and through Mexico. This is very dangerous and some people die along the way. There is also no guarantee that the smuggler will even take the person as promised. The money could be pocketed and the smuggler gone forever. My favorite is the most elaborate. Someone in Nepal can be attacked on their way home and beaten up. They are then kidnapped, smuggled to India, smuggled to Mexico, and illegally transported across the border to the United States. If caught, there will be an official police report in Nepal of the attack, and the person will be awarded a green card or visa to stay in the United States. He said he knows people that have used each method successfully. It was quite a shocking conversation and I laughed so much mostly out of incredulous disbelief.

People in developed countries also find their own sense of honor within themselves. The desperation in developed countries is easily visible by the sharp contrast of home prices from one neighborhood to another. The difference is that desperation from poverty is treatable, but desperation from a lack of or greed for profiting has no end. It is said, "Time is money." On one hand, time offers a cushion to invest resources wisely. On the other hand, money is time in which money can make money and offers stress-free time. It is crucial for businesses to profit and become successful so that society can grow, but it is important that profits do not dig a hole for society to fall into, such as the 2008 economic crisis. Unfortunately, the possibilities for making enormous amounts of money set the table for several unethical business practices. Some examples include real estate gambling on an international level, running sweatshops, unnecessarily removing employee benefits like health insurance and vacations, decreasing work hours, creating health risks by improper waste disposal into water sources and soil, and putting dangerous ingredients into food and health products. If businesses catered to every moral, health, and social rights argument about manufacturing and distribution of their products, fewer products would be on the market today. Money can create desperation, and more money can fuel further desperation.

Our choices are made within a context of our mind's framework. The pressure an individual feels from the local community is within the context of the larger society within which one falls. A society and community full of people struggling to survive will affect how people make choices. Knights and mafia families ruled on a sense of honor, but they don't exactly apply to the average person today. Calling someone chicken or insulting someone's mother does occur, and both elicit an angry reaction. Insults offend someone's honor or something they hold dear such as a religious faith or a family member. Revenge, in contrast, is to recover lost honor after being wronged. Films present many examples of revenge no matter the damages to human life or economic ruin to prove a point.

We say a sign of maturity is overcoming one's need to blame another and taking responsibility for one's own actions. Finding a scapegoat and snitching are ways to avoid confrontation and responsibility. Still, the exceptions do not change that we as a society prefer objectivity over subjectivity, because it provides fairness. We prefer fixed pricing over bargaining, and we prefer science over superstition. Much to our surprise, it all reverses in the context of desperate survival. We will shift responsibility to save ourselves by taking any step to deviate from an objective truth and hide behind a subjective lie. At the end of the day and after all choices have been made, a good quality of life is life itself.

"A better quality of life," as Nina said, "is an enriched one where we live life rather than just survive."

I feel we as humanity must stop in the middle of our fights and take the high road. Otherwise, we will end up in an endless Cold War of terrorism except it won't be blue vs red or terrorist vs citizen; it will be citizen vs citizen and neighbor vs neighbor. People will snitch out their neighbors for their own peace of mind as seen throughout history. The extreme of this desperate behavior is vigilante justice. Sometimes, we admire it and fantasize about it through watching superheroes such as Batman and Spiderman who take justice in their own hands to protect the peace of mind of themselves and others. Other times, we disapprove of it when vigilantes wearing a police badge, a sign they represent the government meant to protect us, take justice in their own hands and mistreat citizens by harassing and abusing them.

Sometimes, desperation arises from the system itself that was created to help people flourish. An example of this was a man arrested for stealing two cans of beer from a gas station and was later financially incapacitated as he fell into a whirlpool of out-of-pocket bills for a lawyer, probation officer, and ankle bracelet services that the government would not fund. The ensuing thousands of dollars in bills overwhelmed the man who stole two beers and it followed he was placed in jail, lost his license, sold his car and lost his job. Our system of government and authority have checks and balances, and we use them, but people that create the system adapt slowly, more so reactively than proactively. The system will also evolve even more slowly for groups of people that have little authority. It takes time to remove as many sources of desperation as possible on both ends of the spectrum to promote an effective honor system so that as many people may benefit for the good of society.

Similar Differences

Politics

I had very interesting and engaging political discussions with people in every country I went to. I liked to learn about royal families, government corruption, and foreign and domestic policies to see how different people try to solve different problems. In Southeast Asia, government corruption was a common topic. In Europe, welfare and employment were common topics. Regarding the U.S., frequent topics were race relations, gun control, and foreign policy to spread democracy geopolitically. Clearly, I was not going to become a political analyst, but I could begin to grasp the values guiding peoples' approaches to these different problems. For example, the drive to balance dynamics for an ethnic group encouraged policies such as affirmative action, but it led to criticism it did not account for individual qualifications. The policy of Title IX arose to reduce sex discrimination for individuals at the cost of certain group sports. Politics is the basis for discussing how to best compromise the needs of different groups.

Without a doubt, anyone that had any grasp of their country's politics was also aware of American politics. Quite simply, U.S. politics guide many global events, so any country with interests beyond its own borders will have some sort of relationship with the United States. Other countries are also of interest to the U.S. for how they affect resources or political structures. In the last half century, the U.S. jumped into the Korean War, Vietnam War, and a multitude of political coups as proxy battles against Communism. Each military conflict had effects around the world.

It is also of interest to people around the world to see how their national governments affected local policy. Nepali friends admitted their government received over a billion dollars in support from India, but the people never saw a penny of development money. Likewise, Indian friends informed me how their government profited from national sports and how speeches of reinvesting the money into local communities were never put into action.

Many discussions were highly memorable. One, I talked with a hostel staff member in Alleppey. He informed me of the popularly-elected communist government in the state and how greatly the people had benefitted from strong, public education, developed roads, and infrastructure. He was highly aware of social needs and government solutions in his community and the United States. In 20 minutes, I felt something I had never thought about anyone I met before, and it was that I was talking to a young man who should be mayor of his city. He had only graduated high school and spoke more eloquently, practically, and humanely than any of the greatest political speakers I had ever heard.

Second, the fifty-four-year-old, English motorcyclist I traveled with around Goa gave me insights about U.S. and Great Britain relations. His information was confirmed by every single British person I met in the months that followed. He said Britain is the "little brother to the U.S.," following its every move and will never say no. England used to be an empire, but since the concessions Great Britain made during World War II compelling the U.S. to join the battlegrounds in Europe, the country apparently never recovered its old standing. When the Iraq War was beginning, the English Prime Minister stood by the U.S. President without question. In opposition, the French neither agreed with the invasion nor sent a large force to Iraq. The U.S. Secretary of Defense at the time called France, along with Germany, part of "Old Europe," suggesting the countries were outdated and lacked the courage to act when necessary. French disagreement may have been fueled by the foresight of the instability it would cause in the region or their regional business interests. Regardless, the propaganda against the French had begun with changing "French fries" to "Freedom fries" and highlighting a weak habit of surrendering which the French seemed to have had throughout history. I know this, because the harassment I received in middle school at that time exploded exponentially with French jokes. They were harmless jokes to my peers, but the rhetoric from adults was not a joke, and I was not laughing after months of hearing the same jokes by my friends and classmates several times per week. After hearing the same jokes for the years that followed, I grew to never view U.S. public opinion sincerely as it could change easily with propaganda.

Third, I began talking at the hostel in Vienna with two Brazilian, medical students. I've always been in the middle of debates between American and European mentalities, but these were the first people I met that told me they, as Brazilians, watch what the U.S. does in North America and what Europe does across the ocean, then their country usually picks a stance somewhere in the middle.

Lastly, I learned a lot from my discussion with a 62-year-old friend that helped care for me when I studied abroad in Montreal and her new boyfriend. At first, they struck me as ignorant. They thought Obama was a Muslim, because CNN, the American news channel they watched, regularly repeated his alleged Muslim faith. The couple had also never heard of Obamacare even though it was possibly the most heated legislation he had passed. Later, I discovered that what I mistook for ignorance was simply misunderstanding through their listening to misleading information.

The boyfriend, another Englishman, wanted all immigrants in England to adapt to the local culture and language. Similar to what I'd heard in the U.S., immigrants lived together in cultural isolation and benefited from social services in London. It sounded intolerant at first, but he admitted there is always something new to learn. He knew everybody wants to be happy, and have a good life for their families. That explanation justified competition from "them," but not the discrimination they legally received and morally did not deserve for simply being immigrants. He noted how immigrants first came as cheap labor, but their children did not want their parents' labor jobs and resorted to mugging and crime as a source of easy income. He thought it was crazy to kill Saddam and destabilize the whole region as it left a power void, and recent history shows who filled it in. He also recounted how the British taught Americans about Vietnam and fighting in the jungle. Unfortunately, "American arrogance" kept American troops there even after the reputable French legionnaires couldn't hold it. I asked him about the Nepali Gurkhas, a regiment of Nepali men in the British army I learned about in Nepal. He said they had more pride and loyalty to the Queen than British soldiers themselves.

He also told me how young people have it better today, because they have laundry machines and dryers. When he married, he had nothing to his name, and his parents bought window curtains for him. He didn't eat out for five years to pay off the new house.

"Now, kids have everything," he noted.

My generation complains about the opposite: how they are forced to live with debt and are unable to attain a livable salary and become homeowners like our parents' generation could."

Both points of view are actually right, since "kids" disagree that they have everything, because they feel they don't, but they do have more than their parents did in a fully globalized market. Compared to thirty years ago, we do have more technology and convenience than our parents, but my generation disagrees about what the future holds as our outlook is bleaker with fewer perceived opportunities. Both sides disagree and yet both are right.

I enjoyed discussing politics around the world until I returned to my home country. I stopped then, because no one wanted to talk politics or were completely unaware of local, political issues that youth of the same age in Europe followed eagerly and fully understood. I began to inadvertently offend people by trying to discuss politics. In Chicago, I sat by a fireplace in a bar with my brother when a couple in their late-20's asked to join us by the fire. I am unsure of how it began exactly, but the boyfriend, my brother, and I ended up talking about social security, and the couple agreed that they were not going to rely on the failing system at all and preferred to depend solely on personal investments upon retirement. I was highly vocal in the friendly debate having been in the habit of discussing these affairs for months. After my brother and I left the bar, he told me that when I left to the bathroom earlier during the debate, the girlfriend said discussing politics had ruined her evening and she wished to discuss something else. My brother advised me to talk about other topics instead of politics to raise fewer red flags for the average American.

I've also had countless conversations only with Americans where I bring up a topic to talk about, and the other person shuts down and refuses to talk. It is only after I explain myself as curious about their point of view rather than wanting to argue that a discussion can ensue. I realized disagreement is perceived as offensive which is why talking politics can "ruin the evening." I was both shocked and disappointed to learn that the last country of my journey was the only one in which I could not greatly share what I learned from people I had met and what I wanted to talk about.

A willful disregard for greater awareness reduces the number of dimensions that a person can use to think about an issue. Being less multidimensional is good for specific jobs. Employers do not want people who are underqualified meaning they know too little to adequately fulfill the requirements or overqualified meaning they know too much and feel underutilized and bored. Being less multidimensional is terrible for citizens. Teaching moral, legal, and civil duties to middle school students in Nepal taught me this in return. A civil duty involves voting and taking part in community issues be they local or national. I taught this in Nepal, a developing country, and I reflected on the United States and saw the lack of public interest in government policies as a problem of the people and for the people, not a symptom of bipartisan strongholds. The lack of faith in the peoples' voting power in comparison to the strength of corporate influence in politics is perfect for corporate influence via lobbying to perpetuate and continue doing it their way. We have feared previously the threat to society if children listen to violent song lyrics. What about adults who can vote and are also easily susceptible to external material including songs, jokes, commercials, and news shows without filters or understanding? Not only disbelief in the political system, but a complete resistance to healthy discussion of what a government should do is the finishing touch on a recipe for an elected government to act independently of the peoples' wishes and turn into a government by some of the people and not for the people. While it seems like this is the worst environment for elected representatives to represent the people, America can always outperform itself. We the people have seen our Congressional representatives lack basic understandings of elementary topics when it comes to health, undisputed science, and how a woman's body responds to rape and pregnancy. The dimension the public sees and gets flustered over is Congressmen entirely relying on ideological interpretations and ignoring the facts when debating policy that will factually affect millions of people. The dimension that is kept hidden is the rejection of scientists from advising politicians on scientific policy and influence of corporate interests on these same politicians to affect millions of American lives. People are often stunned on how supposedly common-sense legislation does not pass into law. For example, the Sandy Hook Elementary School shooting of 20 children and 6 staff led to 90% of the U.S. population in favor of background checks for new gun owners buying at gun stores. People were shocked that 90% of the entire American population supporting a bill was not enough for it to pass into law. To explain, there are heavy, financial interests and defenders of the 2nd amendment of the U.S. Constitution that prevented the legislation from passing. If the same 90% of Americans publicly agreed not to vote for their Congressmen until background checks were put into law, no amount of lobbying could stand between a Congressman's seat and a public vote. That same power to immediately change legislation is held by the people on every issue, and it is very strategic to convince constituents to actively ignore their political power. Whether it is a lack of citizen's will power to get politically involved or lack of space to process political issues, I would call the high lack of involvement a social problem, because the politics will always affect the people directly with or without their knowledge.

History

People manage the past with museums and literature, the present through services and production, and the future through development, research, and technology. The present constantly changes and adapts as it accelerates even faster with technology towards the future, but the past remains constant. History is full of lessons and stories of hate, love, kindness, cruelty, compassion, and behavior geared for survival. The greatest stories transcend all time and history. Stories of Odysseus or Romeo and Juliet do this by offering lessons in what it means to be human, and this extends beyond values, culture, and language. Most of history's events are not universal like those fictitious stories of adventure and love. Rather, history offers examples of people treating each other in ways that are heavily dependent on local culture and awareness. Before globalization and global immigration, most cultures were fairly uniform and lacking significant diversity. The dimensions of awareness never extended to be as universal as they are today. For the first time in history, recent history shows people on one side of the planet empathizing and supporting people in times of crisis on the other side of the planet who differ in almost every way.

We can pick and choose to see good people here, bad people there, good policemen here, bad policemen there, heroes of humanity there, and evil people there. We can do this for as long as we live. Indeed, that is all our ancestors have ever done in history for as long as societies existed in places where different groups clashed together. Recent history shows previously ostracized groups in society gaining social recognition and political power, but many misunderstandings continue to perpetuate in the form of the symptoms described earlier. The only great changes in history have come about through unity, not division and categorization. Humanity is undergoing a revolution of awareness. As a priest would try to make sense of the seemingly senseless loss of a child to distraught parents with what they can learn from it, humanity can make sense of the chaos it has undergone in order to learn from it. I learned in elementary school that I learn history to avoid repeating prior mistakes, and I see now that I can only do that when I fully understand why the mistake was made in the first place. The why is made up of all the dimensions described throughout this book.

I recall when my friend in Montreal was reviewing a lecture of epidemiology, the study of how disease spreads, but she was not interested in a PowerPoint slide that mapped out the historical spread of a genetic mutation around the world. History is not as big and complicated as it seems. Do you remember the last food you tried and didn't like, so you decided not to order it again? That is learning from your own history. The entire subject of history simply includes the mistakes and successes of people from all over the world. Choosing to ignore a part of history, like the spread of a genetic mutation around the world, is to ignore the methods in which the next genetic mutation of tomorrow will travel among a population.

I think most would agree a multidisciplinary team of engineers, biologists, mathematicians, and physicists tackling the problem of how to land on the moon is better than using only engineers. It is difficult to be a productive and functioning citizen without the multiple disciplines of basic knowledge in history, English, mathematics, and critical thinking. Learning history adds a dimension to the person's understanding and empowers future choices.

People were surprised recently when presidential campaigns intentionally squeezed supporters together in small venues to appear overcrowded with support. However, this is an old tactic which was used 50 years ago by presidential candidates who wanted their support to appear overwhelming in photos.

The idea of a multidimensional team can be combined into one person. When that person learns more, it makes that person more powerful and valuable to society.

After traveling through central Europe, I learned from city tour guides about different experiences under Soviet rule which are now remembered as different versions of history. For those who were oppressed under Nazi regime, Russian liberation was a godsend for the victims. The other citizens who were not targeted by the Nazis viewed the Russians as conquerors who stayed and imposed their own political system to expand their influence. The Soviets were not the first ones to occupy another country and would certainly not be the last ones either, but it was interesting to see how the same history was different depending on who was asked.

Many events in history could tarnish the positive image a country would like to uphold today. I never learned about the deals the USA made with Great Britain during WWII until I finished history courses in school and talked with Brits. Japanese-American internment camps during the same era also receive little acknowledgement. That was seventy years ago. What about whistleblowers today about the poor health services in the hospitals of Veterans Affairs? What about the National Security Agency imposing itself in the private life of its citizens? Who do we as a people choose to listen to? Who do we try to shut out? Why? Textbooks in the Southern United States wanted to tone down their rebellious role during the Civil War, so that those states will only be known now under a more pleasant light. The museum in Vietnam showed historical artifacts and images portraying the twisted behavior of American soldiers towards a people they were indoctrinated to have no respect for. That was a dark side of history, and I can understand why it is never taught within American borders. Events like these are not unique to the United States. I only know more of them, because I grew up here and have taken a harder look at this country. The debate of how to record and act upon one's history is everyone's responsibility. It is up to each individual to hold one another accountable. This happens often, such as in 2015 when President Obama asked for Japan's government to apologize for the use of "comfort women" during WWII.

How much do we let history rule our present and future? A country's government, the largest group that can be formed, must keep face and never forget its history. People can learn from their mistakes and forgive their oppressors, but a government and its people are separate entities. Many people told me it was risky to go to Russia as an American, but I found every single person was ecstatic to meet a Californian and wanted to visit California and San Francisco as did nearly everyone everywhere else. People loved meeting me despite their government's policies. People do not always support their rulers, but many said confidently they liked living in their native country despite disagreeing with their country's policies.

One person even asked incredulously; "How could a country's citizens not like living in their native country?"

The extent of influence a national history and personal history has on our local and national choices is the responsibility of nobody but ourselves, and it would behoove us as people in a society to be in control of both lest someone else writes our history for us. I end this section with words I found at a small museum about the Bridge at the River Kwai and the Death Railway in Kanchanaburi, Thailand. "Forgive, But Not Forget" was written above the flags of Japan and the POW countries of Great Britain, United States, Australia, Singapore, the Netherlands, and on a bomb like the one used to destroy the infamous bridge.

Privacy

The debate between balancing privacy and convenience, or rather the cost of privacy to afford convenience, is an old one. I bought a 10-ride bus pass while I was in Montreal, so I could recharge it and pass easily through check-in on buses and metros. A multi-use pass must communicate with a central electronic system that logs where, when, and how many times one uses a bus or metro to determine how many uses are left on the pass. Tracking is when someone in the system follows that log. By using the pass, I consent to the transportation authority to log where and how many times I use their facilities. If government authorities asked to track my public transit or hackers took over the electronic system, either party could follow where and when I was moving without my consent. In fact, many companies have openly admitted how many times the government petitioned them for client information. A remarkable TED talk that really stuck with me questions who is tracking the trackers' behavior. The speaker described how when he surfed the web, he found many websites tracking his online behavior which was normal for him. His concern heightened when he discovered his young daughter was being followed by dozens of sites as she skimmed across webpages for children. We all agree it is insane to let dozens of people follow us around the streets, writing down who we speak to and what stores we walk into, yet we allow this to occur online.

Where amidst these two worlds do we find a balance where we remain comfortable with the amount of privacy allowed for the convenience of having easy searching and social profiles online. Omar, my friend's brother, mentioned how a flashlight app asked for access to his photos, contacts, and location. Is access to personal information necessary to turn on the phone's flash? Certainly not. Would the additional information aid the app's developer in advertising and tracking users for patterns? Yes. Do people typically care when they learn their privacy is being ignored? Yes. Would it be of the company's interest to make it difficult to understand and navigate a company's privacy policies? I'll let you answer that.

Education about privacy can place the average consumer back in charge of one's information by learning about the extent information is used online. Surely, Orwell's description in *1984* of Big Brother defines complete government oversight into citizens' private lives. Whether it is the government doing so for national security or businesses doing so for marketing and optimizing performance, both are often taking personal information under assumed, not explicit, consent.

Laws often act much slower than business practices. Ironically, many Americans supported the Patriot Act and NSA surveillance by stating they would give up their right to privacy for national security since only guilty people have something to hide. This is similar to assuming only the guilty want a lawyer even though it is everyone's right to have one. Another irony, aka double standard, exists when the logic behind giving up personal privacy over phone calls and messages for national security ceases to exist when the debate shifts to giving up personal freedom for gun ownership for local security. I last heard the term Big Brother used by the Australian girls in Alleppey when I was describing Singapore. Despite government cameras around the city surveilling public spaces, I felt more safe and free to walk through any neighborhood in the city without fear of personal attack. The Australian girls disagreed about how safe and right it was to have so many cameras of public spaces. On the other hand, I felt more threatened by the notion of Big Brother in other countries defined by total freedom where my every move and click online is tracked and used unknowingly without my consent. The Canadian students I met in Tokyo and were studying abroad in Singapore had told me Singapore was possibly the only city in the world where a girl could walk home alone at 3:00am anywhere in the city and she would be safe.

The discussion surrounding privacy versus convenience is only as in-depth as the awareness of those discussing the problem. Public ignorance is the greatest tool for businesses and politicians who use citizens' private information without their explicit consent to give away their rights. In a twisted analogy where a man represents the trackers and a woman represents the private information unwillingly tracked, it is equivalent to a man feeling entitled to rape a woman, because the woman did not explicitly say no. The rape of personal liberties in a country defined by defending personal liberty will continue to happen unless there is awareness of the act and a willingness to learn how to say no.

When I was in Montreal, my friend had lit scented candles that filled the room with vanilla aroma. I had recently read about the hazards of scented candles and lead wicks turning the air toxic. After I mentioned the possible hazards, she didn't like the odor and extinguished the candle. I looked up research articles that added concrete fact to what I had quickly read earlier in a news article. I discovered her brand of scented candle did not emit anything significantly toxic to human health, so I told her the candles were alright to use. Ignorance is bliss for suppliers as consumers may reject products if they learn of something they don't like. Being unaware due to a lack of formal education or self-motivation to learn allows the consumer to be bullied and may lead to unsafe and unhealthy decisions for the family and children. We put seatbelts on our children daily but overlook chemicals and poisons we may expose them to in our foods or cleaning products due to a lack of awareness. There are countless examples in which food ingredients have been withdrawn only after being made public. Some people can choose to ignore new information, but many people do change their minds with new information. Hence, labeling ingredients is an on-going battle, because suppliers know full well that too much or too little information for the consumer affects what they will buy.

Before I left on my trip, I went to buy a microfiber towel. There was another brand of towel with microbial properties which indicated to me there was a chemical inside to kill microbes. A lady picked up this brand, and after mentioning the microbial property that was not clearly labeled on the packaging, she said she "definitely did not want that" and picked up the same brand I had.

We all desire to have control over our own lives. We want to know where we come from and where we are headed. We value and take pride in our ancestors, our lineage, our national history, where our food comes from, and where and how our clothes are manufactured. Nobody wants to be a sheep in a country that prides itself on individual freedom and free choice, but willful ignorance can only assist planned invasions of privacy by government or business. Today, social media and easily accessible information allows for rapid dissemination and social unity. The hypocrisies and double standards arising from decades and even centuries of picking and choosing what information to disclose and share are difficult to defend. This is a unique time in history when people have immense power available to them, but the risk of abuse has never been higher.

Religion

I woke up at 4:00am to walk with Govinda, my Nepali host father, as he did nearly every morning before the daily chores. It was dark, extremely foggy, and the only light shining was a full moon. We walked about 20 minutes in one direction on the paved road branching from the main highway. We walked past one, maybe two streetlights, but we were otherwise walking by moonlight. I tripped on the same speedbump in both directions. I stared up at the moon, studying its dark spots and pondering. Because the moon does not rotate as it orbits Earth, I thought every human being in history has looked at the same side of the moon. Only man, with the capacity of introspective thought, can feel so insignificant when looking into the night sky that he feels his place must be divinely appointed on this Earth. Ancient Greek and Egyptian gods' concern towards mankind explained natural phenomena that could not be well-understood by people of the respective era. Events such as heavy rainfall causing floods or an unwarranted victory in battle when the odds were against them were said to be the act of the gods. The major mono-theistic religions coming afterwards continued to promote positive behavior as a way to please God.

I tried to visit places of worship everywhere I went. I entered Buddhist temples and shrines in Japan, Singapore, and Thailand, Hindu temples and shrines in Nepal and India, Muslim mosques in

Singapore and Dubai, and Catholic and Christian churches in St. Petersburg and across Europe. I entered each holy site with an attitude of respectful observation. In Osaka, Mr. Yano taught other travelers and myself how the Japanese pray by clapping twice and bowing. I removed my shoes to enter mosques and wore a robe in Singapore to cover my shorts. I walked quietly around magnificent, large, and quiet church while listening to majestic choirs and absorbing the indescribable energy inside.

I talked with a recently converted Muslim at the largest mosque in Singapore for two hours while she answered my questions about religious tolerance and why we should answer to a higher power. She showed me a poster that revolutionized how I viewed religion. It was a family tree, if you will, of the 25 prophets and other messengers mentioned in the Qur'an. The major prophets began with Adam and descended from Seth to Noah. After several teachers, the line reaches Abraham from whom the Scrolls arose. Ishmael, the progenitor of the Arabic people, descended from Abraham and continues until Prophet Muhammad brings the Qur'an. Isaac also descended from Abraham and led to Jacob. Joseph extended on one side from Jacob to produce the Psalms. Moses eventually arose from Jacob as well, giving the Torah, meaning law, to the Jewish people. Branching out parallel to Moses is Aaron who continues the line towards Jesus the Messiah and the Gospel. The poster placed all the major religions onto one image and showed how they are all connected and stemmed from many of the same teachers.

She handed me a little booklet that described Muhammad's upbringing, rise to the status of religious prophet, and start of a kingdom based on universal fairness and devotion. Muhammad's early followers sounded nothing like some of the followers we see today that are extremely chaotic and violent. His lessons of being fair to neighbors, treating each other with respect, and killing as an act annulling one's devotion sounded like the same lessons I had heard from other religions.

Just as language is a product of time and location, faiths are social products born at times when specific needs had to be met. People's beliefs are true to them, a truth based on where and how those beliefs are nurtured and interpreted. Mohammad's laws targeted social matters of his time, speaking in terms of camels and stones. His message, on the other hand, transcended time as it still is prevalent today, but it changes slightly or dramatically based on personal interpretation. I began reading the booklet about Muhammad and the beliefs of Islam, and I found a man who taught do not kill on one page and killed his prosecutors in self-defense a few pages later in order to establish his faith. He lived by example and tried to teach others about good, honest, ethical and moral living.

When I asked why people need religion, the lady at the mosque in Singapore said, "People are weak."

In this case, it seems religion is an institution to teach good, ethical living as did my mentors in my life. I try my best to live a good, honest life, and I sleep well knowing that I do. I think people put their trust in God, because God-fearing is universal and without argument. As a result, the same people unite under a common goal and form groups based around their faith.

Lighting candles in a church would make me feel like I have a lasting presence beyond the duration of my physical duration within the church. We all desire to be valued and remembered, and God is the most accessible way for accomplishing just that.

Religion is a tool to teach practical and safe lifestyles. Sinful lifestyles involve less productivity and more personal enjoyment which are counter to what a developing society and community requires to survive, so laws are written for the safety of everyone. Holy books are manifestations of these good lessons, and manifestations of bad lessons are outlawed as heretic and blasphemous. Faith serves a purpose of hope and transition to a better life. To argue its validity is beside the point. People use it to protect what they love, to explain the intangible, and find peace when they wouldn't otherwise have it.

Everywhere I looked in Nepal, I saw signs of Hinduism from shrines to tikkas. The more I investigated into which faith I was drawn to, I found my faith to be personal to me, self-empowering, and strengthening my happiness. My faith in the values I hold dear is close to my essence, and that becomes stronger every day. I grew up going to spiritual camps for teenagers with the same goals as being in the Boy Scouts who also strive to teach responsible behavior through external acts and services. The camps I attended taught responsible behavior by looking introspectively to understand our personal attitudes towards an external or internal situation and how, by changing that, we could perceive a difficult conflict differently and always find a solution. It is much easier and effective to change myself than try to convince someone else to feel differently.

After visiting so many places of worship of varying size, location, and affluence, I concluded they are all equal in power and validity. In a cute analogy, are people not the same? I could feel something indescribable when I stood inside massive monuments of faith, and it didn't matter whether it was a church, a temple, or a mosque. An Easter service I attended in North Carolina was in a contemporary church. My brother and I were meeting people there, and we were greeted with a giant rock concert complete with lights, projector screens, a full band, and incredible vocals. I felt chills in my body as the powerful tunes accelerated my heartbeat and my foot tapped to the beat. In Lyon, France I watched people praying in a church go to different altars in small niches, just as people did in Hindu temples as they prayed to multiple gods.

I was wandering and wondering inside St. Peters basilica in Vatican City how each religion offers the same message. I talked with people from every faith, and the message is consistently pure. When each message is pure, how can I choose? People do pick, clearly, whether they believe largely in the oldest of messages in the Torah, Jesus as the savior in the Bible, Mohammad as the final messenger in the Qur'an, or others. The wife of the English couple I waited in line with to enter the basilica asked me if I was religious. I began to explain my understanding that to me the message of each faith is the same.

A guard within the basilica leaned over and said, "They're not all the same message."

Each person picks a team of choice, but we are all playing in the same league. Getting along with people of other faiths is simple. It is like getting along with coworkers. Employees work together to accomplish their individual responsibilities just as people live together on the planet to make the best of their lives.

A description of how different religions interact today is not complete until we understand how each religion is a group on its own. Inter-group conflict is most commonly seen, because of the easiness to blame the other group for causing a conflict. After talking to both Israelis and Arabs independently about Palestine, I understand why each side sees the other as the problem and themselves as the innocent bystander acting in self-defense. Intra-group issues are harder to identify, not because they are fewer in number but that admitting one's own group is wrong in some way is humiliating and humbling, two qualities that a group does not want to associate itself with when maintaining a powerful image.

I digress now to another Easter sermon I attended in North Carolina. I listened attentively to the pastor speak on the topic of accepting God into one's life and took careful note of the language he used. He questioned the congregation if we were afraid to accept God into our lives, asking what fears did we have that stopped us from doing so? I felt like Marty McFly in *Back to the Future* getting called "chicken" by Biff just to elicit a reaction.

The pastor continued, "We are saved because of God's sacrifice for us," making me feel indebted to Him.

The pastor attempted to explain how to react to enemies and repeatedly used the word "terrorism," legitimately inducing fear in me by making me perceive a great threat nearby. By accepting God into my life, I would have undergone a powerful journey for myself and joined a prestigious group of those who are saved. I found my emotions were turning while listening to the pastor's convincing message.

College fraternities are groups that frequently include hazing into their group's initiation so it is as unpleasant as possible. After completion, fraternity brothers feel incredibly close and bonded for having undergone the journey together. Military boot camp is highly intense and difficult, and recruits understand unity, teamwork, and discipline at the end. New soldiers and new fraternity brothers feel unique and prestigious for sharing in something nobody else did. I admire and respect joining a group preaching tolerance of other groups, but one must continually verify that their group does not teach individual growth at the expense of others' growth.

Interpreting the Bible to have a disgust of Gays has been a religious principle taught in the Church until the current Pope spoke of unity and love instead of hate. It is easy to target individuals as sinners or evil, but the issue arises with how the Church defines these things. We can argue with individuals over their most internal, religious beliefs that they've been taught since they were children, but a true discussion attacks the root of the problem to increase understanding. The Pope did not address individual cases of which Gays and Straights are good and bad people, but rather he condemned the fundamental belief that the Bible condones hatred.

A belief's support base must change for the mentality to change. We target racism by targeting the whole mentality instead of debating individual cases of good and bad people and which race they belong to. This is because there are good and rotten apples on both sides of the debate. Tolerance starts with seeing people in another group reflected to us as people like ourselves. Talking to them increases the dimensions of understanding about them and with understanding comes tolerance. A discussion with believers, non-believers, and enemies opens the door for tolerating other groups and seeing that certain language, like "enemy," is reflective not of the other group but of our own.

War

I had dinner with an American bunk mate in Vienna. He trades gold and silver and travels the world while he trades online. He had some interesting points of view on the market of gold and silver that I had not heard before. He mentioned how the U.S. changed gold prices to benefit itself, how China is stockpiling gold, how countries pay themselves back and forth with either paper currency or gold, how France asked the U.S. to pay their debts in gold back in the 1970s, how the U.S. gave counterfeit blocks of gold as payment to some countries, and how China has stockpiled enormous amounts of cash from U.S. trade that it now is spending around the world by buying land in Australia, mines in Africa, and ports in Greece. Then he continued how the U.S. has its hand in everything and plays both sides of the game. His ideas tip-toed around conspiracy theory. He went on to say how the U.S. and Israel fund ISIS to divide and conquer the Arab world by noting ISIS hasn't attacked Israel. According to him, Italy was going to publicly elect a communist government in the 1960s. The U.S. and NATO came in and said they'd change the people's minds as they did not want a communist government so close to them. Terrorist bombings then began and newspapers stated it was the work of communists, thus shifting public opinion away from communism. The basic idea is rule through fear. To keep power, one must ensure fear exists. Things became interesting when he claimed the Colorado movie theater shooting was the result of mind-control by the CIA. It stemmed from MK Ultra which is a follow up to Operation Paperclip, the giving of U.S. citizenship and CIA jobs to Nazi scientists who experimented on people during the War. He also stated the conspiracy theory that the Boston marathon bombings were staged as the victims were actors. Of course, 9/11 was a set up. And the wildest claim was that the Sandy Hook shooting was a hoax as there were no bodies seen, although I think it was more out of respect for the victims. I gave him the benefit of the doubt for some ideas and looked them up; all the websites describing the claims were conspiracy sites. So, truth or conspiracy? Individuals make up their own minds.

The gold and silver trader also mentioned England as the fairest country as it has given back to the countries it colonized, such as returning to India after its independence to ease the transition of infrastructure and maintenance to Indians. Nonetheless, he compared England to the U.S. as a country that leaves turmoil and chaos in its wake despite claims of spreading democracy.

War is a tool for the interests of big groups. Few would deny this "us vs them" mentality that exists between different groups. The largest conflicts in the world are between the West vs the Middle East and the West vs Russia and/or China. Just as people can be mean as a result of bullying, so can countries be enthused by reciprocating aggression towards one another. The problem with fighting back and forth is that it cannot end. It is like, forgive my French, a pissing contest. Two men standing in the middle of a room see who can urinate the farthest. The first man begins by reaching the base of the wall. The second man outdoes the first by urinating up the wall and leaves behind a yellow trail against the white paint. The first cannot let himself be beaten, so he reaches the top of the wall and begins leaving a dripping trail along the ceiling towards himself. The second man sees his success challenged and races his opponent along the ceiling until both men are trying to urinate vertically. What do we see in the aftermath? Two men urinating on themselves, because neither could stand down.

The Cold War between the Soviet Union and the United States was the most obvious pissing contest of the 20th century. Just as World War II arose from the aftermath of World War I, we saw behaviors repeating themselves under Cold War-like hysteria.

In *American Prometheus*[1], the author quotes American writer Archibald Macleish's 1949 essay that, "although America was the most powerful nation on the globe, the American people seemed seized by a mad compulsion to define themselves by the Soviet threat... [and] in this sense...America had been 'conquered' by the Soviets, who were now dictating American behavior... 'Whatever the Russians did, we did in reverse'." Macleish continues, "He harshly criticized Soviet tyranny, but lamented the fact that so many Americans were willing to sacrifice their civil liberties in the name of anticommunism." These events are repeating themselves seventy years later, not because people haven't seen humanity grow immensely since World War II, but because a constant state of fear against "them" for the safety of "us" pushes people to ignore their better judgement and be more exclusive of diversity than inclusive.

I found that Germans are the most understanding and cautious of blindly hating and killing due to stringent education and awareness of the actions that stemmed from such beliefs during World War II. Unfortunately, the German people are unique in this regard. Their personal experience in the matter was their strongest lesson. People from other countries that were not directly in touch or held responsible for the war are far more eager to kill a group different than their own. Personal experience helps people understand and learn from their lessons. The opposite is also true. A lack of personal experience hinders people from learning lessons they never had. Therefore, the more I experienced with people, the more dimensions I could see and the larger my perspective became. It became critical for me to not repeat the same mistakes I knew I'd made in the past or the mistakes of others I'd seen applied before.

I returned to California after my voyage and met with two of the brightest men I knew who worked in scientific research. The wealth of knowledge they have in their fields is astounding, and they have my utmost respect. They asked about my trip, and I briefly discussed how surprised I was to discover among all the groups I met that Germans were the most keenly aware when it came to killing people as a solution to a problem. My words were met with dry agreement with a tone of stating the obvious. I felt that they thought the German awareness I'd observed was too simplistic. These minds were brilliant in their specialized fields after years of study and dedication, but in other dimensions of life, I realized they were trying to piece together a rational explanation of people just as I was. It may be simple, but it is important to add that German culture today now teaches a healthy, extreme caution about killing people, a hesitance American culture does not reflect.

Oppenheimer oversaw the design and construction of the atomic bomb using U.S. military resources. As a young man searching for answers to the labor problems in 1930 America, he found his answers were in association with some communist ideas. His strict national loyalty and behavior in the early 1940's was clear to his military commander, General Groves, who approved his security clearance in 1943, and the Atomic Energy Commission, a nuclear arms regulatory committee formed after achieving control of the atom, which renewed it in 1947. Things changed in the early 1950s with the House Un-American Activities Committee, HUAC, which hunted and hung purported and often wrongfully accused Communist sympathizers out to dry. Oppenheimer's name came up with HUAC due to incidents previously known and accepted by General Groves. Also, Oppenheimer's view, largely echoed by the elite, scientific community, was for the U.S. government to form joint, international control of atomic weapons with Russia. The scientist and humanist Oppenheimer felt it would be a sign of good faith to prevent a predicted arms race and possible nuclear annihilation if both sides decided to use the new weapons against the other. The biography explains the people "of Oppenheimer's opposition...reflected the depth of McCarthyite hysteria that had enveloped Washington. Equating dissent with disloyalty, it redefined the role of government advisors and the very purpose of advice." Indeed, scientific advice had been legally bound to political loyalty which created a newfound lens for people to measure science in terms of personal, subjective policies instead of fulfilling the potential of an objective science.

I visited my ninety-one-year-old grandmother in southwest France. She was reading a book describing events of World War II that occurred in her area. She said she knew the names of the people she was reading about. She knew how they died. In addition, she told me how the French snitched on each other to the Germans for money. Some denounced their neighbors out of nothing more than jealously. Denounced neighbors during the French Revolution in 1789 met the guillotine, and denounced neighbors in 1950 America met HUAC. She continued to describe how Jews had to wear stars on their arms. One Jewish boy in the neighborhood walked around a lot, and everybody came to know him. One day, nobody saw him walking on the streets anymore. Afterwards, my grandmother told me about when my own mother stayed with a German family 30 years after the war. Her host mother brought my mother to the cemetery where young people were buried and spoke of how young German soldiers considered it an honor to die for the Fuhrer. Did they really know what it meant? It was not the first time I had heard of the honor in dying for one's country. I still see and hear it every time American war movies pride themselves in the honor in which their troops now rest in peace. It is the same rhetoric used by any military to motivate people to give their greatest sacrifice for their group.

Conflicts have always been wars of ideas between people, but warfare has changed. Historically, enemies wore recognizable uniforms and met on a battlefield. Today, wars are battles of radicals and extremists hidden among civilian populations, begging the question of how to eliminate terrorist threats without demeaning ourselves. As the opinion piece I read while in Montreal suggested, radicalization is not organically grown. It is created. Many communities around the world lift themselves from poverty and insecurity with education and training necessary for better jobs, because a balanced education produces enhanced awareness for jobs that stimulate the economy rather than stimulate war. Balanced is the key word, because an imbalance weakens the fight against radicalization by empowering radical ideas. Traditional warfare between armies in uniform is now ineffective; wars of ideas between people must now be strategically fought by better addressing how radical ideas originated in the first place. Providing balanced education gives people ideas which lead to choices away from radicalization. An imbalanced education gives people different ideas that can lead to choices towards radicalization. For example, assaulting the identity of a group of people drives each one in the group to evaluate how best to respond, and as much as I hope each one takes the high road, I know every group has a few people more inclined to violence given the right reason.

Wars are always fought to make a safer and better home for the future of our children. Just as my Caucasian peers felt uneasy learning how their unlimited possibilities in society were built upon centuries of discrimination of minority groups, I am uneasy learning that the safer and better world we are creating in the 21st century is built from the blood of innocent men, women, and children that are slaughtered by bombing cities to oust a handful of terrorists. It can no longer be called a war when 4,000 soldiers die next to over 100,000 civilians in Iraq. Consequently, the large imbalance in numbers of experienced loss by wartime survivors creates more anger than gratitude, an anger that will likely lead to future conflicts.

Terror and Fear

Every time I pass through U.S. airline security and customs to return from abroad, I can't stop smiling.

1. Non-priority passengers check in with a machine. Priority passengers check in with a human being which make it seem like a special courtesy to speak to a human. Every other airline in the world has human contact as the norm. It might sound extreme, but keep reading. I check in at the machine. It asks me if I would like to change seats, check in baggage, etc. Then it asks me if I would like to give an emergency contact. This only makes me think that they need to contact family in the event of my death or disappearance, something I wasn't considering until now. Geez, maybe I will die on my flight now or an emergency will happen. I wasn't thinking of that before you asked me about my emergency contact. This is the first time I've ever been asked that after a dozen different airlines around the world. It's a little disturbing to read before departure.

2. I continue through the check-in process, and it prints out my tag for my luggage. Thankfully, an airline assistant was there to assist me in putting it on. Do I want to fumble around figuring out how to peel this long piece of tape and not mess it up or tear it at 9:00am? Not really. Then I carry my bag over to the desk where they hand me my customs form and check my boarding pass.

3. Then I carry my check-in bag over to the security machine where it swallows it away after another assistant double-checks and

scans my boarding pass. I stop and fill out my declarations form. It asks for the countries I visited before returning to the United States to be written on two small lines. I giggled inside and wrote the last few European countries I visited. I realized afterwards it might cause problems if they open my passport later to find visas to Russia, India, Nepal, and Vietnam and stamps from all over.

4. On the way to security, another assistant checks my boarding pass for my destination to direct me to the correct security aisle. Then I go through security where I undress partially. Another security guard scans my boarding pass again and passport. Then I go through the metal detector. Another security guard wipes my hand and belt region to check for any explosive residues. He did this to the man in front of me, so I assume it is standard procedure. I would only receive such luxurious attention when I would opt out of full body scans which are only legal in the U.S. to receive my full body pat down and explosive residue check. And I mean full body.

5. I grab my belongings and head to customs. I check into customs with another machine. It asks me again via touch screen the same questions I filled out on the customs declaration form. Then it asks for me to pose for the photo. I have to stand within the slightly silhouetted region for it to take my photo. I'm too tall, so I take a step back to fit. I'm still too tall for the photo, so I squat a little to bring my head into frame. Then I wait a second to hear a click or something. Nothing. I see a button on screen I need to press in order to take the photo. So, squatting with jackets in my arms awkwardly, I reach out and turn my body sideways to reach the screen. This all seemed like an awkward series of events to me, so I was caught grinning in the photo. It prints a receipt which allows me to pass another security guard so I may finally meet the customs guard. He rescans my boarding pass, holds up my passport photo to my face, and asks me the standard questions which I pass.

I made it to the gate! I met an American before who told me he feels safer when he sees guards with automatic weapons in public spaces. I also met a non-American that on a separate occasion told me seeing automatic weapons makes him nervous, because he feels a proximal threat he did not sense before.

I have traveled through many countries and been in a variety of environments, and I can honestly say I have never once feared for my security or safety until now even though I had been flying a lot around the times of airplanes crashing, disappearing, or being shot down. My view is that of a Germanwings pilot who spoke with his passengers following the suicide crash by another Germanwings pilot. I paraphrase his speech to what I found memorable. He said he and his crew members have families, and they have every intention of seeing them that evening. Fear is something to be controlled. I controlled my irrational fear of any statistically improbable flight issues and flew alongside the tens of thousands of other voyagers every day that make the same trips in the air. Fear is something that can also control us. Either way, I felt more fear after experiencing the heightened security here. It wasn't in my mind before the process, but it sure was there afterwards. Hence, I have to smile in awe at the whole affair.

I did not sense general feelings of terror and fear until I returned to Europe where looming terrorist threats were on everybody's mind. It was such a shock to enter the developed world after five months in the developing world. I was expecting to leave a world of poverty and unpaved roads and enter a world full of comfort and convenience, but a growing ISIS threat in the Middle East petrified everybody. The attacks on cartoonists at Charlie Hebdo had just occurred, and everybody was talking about that. Nobody talked about threats of terrorists in Southeast Asia, so I did not feel the intense fear I found upon entering Europe. Indeed, I was borderline ashamed to find the developed world amid its wealth and power buckling completely under fear of terror. How could I explain to my adopted Nepali family that I had returned to the West to find everybody living in fear?

Fear is fear no matter what form it takes. It is the sense of being highly uncomfortable in any given place or situation, often so much so that one loses one's sense of confidence and control. Statistics say what we want them to say. We fear not knowing whether our community is safe for our children, family, and friends. Nothing is a greater motivator than instigating fear within a community. The greatest challenge comes from identifying the problem causing fear, and then proposing an easy solution. Albeit all too often, the solution is to point to a different group causing our fear and instability.

The greatest freedom, I found, is the release of said fear. The rights of privacy and free speech come after we no longer fear being imprisoned or executed for owning a particular book or criticizing a particular person. Only by understanding the environments surrounding us can we shed fear of the unknown. Everybody can make up a reason for doing something or nothing. Only after understanding said reasons is it possible to address the issue at hand. ISIS beheaded certain journalists after the journalist's respective country declared war on ISIS. Israel attacks Palestine repeatedly for reasons that go back to the peace agreements after WWII. Even the crazed Batman shooter in Colorado had reasons for doing a supposedly unexplainable act. It captivated society, because we could not figure out why it was done. It is easier to fear your neighbor than love your neighbor. It is easier to lock a door than open it to a stranger. It feels safer, but it is based on the internal assumption the neighbor is dangerous. Short term, fear works for survival, but long-term, it slowly wears away a society. The saying about "Faith in humanity" receives enormous praise as it is proof most people prefer safe, co-existing living beyond fear and judgment.

Many Europeans following the attacks on Charlie Hebdo expressed anger, confusion, and desires for revenge at those responsible. The intense level of emotion reminded me of those that arose following September 11, 2001, in the United States when killing and death became highly tangible for everyone. These were not images of bombings on a television happening around the world. It was in frontal view for every American that, prior to that moment, felt safer walking in America than they ever would again. The attacks on January 7, 2015, brought the same terror right to the doorstep of every European.

I then wondered how do human beings respond to violence? We defend ourselves, surely. It is instinct to stop a punch. It is also survival instinct to ensure the attacker cannot punch again, so eliminating the attacker is critical. The animal kingdom shows us that elimination is the physical attack on an attacker. A buffalo will kick back at a hunting lion. A hyena will bite a crawling snake. We as human beings are not often categorized with other animals, because of our ability to think, speak, and create. Still, history shows clans and tribes killing entire rival groups. Dynasties and empires ruled through killing their opponents so that people inside their borders were safe to trade and flourish. Indeed, this was the way life survived. The "Kill them to protect us" survival instinct has not gone away in this modern day. "You are either with us or against us." "The enemy of my enemy is my friend." We still pick sides and group together to fight common enemies.

A consequence of global migration and mixing of people from different groups is that groups overlap. For example, the United States is often referred to as a melting pot. When it began, most settlers were European and Caucasian, so it was easy to identify and eliminate Native Americans because of different appearance and language. After September 11, 2001, people were angry at anyone of Middle Eastern descent and held them responsible for the act of terrorism and thus targeted them for revenge. Under intense emotions of fear and hatred, people revert to survival instinct and group terrorists as anyone who appears similar in appearance, language, and culture. It was widespread and overarching as Indian Sikhs wearing turbans and many Arab-Americans from unrelated countries were threatened. After the Boston marathon bombings in April 2013, the bombers were identified as having roots in Chechnya. People began to hate Czechs so much that the Czech Prime Minister had to correct the target of the immediate hatred that Czech Republic is a different country than Chechnya. Again, intense emotions of fear and hatred stemming from survival instinct were misguided.

Prior to globalization, enemies were often lumped into easily identifiable ethnic and national groups. Post globalization, enemy terrorist groups consist of unknown individuals hidden among a larger civilian population on friendly soil. Old tactics of trying to wipe out a group defined by ethnicity, nationality, or geographical location are no longer sufficient in a world connected by internet and international opinion. During World War II, the United States placed the ethnic group of Japanese-Americans on the West coast in camps to quell fears of espionage. After September 11, 2001, it did not do the same for all Arab-Americans, because the country knew it was inefficient, heavily inaccurate, and would seriously undermine the civil rights the country upholds for its citizens. The Israeli-Palestinian conflict has been a mess since 1947. Israel tries to eliminate a handful of individuals hiding in a civilian population by bombing buildings that house both real threats and innocent civilians. It has received negative, international press because of the number of innocent killings. The United States was also heavily criticized for the Iraq War and the loss of innocent lives there as cities were bombed with little regard as to who was being bombed. The Vietnamese museum about American involvement in the Vietnam War showed American soldiers smiling and posing beside decapitated Vietnamese. The enemy was perceived as all Vietnamese regardless of guerilla involvement, and there were many calls from Europe and American people at the time to prosecute U.S. war crimes for the innocent killings of civilians.

Things have changed. Enemies are no longer groups defined by race or nationality. A civil movement in the United States targets prejudiced police action towards African Americans to show some law enforcement practices are highly inaccurate and unjust. African Americans in the U.S. are not all enemies just as the group of Arab-Americans or Japanese-Americans are not all enemies because another group is terrified that they are.

If a tree falls in the forest and no one hears it, does it still make a sound? If a prejudiced killing occurs in a black neighborhood and the media decides it's not news worthy enough to share, did it happen? Laws are written to penalize people for littering, but there are no laws to monitor how we litter fear onto our society.

Despite laws about underage drinking, when the number of intoxicated youths at an event far outnumber law enforcement personnel, police officers become more concerned with safety than prosecuting drug and alcohol crimes and will only pursue whoever is being unsafe while intoxicated. Opinions about situations can vary depending on what the interests are and what the intended goal is.

Killing enemies is a temporary band aid that will reduce the symptom but not cure the disease. It is critical to address why someone is attacking another. The previous statement exists under the idea, based on personal experience and global history, that a long-term, socially acceptable agreement is the goal for diverse societies. It is possible to resolve issues by eradicating the other entirely, but that is internationally frowned upon today. Geopolitical reasons are used to justify acts of war to ensure the survival of the nation, but never is senseless killing or massacres of innocents a necessary act for success. Most violent acts around the world, both purposeful and senseless, all point towards a single solution. Fix the environment in which violence develops to kill the violence instead of the people. Computer programs won't work if there are too many bugs in the code. Fruit won't become ripe if the soil is nutrient-depleted. Effective leaders are unsuccessful without necessary skills and charisma. A car won't run if time was not spent filling the gas tank. An unloved child turned bully, a scared puppy in the street, or an opportunistic drug user each have a reason for being an abuser, feeling scared, and finding solace under the influence of drugs or alcohol. Often, a lack of time to prepare or understand a situation for an adequate response is also used to excuse violence. The same solution applies to most rapists. Anti-rape culture has grown in recent years and has proven rape is largely an individual choice that stems from violent cultural attitudes with power-seeking behavior that can mostly be altered through education and awareness. Some rapists are naturally prone to urges without external influences meaning those individuals need the most attention to control them. Crime will always exist among a small portion of society's members due to simple variability of human nature, but motivated people together can reduce its effect on daily lives to a minimum.

I return now to the original question of how do we respond to violence today? The way we have done so in the past is quickly becoming stigmatized and outdated for being inefficient and murderous. Time and time again, I hear of stories in which increased access to education led to healthier communities as demonstrations of the upcoming and effective way to fight the new type of enemies which societies face today. By building schools and offering a balanced education to children, the children are given a lifetime of opportunities as a skilled workforce. The mentality available to them changes. Children, then families, and then communities begin to understand how education could remove desperation and poverty and offer them a better life. There would be no void to fill with radical, hateful ideas, and there would even be resistance to institutionalized hatred as people would prefer the positive consequences from an education rather than a mentality of terror, fear, and hatred.

If fear can be both a survival instinct and a weapon to control people, how does one control fear rather than the other way around? It is the basis of any rehabilitation to stop consuming the poison that consumes one's mind. In other words, we as a society can choose to stop letting fear control us by increasing self-awareness and self-analysis. While these tools stop giving those we fear power over ourselves, they also give us more room for the freedoms we wish to embody and hold for ourselves in the long-term. It is a difficult, powerful, and strong mental shift necessary for fulfilling a nation's strongest potential. It is easy to overemphasize fear by playing on one's instinct for survival with repetitive news about potential attacks. Fear needs an enemy, and there is no greater example in recent history than giving the name of terrorist to several small extremist organizations and then extrapolating to the entire Muslim world.

Growing up from adolescence to adulthood requires change and mental development. Winning a war of ideas as adults requires mental development. To acquire a professional job, it is imperative to be well-balanced in skills and personality. If society is a spectrum from poor to rich, most criminals historically come from those that live on the extremes of society with corruption and desperation when the majority as a group decides to live somewhere in the middle. If multiple linear spectrums, or dimensions, of values and cultural awareness all intersect at one point, that point is a multidimensional human being. It is easy and instinctual to identify someone based on one dimension, but there is always a story the observer does not see. We fear bombings more than the frequent automobile accidents seen daily, because it is easy to let fears become irrational from monsters under the bed to a terrorist around the corner. If fears were true, many more children would be eaten by imaginary creatures and bombings would be happening every day in every city. Clearly, neither occurs. Today, threats are changing from the extremes of society to average people who find themselves at a low point in their lives and resolve it by easily resorting to violence.

An analogy is that of children who want more milk or juice. They do not yet know the words to communicate effectively, so they bang on the table, scream, and point at the bottle. The world begins to see this type of immature behavior grow as radical acts are perpetrated by people who are mentally unstable often despite appearing stable previously. People almost universally try to solve this rash of violence by calling for more preventative measures such as more thorough mental health check-ups. Society feels this will ensure the average college student does not go on a vindictive shooting rampage or a pilot doesn't intentionally crash a passenger plane. Realistically, there is no way to identify who needs acute mental health care until it is too late. It would be more effective if we chose it for ourselves. We do need to assess the mental health of the people of our nation and culture to ensure our environment is cultivating the mentality and values we desire for our children. I noticed that simply reaching out to friends who offered valuable and helpful advice in my times of need was my primary way of caring for my own mental health.

Even perceived threat is stressful. I used to think I could not imagine being a minority in society before traveling around the world where I was constantly reminded I did not fit in. I am also told my life is valuable by anti-suicide campaigns, family, and friends, but the constant stress of never fitting in wears away on one's bodily and mental health. There may be no words or overt acts of injustice done, but the environment alone can be stressful. I was perplexed by how to resolve the notion of fear both personally and nationally as locals informed me Switzerland is small and continually fearful of external attack just as Singapore is afraid of Malaysia or South Korea of North Korea. The term "false flags" describes the act of some people deceiving a group by falsely presenting evidence to shift public opinion. Some historical false flags have been identified while others remain conspiracy theories. Public opinion about U.S foreign policy on terrorism has shifted since the beginning of the Iraq War as well as the lack of concrete results since it ended and 9/11 itself. Opinions turned in the direction that the war was unjustified, illegal, and geopolitical for the United States. American intelligence officers suggest wealthy perpetrators, different from those previously identified, as having planned and perpetrated the terrible act by funding 9/11.

Other countries call for political leaders who had managed the Iraq war to be tried for war crimes now that its basis seems less rooted in fact. In early 2015, an American patriot in the state of Georgia left a pipe bomb in a public park and confessed to trying to spur fear of terrorists. News channels never once identified the man as a terrorist, referring to him only as a "so-called patriot." Statistically, it is more likely that a person will die of a heart attack than from a terrorist bombing, but the less likely option receives much more attention than the other. People are emotional beings, and we greatly fear terrorists and sharks more due to popular media and movies.

On my last flight home to San Jose, CA, I sat next to a middle-aged lady who was visiting her son and granddaughter. She mentioned their upcoming vacation to Hawaii. Having recently been to Thailand, I mentioned how safe, beautiful, and economically practical it was to visit the Asian country. She replied her disinterest due to the frequent tsunamis that happen there. I did not feel tsunamis are a daily risk, no more than hurricanes are in the United States. I teased that she should be wary about going to Hawaii as another Pearl Harbor is likely to happen. Her eyes widened and she asked me about it seriously unquestioning of the statement's validity. I smiled and denied the claim, stating an attack on Hawaii was just as likely as a tsunami in Thailand, but I was surprised at how quickly she believed me. The small interaction alerted me to how easily fear can change behaviors as I'm sure she would have had second thoughts about traveling to Hawaii had I been more adamant. A shadow from something we cannot see can scare us. We can fight a dark shadow, but the real fear is from a human being with complex emotions, feelings, and experiences. I also described some of my travel experiences to her, and I brought up the book I was reading about empowering rural populations through education instead of fear and hatred. I mentioned how Iraqi civilians were killed in numbers exponential to American soldiers killed and how it was nearly impossible to bomb a city harboring terrorists without killing innocent bystanders. She did not believe Iraqi civilians were killed at all. She's not the first one I've encountered either. I've learned many Americans do not know of the Iraqi civilians killed during the Iraq War as many German soldiers and civilians during the early 1940s did not know of the

Holocaust. To further illustrate why many people in the Middle East are angry at the United States, I asked her to imagine her children on their way home from school one day and discover they had been bombed and killed. Or if her parents had been killed taking a walk in the park? How would she feel towards the bombers? She naturally said she would be angry and want revenge on the killers. I turned the table once again to point out that many neighborhoods of non-militant, peaceful people were bombed and children were killed which enraged them against the American bombers. She was incredulous to say the least.

Rhetoric and phrases about new, harmful things being discovered from bad foods, bad diets, bad people, and bad habits attempt to guide our behavior to often irrational limits. I returned to California and spoke with someone who had heard about the people of Dubai being snobby to foreigners. I never saw such a thing, but I imagine had I been unrulier and given reason to attract negative attention to myself, I would have been met with equally unfriendly behavior. I never heard of or experienced attacks on tourists in Thailand while I was traveling, because I remained vigilant and followed one universal rule: Do not be drunk late at night in a dark alley.

As I said previously, while checking into my flight to the U.S., I was asked for an emergency contact. It was the first time I was ever asked for such a thing, and I began considering the possibility of a hijacking. I legitimately felt fear in response to being asked the question. Perceived fear versus actual fear is an important distinction. I've seen how fear in WWII made people do evil things. Fear of neighbors can lead to disastrous consequences. I read about providing names under McCarthyism in the U.S., learned about Hungarian Nazis outing Jews in Hungary, and my grandmother told me how some of the French outed Jews to German Nazis during the German occupation. Citizens turn against fellow citizens. Fear of Russia led to a Cold War spanning generations. Fear after 9/11 fueled a religious and regional war. I have seen how those in control of U.S. policies led the country and exacerbated the fear instilled into the American public after 9/11. This caused them to support foreign policies which continued to support our fears rather than disparage them. Fear of ISIS leads to more extremism in retaliation against ter-rorism causing both sides to fight harder. Information is also a tool to change understanding and emotions. One article described ISIS proposing a truce, and it was the first and last article to describe ISIS as a self-sustainable state with schools and police forces. It was showing how well developed the terrorist organization could be if it became an independent state. Bringing this information up chosen specifically by the journalist inherently changed reader opinions by humanizing ISIS as a productive society. Such articles can be seen against daily reports of ISIS killings to change reader opinion and to justify more bombings of ISIS.

Many fears are irrational and unfounded, but we live our lives confidently within the boundaries of fear rather than letting fear be our choice instead of our mentality. I could let myself be deathly afraid of toilet snakes, but without seeing a likely prominent threat or regular reoccurrence, I control my fear and let it go. I read an article recently that stated 90% of gun killings in America are from small arguments between friends and family that escalate into a gun-fight, because neither party knows how to back down. While not backing down is an understandable reaction, grabbing a gun to re-solve a debate is not acceptable. American culture incorporates standing up for who we are and never back down. The problem is that we inherently are not right 100% of the time, but humility is not a value we express often. Calling someone "chicken" initiates a strong response. When a bar fight happens in a movie, it is always a 3rd, 4th, or 5th party that intervenes to stop tempers from rising into a complete brawl. Why don't others just let them fight it out? Having guns in public homes is to reduce violent crime or for self-defense. The irony of these situations is what confuses the rest of the world. Criticism has arisen when shooters are not criminals on the extremes of society but merely average people who grab a gun to settle an issue. If we put a hammer in every home, I'm sure people would bang a lot more things around the house. I was taught ideas are tools, and critical thinking is a tool to be used with other tools. If hammers and guns are the tools we hand people, it is no surprise people will choose what is available to resolve problems. Indeed, a man texting in a movie theater was shot, because his phone was blinding the movie-goer behind him. This is an extreme reaction to a common occurrence. We do not keep guns out of people's hands as it is their right to bear arms, but we feel the need to protect babies by removing small pieces of plastic from their environment to prevent them from getting hurt.

Enough on that. Let's just take one step further the mentality of backing down. If we apply it to countries at a national level, we understand why international conflicts arise and predominate more easily instead of negotiations which are more difficult to manage. National pride is larger than individual pride as people may feel more pride and a larger identity within a group than as an individual. How can countries back down without losing their pride? They defend their image by retaliating against any offense no matter how slight assuming it comes from a legitimate threat which it always is. Today, this is the constant back-and-forth between the world and ISIS.

It is not guns that kill people. It is ideas about people that eventually lead to their death or eradication, and one's ideas about other people are only as inclusive as one's awareness. How many dimensions of understanding are there towards a different person or group by the observer? If the source of information is profiting by, either literally or figuratively, continuing the status quo, there arises a conflict of interest. This leads to subjective results that repeat history rather than achieve the desired optimal, objective direction for the nation. By understanding oneself and one's enemy better, the cycle can be broken and mistakes can be prevented. It will also raise the standard of what it means to live rather than survive. America thinks in terms of survival, and will do anything to accomplish that. Europeans think in terms of living well and are more cautious about taking aggressive steps to ensure their growth to survive geopolitically. The mindsets of the West and ISIS are so radically different that it requires an understanding of both of their similarities in order to resolve their differences. Ignorance of ISIS about the West is similar to ignorance of the West towards ISIS. The attackers of 9/11 caught the American public by complete surprise, because the terrorist mindset was operating on a completely different mentality than that of Americans. The U.S. military proved this possibility to itself during the Millennium Challenge of 2002 as described in the book

Blink[2]. During a military simulation between Red team and Blue team, Red team acted outside the prescribed rules of engagement understood by Blue team and effectively crushed them with incredibly high efficacy. Red team was so effective at thinking outside the box that the simulation had to be rebooted, and pre-established rules of war, however unlikely realistically, were followed for the purpose of simulation. We can only prepare for a situation as far as we will expect a situation to grow, and we can prepare better ourselves by fully understanding the "what" or the "who" we are facing.

What is the difference between the Batman killer in the Colorado movie theater and ISIS? Both follow rules different from those the rest of us follow, but society wants to kill one and jail the other. A little bit of something different is tolerable but not too much. If some immigrants are okay, too many of them make locals begin to feel threatened. We have built systems to handle small levels of abuse that invariably exist in a population, but too much will overwhelm the system. So, the Batman killer can be absorbed into the system and processed through years of court trials and law enforcement, but a large group like ISIS is overwhelming for the international, peace-keeping system set in place. Much like how a healthy body can handle a minor illness like the flu, drastic measures are taken to treat an uncontrollable, major illness like cancer. Unfortunately, radical measures like chemotherapy to destroy cancer threaten the body entirely, and it becomes a race to kill the threat before the entire system crashes.

The mentality of a people stems from its culture. The culture, rising out of the values held by people, can be an indicator for what the values are. For example, popular media presents clearly how different people are portrayed and understood. It is also a two-way street as different mentalities can change the culture and later the values held by people. An example of this was the prominence of Gay celebrities in television who promoted the Gay community as prominent individuals in society for over a decade before Gay Marriage and Gay Rights became more widely accepted.

Movies offer the easiest and most direct channel to understand a people's mentality, and no experience taught me more than watching the film *American Sniper* with German friends in a small village.

It was in German with no subtitles, but I didn't need to understand the words to understand the film. To me, it was a typical American film. During a self-proclaimed bathroom break, Felix told me that even in German the film is boring. At the end of the film is the memorial scene with emotionally moving music and streets bordered by Americans waving national flags. Everyone else in the room started laughing at that moment during what was meant to be an emotional scene. I asked them why they were laughing, and their answer blew me away. First off, the idea of military heroes is foreign to their generation. Praising a killer sounds crazy. Second, they couldn't believe such a movie was entertainment for people. If people want to learn about the war, they should watch a documentary about it. Third, they didn't show any bombings of the city killing civilians or any innocent civilians at all. Every Middle-Eastern local was guilty of trying to kill Americans. Even the nice local man who hosted the troops for dinner was found to be harboring weapons. My friend even had trouble seeing the character on screen carry a toy gun into his home with his family. That's when it hit me. The film was not just entertainment. It was propaganda as it showed a completely one-sided view of the war by making everyone from our country a hero and everyone from "their" country an enemy. The Germans watching it with me saw the bias right away and were shocked Americans saw this praise of guns for killing people as entertainment. Of course, Europeans share a different mentality towards carrying arms than Americans, but I was slightly embarrassed they could see straight through an American film, and I couldn't. This isn't to say the film is bad or attacks soldiers for doing their duty, but it is important to understand how our mentality affects our perception of the events around us.

American Sniper was ridiculous to my friends because of too much senseless violence. "You're a hero if you die for your country" is a bogus idea to those that have been taught annually about the horrors of following the Third Reich blindly. My friends hated the violence. My German friends had never noticed someone be unfriendly if they are being friendly to them, so it made sense to try to always be friendly to others which seemed simple enough. Emotional soldiers who feel for killing the enemy also seemed odd for them. Germans are raised to not repeat their past, making their commentary even more appropriate.

Upon my return home, I watched the latest *Transformers* movie. With a greater understanding of how language and images can influence mentalities, I keenly observed many American flags, language of "us versus them," the need to defend American lives against aliens, beliefs that Americans cannot be abused by their own government, illegal operations occurring in the name of national security, and the rhetoric of protecting American lives to justify profitable businesses.

Scripts, like "our world will never be safe until all of them are gone," do not leave much room for interpretation or understanding. Unless someone really believes there is a common enemy just like it is reflected in the film, eliminating "all of them" sounds crazy especially when we know some of the Transformers were good. The American thing to do is to call the government to report something when one observes a danger or threat. A character couldn't believe his rights could be abused because, "I'm American," as if this protects him from being labeled a national security threat. There was also a secret deal behind the President's back to cater to conspiracy theorists. Perhaps the analysis is overdone, but there is a line between my German friend looking away from the screen upon seeing the American soldier pointing a toy gun at his children and repeated images of young American soldiers constantly surrounded by explosions and gunfire. I wonder if American culture contributes to a highly violent and drugged up population? I don't have an answer, but I know the country incarcerates the highest numbers of violent criminals in the world. A favorite film of mine, *The Siege*, shows the extremes to which Americans go to protect themselves from national threats. Denzel Washington's character must fight to limit the military from becoming tyrannical under the title of martial law, stating the values they fight to protect are lost if they stoop down to the level of the terrorists. In conclusion, what seems to viewers as a normal movie script shows that viewers in fact share the same mentality our enemies hold towards us.

The entire notion of fear and terror as a tool to manipulate within the developed world I come from did not seem to be a problem until I left the developed world and became accustomed to living without fear. Upon my return, it struck me as something abnormal, because my sense of what was normal had changed. At the automated check-in of the American airline, the decrease in human services stood out in comparison to other airlines for which human check-in was the norm. If I had not seen other airlines, check-in via computer would be my norm. If I had not flown other airlines where I received complimentary meals and drinks on a short flight, not receiving even peanuts would appear normal. If I had not left the developed world, living in fear would appear normal.

Similar Differences

Humor

I went out with Tikaram and Hindrijit, two Nepali teachers, to a restaurant for some light drinking, story-telling, and joke sharing. Their jokes consisted mostly of everyday scenarios. The punchlines were no more exciting than a slightly clever line of dialogue. I went out again with Tikaram, Jai, and Sabrina another day. Sabrina and I discovered our jokes involved connecting ideas and information and varying word meanings. Nepali humor included one-liners and less of what I would call critical thinking skills. It was extremely disheartening when we told a "black story" to witness the mental paralysis they encountered as they did not understand the jokes. A "black story" offers a scenario, and the audience must ask yes-or-no questions to gather information to fill in the events leading to said scenario. Our teaching friends were incapable of asking any questions, suggesting to me they were not used to this way of thinking, a skill I trained and practiced all through college. In retrospect, I think we just had different senses of humor. Another volunteer in Nepal said he shared "black stories" with children, and they were quick to analyze and decipher preceding events to a given scenario, so I should not be too quick to generalize.

Humor is a magnificent tool to enlighten sad or dull topics. A human smile is universally known no matter what country or village you enter. Happiness is expressed using the same facial muscles that draw the cheeks up and back to form a smile. Humor, often the

309

precursor to smiling, did not seem as universal. The sense of humor in Nepal was vastly different from the sense of humor in the West. That is not to say I did not share in constant laughter with my Nepali family and friends over comedic experiences or conversations. Simply, the memorized jokes the Nepali teachers carried in their back pockets were incredibly different from their counterparts in the rest of the world. I began to look at humor from a cultural perspective, and many examples arose in which humor varied not only between a developing country and developed countries but between different developed countries themselves.

As stated before, movies offer an immediate and easily accessible outlet to glean into a culture. A French film released in 2014 called *Qu'est ce qu'on a fait au Bon Dieu?*, translated to *What have we done to God?*, describes a French family of four daughters that marry a Muslim Arab man, a Jewish man, a Chinese man, and a black man. The pursuing relationships that ensue comically address their differences and as most movies end, everyone becomes family and live happily ever after. The popularity of this film in France demonstrated the blunt humor of the people there who directly address ethnic and religious differences. The film was banned in the United States and United Kingdom for being too politically incorrect and racially offensive.

Conversely the United States released a comedy titled *The Interview* in which two filmmakers are persuaded to attempt an assassination of the leader of North Korea. Following threats from the actual country and a cyber-attack on Sony, the releasing company wanted to cancel the film's release. Pressure to stand up to these threats overturned Sony's decision, and Obama praised the decision, stating to block its release would be a mistake in a country of free expression and artistic speech. Critics of the film cited it for being offensive, but defenders supported it for only being comedy.

Given the two examples above, one can see how humor varies based on subjective values of what is appropriate. Comedy about ethnicity and religion in countries where both topics are touchy is frowned upon, but comedy about killing an unpopular country's leader is appropriate. Some critics denounced the American comedy for its irony since similar language about killing the U.S. President is illegal and prosecutable. Again, it is all just humor and should be seen as such, but the fact they are viewed differently proves that they are not just about humor or that humor is inherently biased and not universal.

One can hardly address humor and sensitivity about humor without talking about the horrific events in January 2015 in Paris. The brutal terrorist attack on the satirical magazine Charlie Hebdo shocked the world for it was a blatant attack on freedom of speech. World leaders immediately took charge and marched for their common values and pride in the following parade through Paris. If this attack were an isolated event that had happened only once, it would not have been addressed that strongly. Unfortunately, such momentous events create a paradigm shift that is too large to fade into the pages of history.

I was in St. Petersburg, Russia, at the time coincidentally with a French man I had just met and who lived 40 km from my family in southwest France. He gave me the opportunity to discuss the events, and his arguments offered me greater insight into the values of the French mentality as did the conversations with a variety of Europeans over the following two months.

Some might consider my words harsh, but I was shocked to return to the developed world and find it at times oddly medieval in thinking compared to the developing world. I had spent almost five months of great joy and happiness in developing countries and had expectations of returning to a world of luxury and comfort which leads to pleasure and happiness. Instead, I discovered one continent defines itself by the quantity of happiness, and the other does by the efforts to eradicate fear. After my conversations with people, I felt the attacks on Charlie Hebdo did to Europe what 9/11 did to the U.S. It attacked personal, core principles of freedom that made people feel the most threatened and consequently live in tremendous fear and hatred of those responsible. This was something I had not witnessed in Southeast Asia. The negative emotions directed at terrorists only heightened with the new and growing ISIS threat in the Middle East.

After the event, I began to have discussions about who can say what and when it is appropriate. One evening in St. Petersburg,

I sat down and discussed the Charlie Hebdo issue with Jean-Philippe. He felt a controversial cover portraying Mohammad critically was justified on the grounds of freedom of speech surrounding comedy. In France, there are laws against hate speech, but generalized humor and satire is permissible. He thought grabbing a gun in response to a comic was absurd. I agreed. Nobody should be shot for expressing themselves no matter how outrageous the statement.

But how does one gauge a reaction? Can I be upset but not outrageously angered? Reactions are personalized reflections based on past experience and present awareness. I know grabbing a gun is never justified, but that's me. Someone who does not know better may disagree and will indeed reach for a lethal weapon in response. Now, should we limit free speech to avoid distressing those who may react poorly?

The march for free speech by world leaders immediately after the shooting shows these leaders representative of their respective people say, "No, we should not limit our free speech."

Often, silence is a weapon against ourselves which is why people have to take an active stand to defend their beliefs and values for freedom of speech. If I go on about how much I hate tables and how useless they are, and a nearby carpenter of tables is offended that I am attacking his livelihood and identity, I can't un-justify his personal reaction. As an individual in a world of different ideas, it is better to be proactive and control oneself and how one reacts to new situations. Otherwise, we would fight everyone we disagree with, spend a lot of personal energy fretting over moot points, and our world would be more chaotic. But perhaps tables are extremely personal to this carpenter and he yells at me. Or he punches me. Or he shoots me. Each is a reaction, and we agree some reactions are more reasonable than others. For people who do not know how to verbally argue or control their emotions and instead resort to violence, it is understandable they are likely to punch someone at a bar if someone slanders their mother.

Around the same time, Fox News in the United States explained the presence of "no-go" zones in Paris and an entire village in England where non-Muslims were not allowed. Their gross inaccuracy was obvious to the people exposed to these areas which led to ridicule on "Le Petit Journal" in France, a comedic talk-show equivalent to satirical news anchors like those on Saturday Night Live in the United States. The public response led to a call for Fox News to admit their mistake and apologize. To the astonishment of many, Fox News quickly retracted their previous statements and admitted they should verify their facts before presenting them. In retaliation, the mayor of Paris wanted to sue Fox News for slandering her city. She was angry, because it felt like a personalized attack on a dimension of her identity. She wanted legal recourse, because she was a public figure. Her tool was the law. It would have been highly unlikely for the mayor of Paris to bring an assault rifle to Fox News headquarters to demand retribution. Others unfortunately may not be as aware of civil recourse or they do not believe the system will defend their group's rights, so they take matters into their own hands. Perhaps the shooters see themselves as vigilantes. They see an issue they deem as unjust and personally seek to correct the matter. Not all vigilantes are like Batman. Some are harshly perceived as thieving bandits and some are graciously perceived as Robin Hood. Some are good, and others are bad for society. It would be easy to dismiss violent individuals as odd coincidences, but repetitive events establish a pattern and the causes for that pattern point to the environment they come from. What kind of internal and external beliefs do individuals have? What kind of beliefs does society have of the individual? What are the values a culture cultivates? How are children, the adults of tomorrow, taught to resolve their issues? How do adults solve their issues? Do we like the solutions? What is the awareness of the mental and systemic tools available for resolution? The shooters' tools were guns. Paris' mayor's legal recourse via lawsuit comes from her education and background. Unaware individuals sometimes know better from personal values of ethical behavior, and sometimes they do not.

Did both the terrorists and the mayor react similarly to what was perceived as a personal attack due to a damaged sense of honor? Yes. Both were angry and wanted retribution. Is one reaction more justified than the other? Yes. Shooting people and suing people show different levels of maturity. Can observers understand why both reacted the way they did? Are the reactions different, and do we know why? Yes. Considering each person's past and current environments, each reaction can be broken down and linked to an experience when the person learned how to react to a situation. We can apply the same logic for what happened at Charlie Hebdo to rape prevention. How do we prevent rape nowadays? Do we teach women to cover themselves up? Do we arm each woman with pepper spray, a knife, or a gun to grip tightly every time she walks at night? Or do we teach men how to respect women? Rape prevention involves more than instructing people to respect each other. It offers the steps to do so. Nobody teleports from mentality A to mentality B. There is a journey of thought called development in which people learn and understand why rape can happen. I would imagine it is possible to use the same methods to reduce the possibility of public shooters or institutionalized criminals attacking innocent people. Somehow, they need to learn how to become better and more constructive citizens. Perhaps it's naive to think there are solutions to problems that seem to persist decade after decade, because there are always extreme people who will do extreme things. I look at the majority of school shooters and terrorists, and I don't see extreme people. I see commonplace people placed in non-commonplace environments where their personal awareness and space for full development was limited which set the foundation for lashing out in the future. Social movements about what rape and consent mean are brought about because the public is confused about what proper, constructive behavior look like in certain situations. Maybe the same group is confused about how to simply fit into society? Which words should we use to describe people: extreme, crazy, confused, or misguided?

By attempting to understand why people react in different ways, humor becomes an example of how people process new information in the form of a joke. Comedians often joke about several taboo issues to avoid anyone taking offense personally on one issue. It remains general and directed at the public. Attacking one idea or one ethnicity would be a targeted rant that is both racist and offensive. That's why laws on speech in France limit personal attacks but allow generalized humor. There are no laws against personal attacks in the United States other than it being socially frowned upon. When I met with my grandmother in southwest France two months after

Charlie Hebdo, she handed me the edition released immediately after the shooting and some other articles she had gathered about the incident. What struck me is that while my French friend in St. Petersburg said the caricatures were protected and justified as purely humor, my grandmother told me she thought the caricatures were "pushing it." The material could offend somebody not because of over-sensitization, but because it is simply offensive material. Coming from the same lady who read World War II history books about people she knew personally getting killed, I trusted her judgement on how people can horrifically treat one another which is why I talk about it now. I wondered that even though caricatures, no matter how offensive, are legally protected as a right, they may be socially justified as either humor or personal targeted attacks. When is it appropriate to be sensitive to material and when is it appropriate to dismiss it as a joke? Racial slurs like the n-word were surely used humorously in addition to derogatorily during the slave-era, but people do not laugh about it today. People may be sued today for offensive verbal harassment during a social encounter. How humor is received is unpredictable. A documentary of Muslim comedians traveling around the United States to dissipate misconceptions about Muslims offers a great example of this. An Iranian, Muslim comedian offended fellow Iranian Muslims so much that they walked out during her set, because they did not find jokes of their own culture and religion funny within an American audience. The comedian was hurt to see people she identified with dislike her material. However, walking out during someone's stand-up is a smaller reaction for a lesser offense than violence in response to aggressive caricatures.

It is much more difficult to receive criticism than to dispense criticism. The sensitivity is also seen towards the film about the four French daughters that marry different races and religions. It should come as no surprise that when sharing a sensitized sense of humor and being prone to violence are mixed, the individual reacts violently with weapons instead of a sign on a stick to express discontent in protest. What is the difference between mocking and satire? One is despised and the other is acceptable? Nobody enjoys being mocked, but satire is often well-received for addressing flaws in common sense.

I shared a joke that combines the darkest times of American history with those of WWII with Americans, Brits, and Germans. I was surprised at the reactions at first, but in retrospect, I understand why each group consistently reacted the way they did. Americans and Brits found the joke hilarious in the category of dark humor. Germans did not find the joke hilarious despite my prefacing it for being in the category of dark humor. Both groups perceived the joke differently as both have a different history and consequently different awareness. Just as any Muslim killer is quickly identified as Muslim in the United States but Christian killers are not readily labeled as such, people naturally pick and choose their reactions. Even humor requires social feedback and education to appreciate it appropriately. Any social movement is a spectrum, and oversensitivity can sometimes prove wrong. Critics of Disney characters state the cartoons are "too Caucasian," but the geographic locations where the fairy tales originate lay mainly in Europe which is characteristically Caucasian. Under-sensitivity also leads to mistakes in which people apologize after the fact for their comments, often seen from public figures as they receive more scrutiny.

After learning about a multitude of other cultures and the mentalities that arise from them, I returned to the United States with a questioning mind about the role of humor in this country. A large portion of the American population learns about current events from late-night comedians who entertain their audience with only a smaller portion of them being self-motivated and eager to seek out action. Having honest conversations is difficult on social media because of endless opportunities to troll conversations. Trolling is the act of provoking people to elicit reactions rather than approaching topics seriously. American culture highly values humor over in-depth understanding, constantly rewarding it with new media and social status among friends and celebrities. Humor is necessary for people to function and be happy with what they do, but too much humor can oversimplify and obstruct understanding if a serious conversation never takes place. I recall seeing a picture on social media of a World War II photo of soldiers just before they were overrun and killed, and the most popular comment was a troll with a comedic movie quote. One would not think of being disrespectful and responding with humor to a veteran showing the photo in person. Unfortunately, an increasingly online generation anonymizes humor and introduces room for personal biases and beliefs to roam freely without social tuning or feedback for what is appropriate.

Culture gives rise to popular humor, and in turn humor can change the culture by giving a voice to speak about taboo topics. More importantly, humor changes with education and awareness. Sexism and racism instantly become less funny when people see the harm the jokes may cause. Racial slurs apparently are common in the South, but not in California where there is a larger voice against racial slurs. A group may become misrepresented by the media or a comedian for comedic purposes. The group is then misunderstood, labeled, ignored, and then taken advantage of until the group's patience and tolerance is beyond limit and aggression arises or the group disappears. Society tries to teach people to observe sensitivity regarding hot topics such as race or religion but not how much. It is the latter that leads to an enormously large gray area about what is appropriate and when. No line is drawn in society, because nobody really knows what is universally appropriate and by whom. College campuses are centers for sensitivity-education to teach students how to be aware and culturally-competent. When I hear of several stand-up comedians who stopped performing at college campuses because of anti-racist and feminist heckling about their jokes, I must think the audience has a different understanding of which social commentary should be considered funny or not. I've seen many stories about party-themes based on ethnic caricatures, hanging nooses, and burning effigies at college campuses that are criticized enough to elicit an apology for causing offense to people. Other caricatures mentioned above were defended in the name of free expression solely because the cartoonists were called comedians. I am left to think it doesn't matter who is called a comedian or not but rather how the audience perceives it. When I was showering at my brother's home in Virginia, I came across a bottle of "Dumb Blonde" shampoo. It triggered me to think what if other blondes are offended? Growing up, I heard blonde jokes widely used by blondes and non-blondes alike, but I've met some blondes that did not like them. Blackface was in our entertainment culture at one time too, but it was later found to be offensive and we stopped that. So then, do we find a compromise and limit only hate speech? Hate speech is also clearly cultural whether it is prosecuted or not. The n-word is acceptable primarily in African American culture. The term likely carries a different meaning in Africa where everyone is black.

Humor must come down to intent which still has some gray areas. I would define intent as whether the comedian defends what the joke is implying or not. How can I determine if the intent is malicious or not regardless of whether the joke is provocative or not? When I know the comedian has an in-depth, multidimensional understanding of the topic to make a joke that is based on playful, mutual fun rather than hurtful ignorance, I find I am less likely to be offended. My friends can make horrible jokes about my identity, but I find them funny, because I know their intent is friendly. The use of the expression "freedom of speech" can cause problems when used to cover up malicious humor which offends people.

Can a joke really go too far? If I tell a joke, I hold myself responsible if people smile or do not smile as a result. If I do not tell a joke, I am not responsible if people smile or do not smile as a result of my silence. In both situations, the other person's smile is as valid as any smile made at any point in time. This thinking goes to every action every person makes. There are reasons people smile even if we do not know why or understand. A person's reaction to a joke may be partially dependent on the joke-teller. Both the comedian and the audience share responsibility in the response to a joke. The comedian first needs to be culturally competent to understand whether the humor is grounded in thought versus blasting ignorant remarks with a hurtful intent, and the audience needs to be insightful of the comedian's approach without any a prior bias. Either party may cross the line. Likewise, people can mock others without a second thought, but most of those same people become highly offended when the tables turn and they are the butt of the joke. There is a degree of practicality that is called for so that humor can remain a two-way street for mutual fun.

Humor is an amazing tool for checking society when things just don't make sense. I find a chicken and the egg dilemma towards ignorance. Is the over-simplification of information to make it easier for the unaware to understand helping or hurting people? I visited dozens of museums during the seven months I traveled, but the captions never seemed simpler than those in the United States. In the Chicago Lincoln Park Zoo, for example, the description of gibbons largely as the "acrobats of the forest" made the animals seem more like fun cartoons for children than wild animals for the public to appreciate. I recall a college conservation course describing that wildlife documentaries often have both a European narration script and an American narration script which is greatly simplified.

Our society rewards some people's foolishness with successful lawsuits for hurting themselves while robbing someone or suing the person who performed CPR for breaking a patient's ribs in the process. Any minor mistake or accident in an overly litigious society suddenly becomes a social liability.

There are many ironies, misconceptions, and irrationalities to be dealt with as we try to live in equality after centuries of different groups picking and choosing what serves them best. This provides an endless supply of comedic material to feed our skepticism and doubt of the entire system rather than encourage understanding and a will to repair the broken system.

In summary, humor is cultural. When I visited a family friend in Belgrade, Serbia, we watched a Bulgarian soap opera. The entire set involved three men talking in one room. My friend was laughing a lot, and I laughed too when he explained the bigger jokes to me, but I was blown away at the difference in humor. I had never seen an office-like soap opera with a cast of only three men in one room episode after episode. French films include much more dialogue and less action than American films, and they still keep my attention. In the U.S., there is sensitivity about race. In France, the sweet spot is religion. We teach tolerance as the solution for living among diversity. Tolerance and understanding will benefit the 98% of us instead of giving the 2% of terrorists, mass shooters, and criminals dictatorship of 100% of our public policy. Teachers ignore classroom rascals to avoid giving them power. We can't ignore terrorist acts because we need to focus on the small things lest they escalate to when we are forced to address them. Should we focus on the few terrorists or the entire population? Or rather should we react with guns and bomb American cities to eliminate a handful of criminals. Sure, criminals shoot first to warrant a lethal reaction, but society's bullets and bombs that go off today do not stop the terrorists of tomorrow. We attack people we don't like, but it gives them power.

Putting ourselves in others' shoes before judging them builds a better society, because it empowers everyone to act in ways that end conflicts without perpetuating them. Making judgments about police officers before understanding the environment they face is naïve. Having straights tell gays how to live is unwelcome and unappreciated. Having men dictate the rules that guide women's behavior is unfair. It is only when we invite input from others outside of our group that we begin to put ourselves in their shoes and realize that perhaps we need to add some chairs to the dinner table of a diverse society. I look at those surrounded by comforts, and I can imagine how one's seat can feel threatened if too many people are invited to the table. Most people are not radical in thinking. The few radicals that exist encourage others to reflect and react to the other extreme. Eventually, it leaves two, opposing sides rather than a spectrum of options. Black or white. With us or against us. Extreme ideas that oversimplify people and disregard the multitude of dimensions that people reflect encourage extremism. Doing so is a disservice to society, for it hinders growth and fulfillment of potential for both individuals and the group. As scientists break down complex ideas for the public to understand, breaking down social matters sets the stage to have a serious discussion and crack the jokes afterwards. To have it the other way around is to invite internal beliefs, grown from caricature humor, to impede any serious discussion or personal and social growth from occurring. In biological systems, the solution is the simplest explanation. In social matters, there are explanations that are often difficult to see.

Peace

After attending a celebration for Prem Rawat, a world speaker for peace, I went to the peace temple in Kathmandu. My Nepali friends listened to a speech in Nepali while I watched two recorded speeches of Mr. Rawat in English given at the European Parliament and in London. These activities took place for his birthday yesterday. I never heard of him before, but his speeches were extremely moving and visionary. He explains how it is a basic human need to have peace, and it only comes from within each person. I remember two main points. First, we learn from our historical tragedies and mistakes and if possible, we should learn how to avoid painful lessons. Einstein said insanity is doing the same thing over and over again and expecting a different result. Countless wars and fights over fabricated reasons are repetitive and lead to nowhere in the long run. Second, our sense of prosperity is internal. The idea of an economist telling when you are prosperous or when the economy is prospering is fabricated. You cannot look at someone and determine if that person is prosperous. It is an internal feeling. It is the same concept with peace. He says world peace will begin to be a reality when it comes from within and only when people feel it rather than talk about it. It doesn't matter if someone is rich or poor as peace and prosperity are internal reflections. My happiest moments do not stem from material goods but human connections. I think most people would agree. In the U.S., it seems like many people are having a personal Cold War with their neighbors as to who can amass the most weapons for self-defense. Speaking of Cold Wars, I met a Singaporean intelligence officer while rafting who said Singapore and Malaysia are in their own Cold War. Singapore has air turrets hidden in the tops of buildings which can open and has underground facilities to house and feed the population in case of an emergency. Malaysia also, according to him, flies a daily unmanned aerial vehicle (UAV) costing in excess of $10,000 over Singapore which the small country shoots down to remind the country of its neighbor. From my experience in Nepal, the people are happier and find life much more fulfilling than many people I know in the U.S. Just food for thought I suppose.

Peace is an internal, basic need of every human being. Only when individuals accept it for themselves rather than seeing it as an absence of war will world peace begin to be a reality. Peace knows no economic boundaries above basic necessities. It is only limited artificially.

These limits are the same limits that justify statements like, "Let's bomb them back to the Stone Age," and "I'm going to punch the bully tomorrow when he tries to take my lunch."

The cause for violence is the need to feel at peace afterwards. Killing people for no reason is called murder or slaughter. People want the group they are a part of to feel safe, protected, and with the fulfilled potential to ensure food is on the table and people are happy.

Peace does not fall from the sky. Martin Luther King did not begin the civil rights movement to eliminate racial discrimination by stating, "Racial discrimination is now over." As people learn today about the steps towards reducing and ideally eliminating the racist and rape cultures, people in the 1960s had to learn to reduce discriminatory behaviors. Laws against such behaviors were enacted, and a woman's right to say "No" entered mainstream culture as a new value. In regard to peace, Prem Rawat held a beautiful vision and understanding towards humanity. Peace is the natural state for human existence. It can only arise when people first know what it feels like to be free from fear and terror.

Despite everything that can be offered to people to ensure harmonious, mutual existence in society, people are people. People are hot-headed, emotional, and always wanting to show their strength. The greatest weapon to every fight is peace, ending once and for all every fight that is happening and will happen. Provoking others is not beneficial in the long run. It can cause a fight quickly, and in turn the fight can end quickly, but grudges are held and the fight will recommence at another date in time. What is the mature, proper behavior to stand up for oneself without escalating issues? Let's take an extreme example: The bully stealing lunches could be shot Friday after school, and the immediate problem of lost lunches would be solved. It is hopefully clear to most that other problems would quickly arise from such a short-term solution. Courts and judicial systems cannot process internationally-sized social structures. They are largely designed to handle the group for which it oversees, namely its citizens. International justice is difficult to guarantee, especially with multiple world powers sharing oversight. Justice in that case is found in bombs, sanctions, and threats that lead to Cold Wars. Negotiations often prove futile, but they show good public relations for the country and its leaders. Indeed, when economic sanctions were taken against Russia in response to Ukraine's invasion, Putin gained popularity because his responsibility over the failing economy shifted and those imposing boycotts could be blamed for the country's problems, thus turning Putin into a heroic defender of his country. Taking the high road always lets the enemy wither and die alone, ignored by those that refuse to offer attention and feed the problem.

"People must pay" is the same thinking that causes every conflict. Personally, I have discovered it is better to find happiness with others than power through solitude. Great friendship is immensely more powerful than living alone. Power through solitude has limited use in this world, for this world is a social one. The best skill I have is to remove myself from an issue to think objectively and then return with a mature, long-term solution so I can put it behind me once and for all. Objectivity is crucial in science, and I believe in social matters too. People are so invested in their affairs that they forget what it is like to see anything else. Awareness shrinks. On one hand, this is not always bad; it benefits the task at hand to be extremely focused. On the other hand, being too focused on one issue can make it difficult to adapt when another issue arises. This is the time when I find it helpful to take a step back and view the two issues side by side through the same lens rather than looking at the "other" issue from "my" stance. To do so requires patience and awareness of how to first take a step back and then the awareness of how to look objectively at both issues equally. Few are innocent in this regard. As a young man living in a time with technology that provides so much information, there are many hypocrisies and contradictions that we believe are beneficial, but they only hold true in the short run.

I met an American who had come from central Africa and had pictures of the local Tuareg people which are a nomadic group known historically for being great fighters. Their lifestyles share commonalities with Indian and Nepali culture. Their happiness also seemed to be the same, stemming from so little but growing immensely from the heart. Just like examples from history show that the West can't fight terrorism with guns, Tuareg people can't fight peace. Peace isn't within the rules of war, and that is precisely why they can't fight it. The more we fight with aggression, the more ammunition we provide the "other side" to fight us. The world today is on a verge not of collapse but of the greatest growth and peaceful life we can imagine if people want to enact it.

The reason this dialogue has never succeeded before is that it is extremely difficult to talk objectively and not appear crazy to the other person. Like the American who showed me how the Tuareg try to live in peace and create a better life in some of the most isolated parts of the world, we can work to create a better life tomorrow by living a better life now. Any person can be an example of a peaceful life for others. He was so focused on the intensity and valuable cultural experience through isolating oneself in a foreign world as I was that it became possible to lose sight of how to nurture the same outlook and enthusiasm within our familiar world.

Time

Albert Einstein is quoted as describing relativity as keeping a hand on a hot stove for a minute which can feel like an hour, whereas sitting with a pretty girl for an hour can pass in what seems like a minute. Time is relative to human beings and relative to culture. It seemed to act like bubble gum. On the Indian subcontinent, time stretches out as if it had been chewed and pulled apart. To a Nepali teacher who invited me for tea, I explained I would just stay for one hour. In reality, one hour became three hours for tea and dinner. I joked with another teacher that when four of us went out for one hour, each of us counted for an hour, so we returned four hours later.

In the West, time is nicely packaged into separate sticks of gum, each aligned between other sticks of gum within an entire packet that we may call an hour, a day, or a year. In the state of North Carolina, things move slowly, and people think and do things slowly. In Chicago, I took a 90-minute metro ride from the airport, and it passed by quickly, because it did not matter to me. Time can be a subjective experience. I could have let myself become angry instead of neutral about spending 90 minutes in a metro. If I had been angry about it, I would likely have told people about my horrible experience and dissuaded them from visiting and having a similar experience taking the metro. In the Silicon Valley of California, people think of fifty things at once, and the pace of life is much faster.

It is not a good or bad thing, but it simply offers another opportunity for people who prefer time packed away nicely.

Understanding, Awareness, and Experience

We can see different environments support specific life-styles. I've heard minorities have their cultures of failure as kids in violent homes are likely to be violent. For example, a culture supporting harsh forms of conflict resolution such as catching the bad guy through violence will beget more violence to resolve even minor conflicts. American culture supports guns, because it is widely believed guns solve problems. We are taught to praise the troops who protect us in our movies and video games. Thus, the environment of American culture appears overtly aggressive and seems to be the basis for how we survive.

Our experiences also develop our perception of our environment. Traveling is a fast way to have entirely new experiences. Childhood is a critical time for a human being to develop often long-lasting impressions and outlooks of one's position and role in this world which is why people care for their children so deeply.

Life hands everyone a laundry list of decisions based on new information to process every day. If someone proved witchcraft and wizardry produced better and more reliable results than the medicine and science I've come to support, my entire livelihood would become threatened. I would be left to either attack magic or adapt to learn from it, and I am sure my choice would depend on how strongly I hold onto my original beliefs in science. To make a rational decision, I would have to be in a mental state objective enough to think clearly about the situation. It is hard to write many different ideas in a journal without breaks. If I take a mental break between sentences, I have no problem letting the ideas flow. Sometimes, all it takes is a step back to become more objective about an issue. A lack of awareness or fear which can be expressed as and mistaken for anger can cloud judgments. A good story about this point is the mother who cuts the ends of the roast and throws them in the trash before cooking. Years later, the son asks his mother why she cut the ends off, and she replies because her own mother always did it. Upon asking the grandmother why, he finds out that she cut off the ends so the roast would fit in the pan. If individuals do not develop an awareness for information and how information is used, that person is left vulnerable to accidental mistakes or purposeful manipulation.

Empowering people enhances the natural process of development and allows their will to actively alter their experiences. When people become empowered to take charge of their own lives, we see a spectrum from some people who become extreme to most using their new responsibility as a positive tool to find a decent balance.

Online, public medical resources can create some overly zealous patients who trust a website and defy their doctors' opinions which are grounded in the personalized case of each patient while many others will use it as a reference. A world filled with more information than a human being can process requires filters to decide what information is worthy of registering and learning from. Because those filters can narrow or expand based on one's understanding, it is crucial to provide appropriate environments in society to ensure those filters guide people to paths that benefit themselves and the social society we all live in.

Life is full of human connections and material things. If we limit our awareness to only one of the two, it becomes difficult to enjoy life comfortably and be happy at the end of the day. The most successful and happy people in society are those that learn how to balance the two.

When I was in St. Petersburg in January walking through the cold, I could see I was away from all the comforts of home, but I was happier than ever. I think the more comfort we surround ourselves with, the more we come to rely and depend on that comfort. It protects us from discomfort, and we in turn protect it. This mutually symbiotic relationship does not exist as strongly in the developing world meaning people are free to live without "First World problems." I discovered that people in all countries deal with the same social issues in their own way. Wealthy countries fear too many immigrants, because they don't know what these strangers bring in terms of culture, ideas, and lifestyles while poorer countries may lack the resources to provide empowering societies for their citizens. The so-called "First World," called as such by ourselves, is rightfully fearful, because we have more to lose. We have become so dependent on comfort and luxury that they actually wall us into greater isolation with fear of losing our things if we share them with unchecked immigrants.

Comfort and luxury are not bad things to have. My host mother in Nepal would have loved to have a washing machine for clothing so she would not spend hours daily pressing soapy clothes against the concrete floor. I did not mind washing my clothes by hand while I was there, but I can vouch that pressing a button and letting a machine do the work is a nice comfort to have. Everyone in the world wants to live with those same comfort and luxury, so it is easy for self-perceived "haves" to be susceptible to the fear of being robbed by the perceived "have-not." Personally, I would say it is only when we see our things as tools that benefit us rather than extensions of our existence that we see the threats of loss dissipate without alienating a part of ourselves or our identity. Nonetheless, it is beside the point. Living entirely in luxury can disconnect or appear to disconnect a person from truly living and from society. That is why Hollywood celebrities make front-page news when they go shopping and use a shopping cart like everyone else. Even more worrisome is a ruler who splurges too much and becomes disconnected from the average citizen. If a ruler only reconnects with his or her constituents on a human level at re-election time or after a tragedy, the ruler's credibility can erode. One example of such a great disconnect between ruler and citizen was during the French revolution. Perhaps equally extreme is the continual manipulation of citizens to vote for a ruler's luxurious lifestyle.

Everybody makes mistakes either in times of desperation or simply poor judgment. While one should hold people responsible for their actions, it becomes difficult to blame people when they were unaware and did not know better. It is a lack of shared experience in a situation that makes personal empathy nearly impossible. After experiencing so many aspects of life around the world, I can now empathize with different mentalities to a larger degree I did not expect. This does not mean I excuse people for wrongful behavior, but I can understand why people make their choices and hopefully explain why so the same mistakes are not repeated.

When ISIS began destroying ancient artifacts, Coraline was so angry she wanted to kill them. My reaction surprised even me as I was matter-of-fact about it. They want a clean slate to write their ideas on like Aristotle believed we had a clean slate at birth. In this way, ISIS could fully construct an ideological kingdom based on hatred of others. Destroying a part of history is despicable. Understanding why they commit such a crime does not seem likely that it would stop them from destroying the artifacts, but it is a lesson for everyone to learn about the environment they come from to either address that environment or ensure it doesn't repeat.

Solving problems is useless without raising awareness for long-term durability. Our limitation for humanity is our understanding. Globalization and technology have set the stage for us to be truly great, but without expanding our understanding, we are destined to repeat our mistakes. We can lead a horse to water, but we can't make him drink unless he wants to. We can also give man a fish once to feed him temporarily, but unless we teach a self-motivated man how to fish on his own, he won't learn anything new that will feed him a greater understanding of life. Knowledge is power, but so is the lack of knowledge in the right people. Even more powerful than that knowledge is convincing people they don't need knowledge or awareness.

Inside a turning plane, I could feel the acceleration, but I couldn't understand what was happening to the entire plane since I could not clearly see a reference to the land below. I can go through life simply being tossed and turned by events beyond my control, but learning about why some of the events occur gives me a potential voice in whether the events happen again or not. True, some sheep want to be passive sheep. Some do not, but without opportunity to grow, society is losing its potential for driving growth. Many immigrants, albeit some illegal, want to live life fully rather than just survive, but they are limited by a lack of political power in a new country and can easily be oppressed instead of participating in the civil resource structure for established citizens. I imagine most people would be surprised how much others can accomplish given a chance, but we blame them for failing miserably when they are never given an equal opportunity to succeed.

Appreciating something is a learned skill that takes time whether it be beer, art, music, or coffee. No one is an expert after a single experience. Appreciation grows with more exposure until one learns to compare different styles. That's why I learned how to experience and appreciate new things. Now, I can appreciate just about any topic or field for its representation of the culture and environment it was created for. To verify I learned something properly, I discuss my understanding or idea with people. If I stray away from a reasonable understanding, they guide me back onto a healthy path. It would be unreasonable for me to allow a misconception of someone or something to cement itself into a firm and immutable belief if I would never challenge its validity.

In Switzerland, I gave the train conductor a folded train pass and expected him to glance over it casually as previous conductors had. He then asked for my passport too which was a first. A French conductor even punched a hole in the train pass when there was no need to. The same act of having a conductor check my train pass elicited several reactions, because we are all humans with a slightly different understanding of how to perform the same act. Despite natural variations of people being different, expanding awareness can only push people towards making wiser decisions that will proactively prevent future problems.

Listening to talks online is valuable. They bring into public view ideas from different groups around the world like a Venn diagram, so all groups may find common ground and benefit from exposure to other viewpoints. Even if one doesn't accept the idea, learning about it teaches one at least what is strong and what is weak. In this way, I can appreciate hearing about the latest technology and the process of its development even if I do not directly work with the technology.

Photos offer a good analogy to understanding awareness of other people's actions. The act of taking a photo is between the photographer and the subject. An observer with an external judgment has no impact on the resulting photo. When we see someone taking a photo of something we wouldn't, we cannot pass judgment. Realistically, we are not in their shoes and do not understand the connection or gratification they must enjoy from taking such a photo. In addition, the way people take photos has been under attack. People have made fun of selfie sticks, because they are radically different from the traditional camera being used to take photos with people saying "Cheese." I noticed I met mostly Asian tourists with selfie sticks and Caucasians with go-pros. It is the same act, but Westerners judge selfie sticks. Asians don't consider it weird, because different cultures employ different aesthetics for public outings. Westerners like to say it is good to stand out but apparently not too much. Most behavior serves a purpose for someone else, a purpose often invisible to an observer. Other times, behavior just doesn't make sense. I chuckled internally when a girl asked me to take her photo at the Grand Colosseum in Rome and then proceeded to show me a photo she had just taken of the Colosseum explaining that she wanted it or something similar in the background. I really had no other option for the background except the massive Colosseum behind her which we were both visiting. Soon thereafter, I chuckled when I saw a girl posing for a friend's photo on an ancient Roman wall directly facing a sign that said no climbing on the walls. My cousin and aunt had vertigo in the dome in Florence. I did not understand it, but I acknowledged it and thought it must be a tangible fear for them. I tried to help them as best I could. Similarly, a large Indian man was scared to step on an escalator in Trivandrum. Instead of patronizing him, I accepted his fear was tangible for him, and I remained patient for a few extra seconds until he mustered the energy to jump on. Awareness is on a spectrum, and regardless of whether someone chooses to stay where they are or expand it, it is beneficial for any observer to know why.

Human beings judge what they don't understand with whatever bias they can relate to the unknown topic. I was surprised to learn at the end of my voyage that there were only so many social interaction scenarios out there, and after experiencing a very high number of them, new experiences began to seem like different copies of the few same originals. This means that I had more confidence and less prejudice about new situations, because I could better understand a new situation by relating it to what I had already experienced. I have a strong impression now of what is good, bad, and just different variations of either. I returned to the United States highly opinionated on all the ideas mentioned in this book to a much greater extent than before I left. I now understand why people fear to travel beyond brief road trips, why I receive meals and tea on a public Indian train but not even peanuts on an American flight, and why the United States is not the only melting pot of ideas and people. People can lose hope in humanity, because they haven't met enough good people in their lives. I can confirm good people certainly exist out there. The media is quicker to portray negative events, because they capture more attention. For evolutionary reasons, we fear things outside our understanding. If awareness is expanded largely enough, everyone would see humanity strives for good constantly. The few manipulators and extremists scare the masses, but we as human beings naturally strive for good.

The events that highlight the extent of our awareness are local shootings of innocent, unarmed teenagers by police for which we find no excuses. We are forced to reevaluate who is good and who is bad and whether the circumstances warranted the act. The media or the police describing the victim as a "bad kid" suggests anyone judged bad deserves bad treatment. This is wrong, because it remains the same tragedy when the teenager characterized as a "good kid" is shot. Without individual reflection, it inevitably happens that someone will decide for us if this person is good or bad and deserves this or that treatment. Criticism is not synonymous with hatred. I find it sad when people are surprised over and over again at every tragedy. There are always reasons why criminals and terrorists act. Once we understand those reasons, we can work to resolve the issue at its core. Just as the world united around Charlie Hebdo, I am sure terrorists unite and strengthen around every attack on them. In an oversimplified version of a combative issue, a bully has his reasons for picking a fight, but do these excuses and reasons justify the behavior? Perhaps in the short run. But long term, every war ends with someone firing the last bullet. Either the battles continue, we win on a moral level or both sides claim victory. We try not to discuss school shooters without acknowledging the victims, because it gives the shooters power and glorifies their actions into our history books. Why can't we do the same with terrorists? People repeatedly point out contradictions and hypocrisies here and there. What if the frustration with these patterns of action could go away? It is possible, but it will not change by itself. To drive change in the world is meaningless if people do not know what direction to change. Expanding our awareness shows us the proper direction.

Art

Looking at art in museums is like watching television. I get to pick my favorite channel and figure out the story myself or enjoy the story behind each painting and sculpture.

As cameras did not exist 500 years ago, paintings had to be realistic and portray their environment as accurately as possible. My cousin informed me that once cameras were created, art did not have to be as literal or record memories. People began to indulge in subtle, abstract suggestions for the viewer to develop a personal story about art rather than telling the story exactly as art did during the Renaissance. Again, art differs according to its environment in time of creation like words and music.

Products

Walking can be perceived as a workout or an act of necessity. Marketing is the process of changing the perception of a product or experience. Something small can be made to look as significant as Mt. Everest if zoomed in on or something large can look as petty as the width of a fingernail when zoomed out.

Anything can be bought and sold. Inside the Taj Mahal were signs for no photos or lights. My guide asked for a light from the security guard to show me how the different marbles glowed under the light and then told me to tip the man for letting us break the rules. Making money is a global necessity, and people learn how to do it very, very well. Soda companies know larger portions make for greater consumption by making the product more accessible to the consumer. Similarly, if I keep a large water bottle nearby, I drink a lot more from it just like walking is easier for many people if incorporated into a commute rather than a chore of exercise.

No matter, it is important to keep one's wits to distinguish between the marketing and the product. Losing my toiletry kit in Nepal required me to buy a local toothbrush, toothpaste, and razor. As far as I could tell for an average guy like myself, a 30-cent razor did the same quality shave as a ten-dollar razor.

Before I began staying with friends and family, I washed my clothes for six months by hand with the same bars of soap I used for my body. I also cleaned my brother's kitchen counter with hand soap. Done properly, I felt I attained the same, hygienic results with much fewer chemicals and many fewer products. I go to the store and see hand soap, dish soap, laundry detergent, fabric softeners, disinfectants, and air fresheners. Just as segmenting the market between blue and pink backpacks increases prices for each specialized product over a generic one, segmenting a cleaning product for each type of use increases the market by producing a need. Some products do work better than others, but that does not explain the immense variety of specialized products when a general one could fulfill many of the general needs of a house. If product specialization lasts long enough, the products become part of our culture as brand names, and the corporate profits are guaranteed.

I was sitting in a shopping center in the West Island of Montreal and was overwhelmed by the scale of consumption. It was in complete opposition to the scale of life I had lived in Nepal. I saw numerous shopping bags and products bought whimsically for pleasure rather than necessity where people have the luxury to afford these comforts. A little girl sat at a neighboring table with her father. Her heavy winter clothes visibly from a large, brand factory name separated her from other children around the world who played in the streets by pulling a battery on a string as I saw in India. Her country of birth, her parents' income, and her welfare would help determine the opportunities available to her in life. She looked just like other children I saw in any other country, and she acted like them. In contrast, she can be spoiled with readily available healthcare, education, and a career that can give her financial independence from her husband. Her culture of comfort is the only difference between her and any other child in the world.

Debate

A lot of the ideas in this book arose from discussions and debate with people from around the world. I traveled across three continents but had the opportunity to meet and learn from people from six continents. For most of my travel, I had engaging, respectful, and non-offensive discussions about many topics that are taboo in the United States. Except for the American anarchist in Sofia, every single conversation ended with mutual respect, gratitude, and most importantly greater understanding of the other. The habit of debating respectfully and passionately with people, the habit that had been cultivated for almost seven months, eventually became a problem. I had to stop debating when I returned to the United States and visited the Washington D.C. area, North Carolina, Chicago, Illinois, and San Jose, California. I'd forgotten it was offensive to disagree with people in America. Discussing ideas reflected the bipartisan nature of the country as everything was either black or white. Besides the pun of social conflict in America, it astonished me this was the first and last place after a score of countries where people expressed a genuine disinterest in discussing social and political matters. I inquired about issues in the same way that worked for months previously, but people in my home country shut down and became hurt as they perceived my questions as threatening.

The topics I had with people also had to shift. My first conversation with my brother's coworkers over lunch at a sushi restaurant involved a roast of Justin Bieber, complaints of not enough free food at company outings, and unnecessary speed bumps in the parking garage. "I've a feeling we're not in Kansas anymore." Granted, I know from experience daily conversations among coworkers can be strained for interesting topics, but it was a shock nonetheless. In North Carolina, a conversation among friends broached deeper topics on social matters, and I was asked if I was surprised they were talking about something intelligent. The question reflected the cultural attitude towards debate. In Chicago, the girl with her boyfriend mentioned to my brother that talking politics ruined her night even though her boyfriend brought up the topic, and I engaged him in a debate for a little bit. I learned not to bring up touchy topics by then.

One of the biggest illusions I discovered is the belief in completely artificial and fabricated stories as real. We indulge in mixing reality with fantasy as people discuss soap opera characters as they would their own families. The greatest divide and conquer I have ever experienced is that of the general public. People have been convinced over centuries to fight amongst each other while ignoring those in power. It is like cats throwing cheese among the thousands of mice surrounding them so the cats can walk away quietly and do as they please. Some social attention has addressed this behavior with phrases like, "Don't be a sheep," in reference to herds of sheep blindly following a shepherd. Regardless of the idea being debated, accepting criticism openly in a debate allows for self-growth and mutual growth if not blocked by the walls of self-defense.

Fashion

There is a balance between fashion and efficiency. Women go out on cold nights wearing little more than short skirts and tank tops. They sacrifice warmth for looking fashionable during nightlife. As a budget traveler, I was left to focus on efficiency instead of fashion by buying cheap things that served my needs. Over time, I should be able to afford both quality of material for durability and fashion.

Fashion is also largely set by gender. An airplane magazine showed advertisements comparing men and women. The man's face was lit from above to show a broad forehead and prominent facial features. The woman's face was lit from below to highlight a soft jawline and fine features of the skin.

The experience that enlightened me to the world of fashion was in Italy. I walked around Florence with my cousins, and I felt I had walked into a fashion magazine. I had never seen so much fashion style before in real life. It continued with my friend studying fashion in Milan who introduced me to the term "fashion victim". When I reached the United States, I saw mostly plain t-shirts, large sweaters, and baggy clothing. I remember being shocked when I looked at a line of people in cold weather outside the Chicago aquarium. I saw a fashion sense arising more so from mass production when compared to Europeans. I observed lots of plain clothing with materials like plastic, polyesters, and athletic clothing. Europeans in general pride themselves in the winter months with more stylized jackets and coats in public and with cheese, chocolate, and food.

Failure

Children that are never told "No" often grow up spoiled and defiant. They know of no limits that apply to them as anything they wish for they can have. I saw this in the children of the volunteer organization's owner in Nepal. They were treated well with gifts, but I felt their luxury was unique to Nepal and offered a false sense of superiority over their peers. Among all the Nepali children at the orphanage and school, the boss' children could be the most disrespectful and rude. They were good children, but they were the only children I sensed arrogance from in my two months there.

As an athlete, I learned the vital nature of failure which pushed me to succeed. Likewise, many businessmen speak positively of their past failures for guiding them towards their present success.

In the United States with our freedom of choice, we have countless appliances, convenience, and abundance. It is truly an ideal example of a world with seemingly infinite resources. Due to its abundance and great protection from its military, it is a safe playground for many to live lavishly and independently. However, too much of any good thing can lead to negative consequences. Candy tastes good, but eating only candy for breakfast, lunch, and dinner will likely have unhappy results over time. In terms of social awareness, Americans have not seen a war fought on its soil in over a century. The result of being one of the greatest world powers means that there is no mentor to look up to for feedback. Some Americans are like the children I mentioned who are never told "no" and thus are quick to entertain violent means without foreseeing the full consequences of such means.

Living with others that are equally comforted without room for failure creates a highly proud community that continually elevates itself to believe it deserves the best. This sense of entitlement is used to explain the lower academic prowess of native-born, American students in comparison to foreign students who had to travel and invest in an education. Ivy League alumni received criticism for being naively overconfident in their abilities as a result of rarely experiencing failure since any deviation from the perfect path towards graduation had high repercussions. A sense of entitlement appears generally in extremely pro-American culture and with political representatives who use their positions to cater to personal interests instead of to their constituents' concerns.

Investment

Investment relies on the distinction between short-term and long-term. In developing countries, people have to think short-term survival, so any solution that quickly solves a problem is good enough. As a result, social media loves to report on the crazy ways in which people in developing countries perform tasks, often in surprising and ingenious ways.

In the developed world, we also give up our potential to profit from long-term investments by focusing on the short-term. Some examples of short-term investments in the developed world can be disconcerting: Government funds for schools are diverted towards short-term needs like military contracts and harvesting natural resources. Short-term consequences of reduced government funding for education opens the door to corporations developing a presence in schools and offer school administrations supplemental income by promoting soft drinks and fast food on campus. Children quickly become regular consumers at an early age with long-term health costs. Such excessive youth consumption of unhealthy foods drew so much attention that Michelle Obama addressed it with national exercise programs. Hospitals which represent the utmost care for health can notably be bad for one's health as some ironically supply cheap, unhealthy foods to their patients. Healthcare pursues short-term profits by investing more in acute, specialist procedures that leads to the high costs of healthcare today. The meat industry prioritizes expediency and profit over safety relative to other countries which leads to lower quality of meat and frequent disease outbreaks. Big pharmaceutical companies must remain competitive in a rapidly changing market by accelerating drug testing and production which has led to some drugs being pulled from the market after human damages were reported.

Profit is short-term, and short-term investments can quickly produce secondary, long-term problems. America is a short-term, reactive country instead of a long-term, proactive country. Wolves were reintroduced to Yellowstone National Park in 1995 after 70 years, and scientists observed the ecosystem flourish even greater as the keystone species affected all tiers of nature. Long-term benefits are not always visible in the short-term even if they may be equally if not more beneficial for society than short-term benefits. By nature, the U.S. houses and benefits from much of the rapidly developing entrepreneurial creativity and entertainment culture around the world. Europe invests more in long-term projects like education and healthcare, and while salaries for the wealthy are less, a greater portion of the population partakes in reasonable opportunities for success.

In-depth analysis points to the benefits of long-term goals. Childcare is a long-term investment that has been shown to produce more productive and efficient adults 20 years down the road. IRAs are one of the few long-term investments Americans make, probably because, as the young couple I met in Chicago said, they expect government resources to shrivel up. They wished to be completely independent financially.

The honor system fails with short-term thinking. Cheating is a short-term solution, and the arguments against it are thought in terms of long-term effects. Eating healthy is an investment involving long-term thinking. It is the equivalent of taking care of a car with regular oil changes. I eat healthy, so my body is not crumbling at a younger age than I would expect, and I can enjoy my life to its greatest ability. The British guy in Montreal told me how the English people were healthiest when they rationed food during the 1950's. His dentist told him tooth decay was virtually nonexistent at the time.

It only reappeared after the ration books disappeared and people began enjoying life with excess sweets. Investments, both short and long, have their strengths and weaknesses. A good balance of the two would seem to solve both problems we face today and prevent predictable, new problems from arising in the future.

Similar Differences

Conclusion

I began my travels blindly thinking each country would be a different experience. I did not expect to find similarities extend beyond cultural and national borders. I did not expect my understanding of people to grow like it did. People, no matter their background, inherently share many basic, underlying social qualities beneath the layers of cultural differences. Once the first layer peeled off, I realized people are also inherently complex, multidimensional entities whose presence and potential cannot be defined by a single impression. Similarly, larger entities, like governments, became much easier and tangible to engage with once I understood they were merely groups of people whose actions depended on their understanding of themselves and others. Appreciating these multidimensional traits in others helped me learn about and value what I can contribute to this world. When I look in the mirror, I can identify elements from mostly everyone I have met thus far in my life, like wisdom, appreciation, compassion, empathy, understanding, awareness, hospitality, energy, kindness, helpfulness, foresight, analysis, and patience.

Life, at times, puts people in situations which they have no control over. We can neither control what other people do nor can we control time or the elements. What we can control is how we perceive, process, and prepare to react to unforeseeable personal and social circumstances. I've met many pessimistic people who have given up hope in the betterment of humanity and state the amount of violence and crime in the world overwhelms the good that humanity can produce. Quite frankly, I believe our species is better than that. I have seen extremes around the world, but without a doubt, I saw an indescribable kindness always appear if we smile, greet, and introduce ourselves in a culturally respectable manner. I met more good, kind people from more countries than I can count, many more good than bad. I see an enormous, trending positivity reflected brightly by people worldwide, a perception which may be harder to acknowledge from a single geographic location. Inevitably, to ignore good people is to leave voids for hatred to perpetuate. The killing of groups of people cannot bring peace to a society, especially today as the world is connected through technology and extensive sharing of ideas. When war does exist between groups of people, we need to reflect on our own role and how it impacts the environment we all share in order to address these issues before fear and terror take over and become the acceptable response. Regardless of whether individuals actively engage or deny their roles, proof that our behavior matters and our groups are increasingly interconnected at this time in history is the shared pain of loss or joy of success as a result of current events all around the world.

Since I was a child, my interests developed to make people healthier physically and socially. As a teenager, I never understood my friends who idolized sports players as their role models until I consciously identified my own role models. The kind of person I wanted to emulate was best reflected in TV characters like Hawkeye and BJ in MASH and Dr. Cox in Scrubs. My role models did not glamorize killing. They condemned it from within. I learned that in any war both sides lose. I can't support the notion of protecting the children of one country while allowing the killing of children of another country. Perhaps I was heavily prejudiced to see the world this way and only saw what I wanted to see while traveling. Perhaps not. Although wars are about imposing ideas and principles that extend beyond national borders, we are an international planet with no nationality superior to any other, no group or race better than any other. The differences between men versus women or one race versus another are reflected by the rules they live by, whether by choice or not. Our security will not be found in the death of our enemies but in three points leading to peaceful co-existence: the awareness and embracing of each other's multidimensionality, the enrichment of everyone's lives through multidimensional education, and the respect for everyone's basic human rights. As a future physician, my aim is to care for everyone. Understanding who they are helps me do that. Traveling helped me appreciate the first two points and see the consequences if we forgo the third. As a society, these achievements are up to the people and the few people that rule over them.

I find there is a spectrum of existence from survival on one end to "civilized" growth on the other end. We are emotional human beings built on survival, but only with proper space and freedom from survival can we expect ourselves to evolve further through societal growth; else, we limit our growth and destine ourselves to fluctuate back and forth and repeat our mistakes. Treating people well extends beyond survival. Medicine treats people to help them survive physically, but living fully is beyond what medicine can ever accomplish alone.

Ancient civilizations were marked by scholars as "developed" when they could specialize their work force, such as making some people farmers and others artists. These artists made early pottery, jewelry, and paintings, and they marked the development of their early societies. Today, our society is no different. A natural or artificial crisis limits our creative expression. For example, a pressing issue like a public shooting, a natural disaster, or a financial crisis captures our attention. The natural reaction is to call for an immediate response to the issue at hand. Naturally, a major loss threatens one's sense of survival, and emotions run high and far away from a sense of happiness that would follow continued growth and living fully. Our capacity to reflect on the many dimensions of what caused the issue narrows as people revert to their internal beliefs for support and strength. This is when education and development of artistry, science, and technology as long-term markers of society's development are often the first to be discarded or blamed. Naturally, it is difficult to think clearly in times of crisis and easier to think when there is time to develop and prepare our ideas. Choices may seem limited, and we are tempted to pick the first survival-oriented, short-term choice that comes to mind. Time and time again, I observed this to rarely be the best choice, because it ends up being merely a band-aid which hides the pain temporarily but does little to prevent tragedy from happening again. It is inherently more difficult for individuals to contribute to society when basic issues of survival are inadequately fulfilled, and they become heavily focused on one-dimensional solutions to survive. It becomes more difficult for society to meet individuals' needs when too many wounds remain hidden by overused band-aids which lead to an unending cycle of additional problems to deal with.

History shows our short-term choices frequently have unintentional, long-term impacts. If the goal is to solve a problem, additional foresight could help evade retaliation and prolongation of the same problem. Does our behavior towards others today reflect how we want our parents, siblings, and children to be treated? Do we want our children to learn from adults who mistreat each other, practice racial slurs, and learn to hate another group or rather be kind, understanding, and curious about the world they live in? Finding answers to these questions can be confusing, because there exists a lot of individualized judgement about others. Does that person from that country hate me for simply being from my country? What situation are they in that pressures or motivates them to use weapons instead of diplomacy? Why are we going to war, and will it really solve or simply delay the problem from re-occurring? I do not presume to know the answers. All I can say is more people than I expected across this world had very similar answers to my questions. Why? Because as different as lifestyles and cultures exist today, we all share the same goals for a happy and decent life for ourselves and our children as we try to understand and navigate the social differences we face. In a uniquely beautiful way, these social differences contain both the problems and the solutions.

People have made tremendous ground forward as we can see the rapid evolution of human thought in the last, few hundred years to increase equality and civil rights around the world. It is not always a straightforward path, but it is always moving forward for the better. Society is not perfect as it continues to evolve in the same way as life does in the wild with the common goal of prospering through constant adaptation. It tries something, and it makes mistakes. Society can unfortunately design circumstances, like discrimination and oppression, that behave as festering diseases. The implications of discrimination for the groups involved is not always clear in the moment as the distinction between illegal and immoral arises only once there is backlash from the discriminated groups of people demanding respect. As long as people in society consistently make efforts to understand why certain groups either choose or find themselves in a particular situation, the solutions to these inter-personal issues will arise spontaneously. Furthermore, without a deeper understanding of how and where, for example, group anger originates, society cannot eliminate it, will oscillate from one form of anger to another, and remain guided by whichever group speaks the loudest or the strongest. For example, the mainstream, racial hatred of the 1960s is similar to how many people feel about racists today, albeit the motion today is to defend equality instead of segregation. It isn't perfect, but it is a step forward.

Today's globalization and shrinking borders connect previously isolated groups of people with many other groups, each with children, grandparents, and many more in between. The world is a beautiful place with many countries and landscapes now connected in unprecedented ways through travel, emigration, politics, economics, and social media. These increasing methods of communication permit us to observe the diverse nature of people for all the qualities and characteristics that make us human. Society and individuals are intricately interactive, and history shows that both grow stronger when individuals can pursue their passions collectively. Individuals have the goal to find success through their own will and desire, and society benefits from taking the next step forward by sharing that success with everyone else. How can individuals attain these goals? I propose a multidimensional understanding of people to learn how to navigate this new, interconnected world we are discovering together.

Understanding others is a powerful tool for two reasons. The first reason is that understanding can mend the division of disagreement and perhaps even prevent violence. In a hostage situation, the first and best solution is always to bring the negotiator to discuss the reasons behind the hold-up, and the second solution is to use violence only if necessary when discussions are ineffective. To understand and listen is not synonymous with condoning or excusing wrong behavior. To misunderstand a person or group by only understanding single dimensions calls for stereotyping, racial profiling, rhetoric, and propaganda. Simple misunderstandings have symptoms of confusion about the unseen dimensions of people. Greater misunderstandings have symptoms of frustration, anger, and deep-seeded hatred.

The second reason is that understanding leads to empathy. Empathy requires an expanded awareness of other people, other cultures, and other values. To empathize is to understand someone else's interpretation of the same experience we partook in and to learn from someone else's experience even if we were not directly involved. To empathize is to witness someone else's values, observe that person's mentality, and foresee the limitations of behavior based on that mentality. Empathy leads to ideas for preventing atrocities from repeating. Empathy benefits me as well as the other person. I traveled, because I consciously did not want my lack of life experience to inhibit my learning and ability to care for people. It empowers me to understand other people from their point of view and control my response to them in a way that saves me energy and makes me more effective. If I meet someone who is upset over an issue, rapidly being able to understand why, including reasons that may not be readily apparent to the individual, simultaneously helps me remain calm and better prepared to help. Traveling provided the experience of living in someone else's shoes long enough for me to develop the skill innately. For example, I'm white, so I visualized what it is like to be non-white. I can afford food and housing, so I visualized what it would be like not to. I have a mother on Mother's Day, so I visualized what it is like for those without mothers on that day. Stepping into others' shoes does not cost anything, yet it teaches patience, compassion, and understanding of individuals as well as ideas about how to begin assisting at the group level. All of the people whose shoes I stepped into wanted to be heard, understood, and treated with dignity by others. I cannot disagree with that since I would like that too. Empathy is what brings people and communities together to be stronger. Most importantly, empathy inherently constructs anger-free patience to listen for the time it takes to eliminate the anger of misunderstanding and feeling misunderstood.

Understanding for the reasons I mentioned above is not easy by any means. Many factors may inhibit understanding. The first obstacle is a lack of interest in clear and compassionate communication to gain greater understanding. I found the opposite of understanding to be "ignorance," a word frequently thrown in the United States at those who disagree and is used to justify disregarding any disagreeing statements. The only ignorance I can speak of is my own ignorance which propelled me to travel in the first place. The second obstacle is time. I found that a deeper understanding between two people usually comes after 15-20 minutes of pleasant exchange to figure out and permit a mutual topic to arise that both parties can discuss openly and passionately. The people's beliefs I came across were simple manifestations of their past experiences and lessons, a valuable treasure for me to learn from. Countless discussions led me to view disagreements as normal and inevitable, and there is nothing to gain from responding to ignorance with anger and disbelief. In fact, anger and disbelief simply perpetuate the disagreement even if the intention is to reach a resolution. Having the intention to at least appreciate why someone holds onto a disagreeing belief creates the environment to encourage mutual understanding and reduce ignorance on both sides. Interestingly, I always found it very enlightening to engage in conversations with people who actively chose to be ignorant, a choice they have the right to make, because I could always locate a reason, given enough time, that made them steadfast in their beliefs.

Many people admire Gandhi's famous quote about being the change we wish to see in the world, but a limited number of people live by those words. Why? It is not easy when we constantly feel that other people threaten our survival and well-being. Naturally, our past experiences create the filters that affect how we perceive and feel about others, yet we often overlook how our perception affects our present behavior and contributes to the world we inherently help create. Through a better understanding of the topics in this book, I can better communicate with people. When meeting someone new, I can simultaneously listen to what words they choose and why they choose them as indicators of their background values, inner and external beliefs, how many dimensions of an issue they understand, and where the limitations are for greater understanding. Nearly all the people I talked to around the world were interested in learning and greater understanding, because they would engage in kind discussion instead of dictating their opinions to me just as I was eager to share with and learn from them. With the discussion skills I developed over time, I could quickly tailor the examples and stories that would, in an appropriate and respectful manner, promote further discussion, answer their questions and expand their understanding. I had to quickly learn if I was serious about finding broad solutions, I had to adapt what I could give and receive in a discussion. To give, I consciously chose examples that applied as broadly as possible to the entire group of interest, not just extreme examples to support my own point. To receive, I constantly adapted my perception to every single fact and story that didn't fit my original view. I also was more interested in receiving the *why*, not the *what*. Anyone can have an idea on the *what*, and knowing *what* someone does is easy, but knowing *why* someone does something is much harder and more important. Learning only the *what* predilects us to repeat history, but learning the *why* empowers us to change it.

It took me some time to figure out what the point of my past discussions might be. Empathy is not a typical super power, but it sure feels like one. I hold conscious respect for numerously more people in this world than before my journey began, respect for the past experiences which influence who they are today, and respect for the potential they have to grow for the better. The best assessment I can make at this time is that while our differences are similar around the world, our goals are even more alike so that when we disagree with someone, seeing common goals puts discussion and compromise on the table when they were not there before.

This book attempts to be the first step in combining all the impressions of a person or people into a common place from which we can effortlessly create ideas and opportunities for the better world we each strive for. Self-analysis may seem underdone or overdone, but the purpose is to share the value in learning from our experiences and in spontaneously developing healthier relationships between multidimensional individuals. With a little understanding, we can travel much further from simply wanting to live in a better world towards actually manifesting a healthier and happier world. Doing the best thing is not always easy, and honestly, traveling around the world out of a backpack is much easier than the admirable leap forward made by traveling beyond the borders of our own minds. I combined ideas from hundreds of people to write this book, because I trust people have ideas of how to solve the social problems they face even if they don't have the means to apply those ideas. I listened to them, and I could never have anticipated developing the powerful and effortless ability to empathize as a result. I hope you listen to them too.

Finishe

3 Feb 2018

Unbeliveoly gross

10 stars

rathr

Similar Differences

Acknowledgements

Words cannot describe the gratitude I have for the countless friends and family that brought me into their homes and lives. To name some of them, thank you to Clint, Molly, Chad, Tomohiro, Kristine, Frank, Nick, Meg, Ead, Bhagawan, Yubaraj, Rashmi, Asok and the Poudel family, Hakum, Vidhu, Jean-Philippe, Vasek, Taliah, Sabrina, Coraline, Kristiana, Yassemine, Pearl, Stefan, Duska, Geoffrey, Antoine, Lala, Jonas, Luisa, Daniela, Nina, Stanko, Alice, and every single one of my extended and immediate family. It was for just a short while, but it was a lifelong gift of memories and treasures that brought this world a little bit closer together. Lastly, a great thank you to my parents, Catherine and Gerard, for supporting me on this journey wherever it took me.

Bibliography

[1]Bird, Kai, and Martin J. Sherwin. *American Prometheus: The Triumph and Tragedy of J. Robert Oppenheimer.* New York: A.A. Knopf, 2006. Printed with permission.

[2]Gladwell, Malcolm. *Blink: The Power of Thinking Without Thinking.* New York: Little, Brown and Co, 2005. Printed with permission.

[3]Krakauer, Jon. *Into The Wild.* New York: Anchor Books, 2015. Printed with permission.

About the Author

Benjamin Berthet was born in San Ramon, California and spent most his childhood at the base of the Santa Cruz mountains in Los Gatos, California. Early interests in psychology, biology, and the mind led him to pursue a B.S. Physiology and Neuroscience from University of California, San Diego which he attained in 2014. During that time, he participated in UCSD Track and Field as a pole vaulter, took several sociology courses, and managed research experiments in theoretical vision neuroscience at the Salk Institute. The travels in this book were completed the year before beginning osteopathic medical school at A.T. Still University, School of Osteopathic Medicine in Arizona with expected graduation date in May 2019. Hobbies include exploring the wild outdoors at any elevation, running, and engaging in community events.

Made in the USA
Columbia, SC
05 January 2018